blaxploitation (blax sploi tation) *adj.* **1.** A commercial-minded film of the seventies for black audiences. **2.** The design of such films drew heavily on the popularity of black actors in screen stories that were often highly sensational: tough crime plots with superhero figures, for example, *Shaft* ('71), were common ingredients.

—*Dictionary of Film Terms,* Frank Beaver

Blax (blak) *prefix.* If, at this point in the twentieth century, you need a definition, it's too late.

exploit (eks'ploit, ik sploit) *n.* To use for one's own advantage; take advantage of: Rulers often exploit the people. [<OF *esploit* <L *explicitum,* neut. sing. of *explicitus.*]

exploitation (eks'ploi ta'shen) *n.* **1.** The act of exploiting. **2.** Selfish employment for one's own use or advantage.

—Funk & Wagnall's Standard Dictionary of the English Language International Edition (1960)

Courtesy of Francois Gaudet.

. . . sigel *means the images*
they've created to fool the world
like the colours on Old Glory
the flag that they unfurled . . .
—from *E Pluribus Unum*,
Jalal Nuriddin, The Last Poets

THAT'S

BLAXPLOITATION!

Roots of the Baadasssss 'Tude

(Rated X by an All-Whyte Jury)

Darius James

a.k.a. Dr. Snakeskin

ST. MARTIN'S GRIFFIN ❧ NEW YORK

This book is dedicated to Joy Glidden,
my friend, lover, and partner in bad taste.

My father and sister, Walter and Jeri
Collette, with great affection.

Bruce Huckabey and Peter Dennis, with
whom I got blasted in the basement.

My Kung Fu Pimp-vined partner, Carey Howell.

My bloodbrother in the ink, Norman Douglas.

My great cradle-to-the-grave friend, Hoodoo
Queen, and Kali cut-up, Sallie Ann Glassman.

My true friend, Noah Seaman.

And, lastly, to a future "Mack of the Year,"
Max Julian Sundiata Holmberg, born 8-29-94,
and nicknamed "Goldie" by his mom, Lydia.

Grateful acknowledgment is made for permission to reprint the following:

"Whytesploitation" reprinted by Michael Will.

Interview with Robert Beck a.k.a. "Iceberg Slim" entitled "Chillin' with Iceberg" printed with permission by Fred Brathwaite.

"The Blackman's Guide to Seducing White Women with the Amazing Power of Voodoo" reprinted from *Love Is Strange* with permission by Joel Rose.

Parody-sketch of *Shaft* printed by permission of author Michael O'Donoghue.

Excerpt from *Groove, Bang and Jive Around* reprinted with permission by Steven Cannon.

Jacket cover from *Shaft Among the Jews* by Ernest Tidyman. Copyright used by permission of Bantam Books, a division of Bantam Doubleday Dell Publishing Group, Inc.

Animated Flip Book courtesy of Rick Trembles.

In altered form, excerpts from *That's Blaxploitation!* have appeared in *Grand Street, Vibe, Love Is Strange, Red Tape #7, Sensitive Skin* and *The Village Voice*.

Design by Richard Oriolo

Library of Congress Cataloging-in-Publication Data

James, Darius.
That's blaxploitation!: roots of the Baadasssss 'tude (rated X by an all-whyte jury)
Darius James
p.   cm.
ISBN 0-312-13192-5 (pbk.)
1. Afro-Americans in motion pictures. 2. Sensationalism in motion pictures. I. Title.
PN1995.9.N4J35 1995
791.43'75'08996073—dc20   95-17149
CIP

First St. Martin's Griffin Edition: December 1995

10 9 8 7 6 5 4 3 2 1

"Remember the phrases 'Power to the People!', 'Off the Pig!' and 'Free Huey!'? Can you stretch your mind back to a time when your hair looked like a meticulously tended shrub on the White House lawn, providing the perfect cushion against the blows of a racist pig's nightstick? Do you remember rakin' out the naps with a metal sponge-cake cutter which you also used to pacify obstreperous, foul-mouthed Caucasians during your high school's springtime race riots? *You do?* You must be one *old-ass* muthafucka then!"

Courtesy of Photofest.

"Jim's got to go bad. *Real bad.*"

CONTENTS

· ·

Courtesy of Photofest.

BLACK GODFATHER'S BACK!
...there's gonna be
Hell Up in Harlem
Samuel Z. Arkoff presents FRED WILLIAMSON . "HELL UP IN HARLEM"
Also Starring JULIUS W. HARRIS · GLORIA HENDRY · MARGARET AVERY · D'URVILLE MARTIN
SOUND TRACK ALBUM AVAILABLE ON MOTOWN RECORDS AND TAPES · A Larry Cohen Film · A Larco Production · COLOR · An American International Release
© 1973 American International Pictures, Inc.

PAM GRIER TALKS

TAMARA DOBSON: PHASION FOTO

Courtesy of the George Trow Estate.

Courtesy of Photofest.

Meet SUGAR HILL and her ZOMBIE HIT MEN!

Devil Woman with Voodoo Powers to raise the Savage Dead! She's Supernatural!

Sugar Hill

SAMUEL Z. ARKOFF Presents "SUGAR HILL" an American International Picture Starring
MARKI BEY · ROBERT QUARRY · DON PEDRO COLLEY
Produced by ELLIOT SCHICK Directed by PAUL MASLANSKY Color by Movielab
Original Music Composed by NICK ZESSES and DINO FEKARIS
"SUPERNATURAL VOODOO WOMAN" Sung by "THE ORIGINALS" Available on Motown Records

Courtesy of Photofest.

Courtesy of Photofest.

Courtesy of "Blacula" Photofest.

FOREWARNING

. . . .

That's *Blaxploitation!* is not an exhaustive, encyclopedic or definitive work on the era and its films. Nor does it pretend to be. I never intended this book to be a serious, indepth study of the 1970s or 1970s black film culture. If this were my intent, a great many more topics would have been dealt with in these pages. For example, you won't find a discussion of the popular black music of the seventies or the soundtracks of films described in this book. I'm sure this seems absurd to anyone even remotely familiar with the period (after all, a few bars of Isaac Hayes's score for *Shaft* is enough to invoke, in most people's minds, insurrectionary images of leather-clad black men poised to challenge the hegemony of whyte male power—a point not lost on Courtney Love in her ironic use of the theme from *Shaft* in the movie, *Tank Girl*); but, frankly, I didn't really give a fuck about music in the seventies.

A whole other area not discussed in this book is fashion. You'd easily understand why if you ever saw me in public. I dress like a bum. In fact, I dress like a bum timelocked in the seventies. And you won't find photos of the customized pimpmobiles that tooled through Times Square in the 1970s. That's a book unto itself. It's also not the function of this book to explain black people, the products created by black people, or those products that are created by whytes and peopled with blacks. I did not write this book with aspirations of grinning in front of a television camera at the next NAACP Image Award ceremony. I chose this subject because:

1. I thought I might be able to pay the rent on my apartment with the advance I received for this book. (I was sadly mistaken. It was gone by the third month of this two-year project).

2. I spend a lot of money on video rentals and cult-movie fanzines. And I want to claim these items on my tax forms. I hoped, too, that this book would encourage video companies to send me preview tapes of forthcoming titles with the idea that I would include it in a later revised and expanded edition of this book.

3. In the libraries of specialist video-rental stores, like NYC's Kim's Video, you can find just about any obscure pig-fucking, psycho-hillbilly-slasher-movie ever lensed in the swamps of Louisiana; but precious little in the way of blaxploitation films. And I could find no *popular* works on the genre in the bookstores.

What this book became was an exploration of what my parents, neighbors, teachers and a battery of psychiatrists have said is my "bad attitude." The foundations of that "attitude" is what I now call *The Trinity of The Pusher, The Pimp and The Panther*; my models of "bad" behavior. I think this is actually an important point to consider, especially after one realizes yesteryear's Superfly cult fathered today's brood of gun-loco, inner-city cowboys. Also, as a child of blaxploitation films, my favorite one-liner is "kill whytie." I *roar* every time I hear it, rolling around on the floor in pissed-pants laughter. Whether it's a movie militant in black beret steppin' up to the "Man," or an anti-colonial African Mau-Mau slitting the throat of a sleeping Brit, it just cracks me up. Don't know why I find the idea of dead whyte people so goddamned funny. On the other hand, I can't stomach much in the more recent cycle of black films. Don't like watching black people kill other black people. Don't know why on that one either. I guess I'm a traditionalist that way.

What you really hold in your hands is a celebration and a memoir. As you skip down the chocolate path of memory lane, you'll encounter loads of unlawfully sarcastic "film comments"; hundreds of mediocre reproductions of black and white movie stills; bizarre, self-serving interviews; smutty comics; paradies; and promotional booklets of the era's most popular films. This book also attempts to recreate the nineteen seventies by portraying the depraved mental state of one particular Afro-American adolescent: *me*. What began as an affectionate look back at my adolescence, and the varied forms of "entertainment" offered in the seventies, gradually evolved into an informal examination of a popular black American pastime: *Signifyin'*. I didn't plan it that way. It just happened. Call me *triflin'*.

When I gave some actual thought to my adolescence, I realized—once the haze of reefer smoke clouding the memories I have of my past began to lift—I was pissed off most of the time (At what? You name it and I was pissed at it. *And I wanted to piss on it!*). My only relief was in the grotesque humor I found in the things presented in this book.

So, other than the unlikelihood of selling jillions of copies, I have only two hopes for this book:

1. It will start an explosion of seventies film & funk fanzines like David Mills's exceptional *UnCut Funk*—a 'zine truly devoted to the excavation of the "BaadAsssss 'Tude."
2. Video companies will release the entire catalogue of seventies black films on the market—and then, finally, I'll be able to watch *The Zombies of Sugar Hill* uncut and without commercial interruption.

DARIUS H. JAMES

INTRODUCTION

· ·

Unlike most of my platformed peers in the 1970s (with whom I spent many semi-conscious hours smoking cannabis by the bale), I wasn't given to dreamlike reveries of floating across the Peruvian pink-flaked cliffs of Superfly Valhalla, encircled by a corona of refracted light, with a mink-lined cape billowing off my shoulder. Nor did I boast aspirations of cruising in the rabbit-fur comfort of a customized "El-D" with a stable of hypnotized hoze under my charismatic control.

No. My teenage agenda was simple:

1. Get high.
2. Overthrow the U.S. government.
3. And fuck big-boobed whyte girls.

My idea of a good time was parading through the streets with Nixon's maimed, dog-jowled head speared on the end of a bayonet. I wanted to live on the streets described in the pages of *The East Village Other*[1]; join a cell of the Weather Underground, blow up buildings, assassinate heads of state and pollute the water supply with the finest LSD manufactured by the best minds the chemical underground had to offer. Unfortunately, until the revolution came, I was forced to wait in the basement of my father's house on a second-hand Castro Convertible sofa under posters of Angela Davis and H. Rap Brown with a square of paper acid dissolving on my tongue. In the basement's cathode-tube–lit darkness, I'd watch Universal's old monster movies on a flea-market Motorola hallucinating the *Famous Monsters of Filmland* terrorizing whyte suburboid populations with Huey Newton's helium-squeak voice. Or, I could be found in the company of my comrades, Huck-n-Pete. With The Last Poets and Funkadelic rasping through cheap speakers in the background, we'd smoke one clumsily rolled joint after the other, while reading Uncle Ho Chi Mihn on guerilla warfare, plotting our teenage coup d'etat.

I'd awake each morning at 6:45—red-eyed with lint-flecked Don King hair and a bouncing, batonlike hard-on—to a Fleischer Bros. 'toon on the tube and a stick of one-poke pot. And, while Koko the Clown leapt out of the inkwell singing those "St. James Infirmary Blues," I'd dress in ragged denim bell-bottoms, needle-toed cowboy boots and red-fisted Columbia STRIKE! tee with a crash helmet hanging off my belt loop. By 7:15, Huck-n-I had hooked up to get fucked up.

Huck was six-one of solid, bushy-headed negro. He had the kind of attitude that put most black men behind bars. But not him. He was smart.

On the lapel of his pea coat, he wore a button with a detail lifted from the cover art of Miles Davis' *On The Corner* album. It read FREE ME. He said it meant he was a political prisoner without a prison.

"Hey, fellas, what it is?"

[1] *The East Village Other* was the one consoling publication of my teenhood. It was a mad mix of comix, poetry and politics celebrating all those values close to the hearts of disenchanted American youth: anti-authoritarianism, unrestricted drug use, unrestrained (and latex-free) fornication and savage rock 'n' roll.

In the instant Huck-n-I locked the joint's stub in the vise of two paper match sticks, scorching it with flame, there was Pete listing forward with his mouth open and his lips stretched out, ready to suck in and share the fumes. Pete was the neighborhood b-ball coolie. He-n-I would stay up until four in the morning, after a long and exhausting day of gettin' "high" in high school, and a longer night of gettin' blasted in the basement, sitting in the front room of his parents' home, talking and listening to jazz, concocting meals out of whatever we found moldering in the rear of his mother's refrigerator, drowning it in Red Devil hot sauce before it had a chance to crawl off our plates. When the three of us finished the reefer fumes, we joined the remainder of our crew waiting on the corner for the yellow school bus.

Slouched against the slats of a white picket fence was the hook-nosed "Volt," a self-styled Black Militant and scowling Lilliputian with a monster-sized 'fro, who we nicknamed after the sixty-five Watts riots because of the ruckus he raised in our high school cafeteria ("Volt" had bounced up and down on the balls of his white Converse-sneakered feet, sliced the air with the teeth of a metal afro-pick and hurled a volley of greasy meatballs, shouting—*"DEATH TO ALL Y'ALL DEGENERATE NO-TASTIN', POTATO-SALAD-EATIN' HONKY DEVILS!!"*); the impeccably dressed, and self-assuredly *cool,* "Honey-Boy Tuna," a Seventh-Day Adventist who wanted to be a pimp; and the three-hundred-pound "Pork Rind," who looked like a gelatinous mold of hog's entrails, or head cheese (a congealed combination of ears, snout and tail), in blue overalls, black leather coat and wide-brim straw fedora with a pair of tinted granny glasses perched on the tip of his pug nose, munching from an ever-present bag of Howards' barbecue flavored, deep-fried pork by-products.

Now, in contrast to the space Pork Rind's girth occupied on planet earth, his voice was a hysterical, fast-paced and country-twanged falsetto— "Look! *Woofmane be blasted!* C'mon, Woofmane, whip out de' woof*bane!*"

My friends, to my chagrin, hadn't apposed an appropriate appellation to my person, a name suiting my "revolutionary" persona (say, for instance, "Chairman Ho Chi Nigger"). Instead, they called me "Wolfman"—that hairy, howling lunatic who crept on raised canine arches. Their reason was two-fold:

1. I had a reputation for talkin' mucho shit, or "wolfin'" (as in *The Boy Who Cried Wolf*) to the would-be Don Corleone whyte boys with the toodged, greased-back hair crowded around the water fountain outside the cafeteria.

2. As a child, I wanted to join the ranks of horror-screen legends Boris Karloff, Peter Lorre and Vincent Price, be billed as "The World's First Horror-Movie Kiddie Star," and appear in movies with titles like *Blood Shriek of the Buck-Dancing Pickaninny* (a surefire favorite with the hillbilly half-wits on the southern drive-in circuit), frightening the popcorn-noshing multitudes in second-run flea-pits across the country.

So, spotting an ad in the rear of *Monster Times,* which promised the secrets of lycanthropic transformation, I mailed five dollars to a p.o. box in Derby, Connecticut; and received, for my troubles, a set of plastic, glow-in-the-dark dog dentures.

Undeterred by this blatant act of mail fraud, I utilized skills gleaned from a special Dick Smith edition of the *Monster Make-Up Handbook* (a Famous Monsters' do-it-yourself guide with complete step-by-step instructions on how to turn yourself into one of Big Daddy Roth's pop-eyed hot-rod demons with just some nose putty and two halves of a Ping-Pong ball), and uttered incantations under the full moon.

With my face clotted with clumps of coiled, beetle-ball hair saved from my last haircut, and a mucuosy mixture of spirit gum and water, I'd leap from a limb of the maple tree in front of my house, and *pounce* on one of my unsuspecting playmates; who, in turn, screamed in cold, uncomprehending terror at the deranged sight kneeling on their chest, a large bubble of snot inflating from both nostrils.

It was a period in my life no one has ever let me forget.

By nine years old, I'd become a local urban legend. Even now, over thirty years later, strange children approach me on the streets on my visits home, their eyes wide with curiosity and fear, asking, *"Is it true you be the Wolfman of Winchester Avenue?"*

THAT'S BLAXPLOITATION!

MELVIN VAN PEEBLES:

"ORIGINAL GUERRILLA"

One afternoon in early January 1994, I sat in a theater located somewhere off of Eighth Avenue and watched a staged reading of a new musical written by the *singular* Melvin Van Peebles.

Some months before, my wife, Joy, and I had attended a screening at the Tribeca Film Center of *Vroom-Vroom,* a short film Melvin had produced and directed for late-night German television, which would be included later in a trilogy of erotic shorts by distinguished directors for the Cannes Film Festival.

Vroom-Vroom is the first instance I know of to present unadulter-

The Story of a Three-Day Pass

(1968)
[On Video]
DIRECTOR/SCREENWRITER: Melvin Van Peebles; STORY: based on his novel.
CAST: Harry Baird and Nicole Berger.

Van Peebles's first feature is the story of a black soldier and a whyte shop girl with whom he spends a three-day holiday in the French countryside. Crisp, funky and literally in black-n-whyte, the film is indeed the product of an African-American and French marriage—*underscored* by Van Peebles's wit and genuine insight into the subtle mechanisms of interracial romance.

ated Black erotic folklore in an American film. The only films I can compare it to are the animated *Lemon Cream* shorts produced in Japan.

Its simple story concerns a virginal rustic, derided by his pops for his "pussy" bumps, and suffering rejection by the booty-shakin', big-legged gals at a neighborhood barbecue. No matter how hard he tries, m'man couldn't get hisself any.

Strolling along a back road, our hero saves a local hoodoo woman from getting squashed by a truck. She grants him a wish. He wants two. They huddle in negotiation. The hoodoo woman compromises. And our hero ends up with a motorcycle that morphs into a woman.

If Melvin's new musical blackened the Great White Way anything like his first, *Ain't Supposed To Die A Natural Death,* it promised to be an adventure. I looked forward to a rousing time, complete with Big Bird on crack! But, due to a prior meeting, I arrived late.

I entered the theater, sat down, and, to my bafflement, found a stage *loaded* with whyte people reciting some Brit-accented, Anglophilic *Brideshead Revisited* PBS bullshit!!!

Either Melvin had lost his fucking mind or my black ass was in the wrong theater! As it turned out, the man who had produced such subversive and wholly outrageous works as *Brer Soul,* the "Rated X by an all-whyte jury" *Sweet, Sweetback's Baadassss Song* (Or Another Mother's Come To Collect Some Dues), *Ain't Supposed To Die A Natural Death* and the novel, *The True American*; as well as conquered Wall Street, and sired *New Jack City* director Mario Van Peebles, had written a musical adaptation of *Vanity Fair,* entitled *Becky.*

To my own surprise, not being an Anglophile, I found the experience quite enjoyable, and thought the musical would be an enlightening treat for Broadway theatergoers.

At the time of this interview, Melvin was just completing a draft of the script for *Panther,* the film directed by his son. We opened the interview with a discussion of health and jogging.

MELVIN: . . . I'm the world's greatest degenerate but I discovered a sly secret long ago: if you keep a modicum of sensibility about what you do, you can really eat shit. I hate running. I hate exercise. But I manage to stay in great shape, which allows you to do a lot of other things.

I like greasy food. And *rice*. You can keep the rest. That's all I'm interested in. That's what I eat so I have to pay the price. I'm up at five o'clock in the morning. Five-thirty I'm out of here.

DARIUS: Over the telephone, you said you started out as a writer. *The Story of a Three-Day Pass* was based on a novel you had written in France. And you were able to get your director's license there as a result. Had you written other novels prior to that?

MELVIN: Yeah.

Melvin leaves the room and comes back with a photo book on cable cars in San Francisco.

DARIUS: You used to be a cable-car operator in San Francisco?

MELVIN: Yeah.

DARIUS: And *The Big Cart* was your first book?

MELVIN: Yeah.

DARIUS: What years were you employed as a cable-car operator?

MELVIN: That would be about 1957. I was about twenty-five, twenty-six.

DARIUS: How long did you do this for?

MELVIN: I guess about a year.

DARIUS: So you came out of Chicago with aspirations of being a writer or a filmmaker?

MELVIN: *Oh, no no no no no no no!*

I came out of Chicago with aspirations of getting away. Just to get away from home. You didn't graduate out of the schools I came out of. You had to be big enough to climb over the walls.

I just left home and went to college. I didn't know sophisticated things like SATs or this, that and the other. Nobody in my family ever went to college. I didn't know that these cats passing out these tests were going to be giving me scores and stuff. [Warm chuckle.]

There was a nice guy who talked to me once when I was in

Courtesy of Photofest.

Watermelon Man

(1970)
[On Video]
DIRECTOR: Melvin Van Peebles; SCREEN-WRITER: Herman Raucher; MUSIC: Melvin Van Peebles.
CAST: Godfrey Cambridge.

Melvin's first Hollywood feature is a turnaround on the minstrel tradition with lead Godfrey Cambridge in whyte-face makeup: suburbo-businessman wakes up, stares in the mirror, screams in horror and reaches for a jar of Ro-Zol bleaching cream.

And it was not the first time Cambridge donned whyteface for a switcheroo coonshow. In 1961, at N.Y.C.'s St. Mark's Playhouse, he was a cast member of the original American production of Jean Genet's *The Blacks: a clown show.*

Sweet Sweetback's Baadasssss Song

(1971)
[On Video]
PRODUCER/DIRECTOR/SCREENWRITER/MUSIC:
Melvin Van Peebles.
CAST: Melvin Van Peebles (Sweetback); Simon Chuckster (Beetle); Hubert Scales (Mu-Mu); John Dullaghan (Commissioner); Rhetta Hughes (Old Girlfriend); Mario and Megan Van Peebles.

> You bled my momma . . .
> You bled my poppa . . .
> but you *won't* bleed me!

In February 1970, something was troubling Melvin Van Peebles—an idea lurked in the shadows of his brain waiting for the coast to clear. So, to seduce the muse with an experimental crash method for his UP-FRONT AIMS PROGRAM, Melvin hopped into his car and drove into the Mojave desert. He said he had this thing about "communing with (himself) in the bosom of wilderness."

He turns off the highway, driving over the rise of a hill. He parks the car, gets out and squats down facing the sun. Then, unzipping his fly, he whips out his weenie and starts to *pound his pud*! They had electro-shock, he reasoned. Why not *semen*-shock?

He'd even seen this jive-ass movie once where this doctor used racial-shock. Called a cripple a *nigger!* And the cripple couldn't get out his wheelchair fast enough to beat the doctor with a crutch!

college. I was having financial trouble, you know? I had a partial scholarship and I mopped floors and things like that. This guy gave me seventy-five dollars a month just to study. That was great!

Except when I got out of college, he said: "Okay, now you're in the *Air Force!*"

I was in the R.O.T.C.! It was peace time and I didn't think there would be any more trouble. *Right!*

I was out of college thirteen days and I went into the Air Force as an officer. When I was twenty, I was already an officer. You didn't have to stay in long, just eighteen months.

They kept me three-and-a-half years. I learned the hard way.

DARIUS: Is the Air Force where you learned photographic and motion picture skills?

MELVIN: No. No, nothing like that. I was in radar for a bombardier navigator on a jet bomber. You see *Dr. Strangelove*?

DARIUS: Yeah.

MELVIN: That's what I used to do.

One day, I got tired of being inside. I lived in Mexico for awhile, where I was a portrait painter. Then I came back to the States. Even though I had a high specialty, the airlines wouldn't allow minorities into the cockpit so I ended up doing your basic old manual labor driving cable cars. And riding cable cars, people got on saying [speaking in the voice of a castrato Mickey Mouse], "Oooh! Oooh! Look at this! Isn't this wonderful! I wish I knew more about this!"

I thought, *hmmmmmm . . .*

So I wrote an article and the article grew. I had taken some pictures and I put them all into a book and I published the book.

One day, somebody got on the cable car and said, "Oh, this is a marvelous book. How did you do this?"

"Well, I put some biography here and a photograph there . . ."

"Oh!" she said. "It's just like a film. You're a director!"

"Is that what that is?"

Hmmmmm . . . so I made a movie. I made my first movie in 'fifty-seven.

DARIUS: What was it called?

MELVIN: There were three of them, each shorts—I thought they were features. Each one turned out to be eleven minutes long.

I was trying to do features. I knew nothing. *Nothing!* You can't even understand how *nothing* nothing is!

When I said to the guy, "I want to make a film," and the cat said, "Well . . ."

Let's see if I remember what he said.

"Do you want to make it in sixteen or thirty-five?"

"What's that?"

"Millimeter."

"What's that?"

"Two feet or one foot wide."

"Which is better?"

"Thirty-five is more professional but I have a sixteen millimeter camera."

"So how long is a feature?" I had been going to triple features all my life.

"About ninety minutes."

"How much would that cost?"

"I don't know."

So I added it up and figured I could make a feature for five hundred dollars. That was the cost of ninety minutes of film.

I didn't know anything about shooting a film sixteen to one or ten to one or none of that shit. Then I forgot you had to develop film. And I didn't know you needed a work print. All I can say is that after I did one thing he would say, "Well, aren't you gonna put sound on it?"

And I would go, "Oh shit!"

That's all I could say.

"Oh shit! Oh shit!"

And my car—"Oh shit!" I haven't had a car since. My wife—"Oh shit!"—and I weren't getting along. All I could do was go—*"Oh shit! Oh shit! Oh shit! Oh shit!"*

When I finished those films, I took them down to Hollywood. I asked them for a job. They said, "Yeah, we can offer you a job."

So there's Melvin crouched against his car in the Mojave desert, jacking his johnson.

"Yum-yum (pound, pound), yum-yum (pound) . . . Yum-yum (pound, change hands, pound)."

"WHAM, SHAZAM . . . the muse had rolled the stone away from the cave . . . *I was going to do my OWN movie.*" [Italics mine]

What do I want to accomplish with my script? he asked himself. Answer: to take another step towards getting the Man's foot out of our collective asses. The first beachhead was to reconquer our own minds.

"The biggest obstacle to the Black revolution in America is our conditioned susceptibility to the white man's program. In short, violated, confused and drained by this colonization . . . from this brutal, calculated genocide, the most effective and vicious racism has grown, and . . . the intention [is] to reverse the process."

He decided on the direct approach. His *own* movie was going to be "about a brother getting the Man's foot out of his ass"; realizing if "Brer is bored, he's bored. One of the problems we must face squarely is that to attract the masses we have to produce work that not only instructs but entertains."

The film inspired by his blob of desert-spent jism is the parable of a modern black fugitive/runaway slave told in the raw, liberating language of a poet-warrior, the highly regarded (and "Rated X By An All-White Jury") *Sweet Sweetback's Baadasssss Song*—"dedicated to all the Brothers and Sisters who have had enough of The Man."

New York Times film critics cut the fool trying to figure out what this semen-spewing Black man was up to. ". . . Behind this busy technique is a slight, *pale* [Italics mine] escape drama, about a black man"—Canby

"A disgraceful and blasphemous parade of brilliantly precise stereotyping . . ."—Clayton Riley [a black commentator]

But *The New York Times* could kiss Van Peebles's happy black ass. None other than Huey P. Newton himself came out in full support of the film, devoting an entire issue of *The Black Panther* to the film's revolutionary implications (a guerrilla filmmaker, like any other kind of guerrilla fighter, needs the support of the masses to win in revolution). And *Sweetback* went on to gross $4,100,000 dollars, which doesn't include the additional revenue from the movie's soundtrack and book tie-in.

Hollywood didn't waste any time churning out the excretions of its brainless machine—both exploiting the untapped black movie-going market and inverting the revolutionary precedents set by the film in the process.

But that was then and this is now. As the movie says at its conclusion—"A BAADASSSSS NIGGER IS COMING BACK TO COLLECT SOME DUES."

Dig?

"Really?"

"As an elevator operator."

"What do you mean? I want to *direct!*"

"Well, we'll get you a job dancing."

"*Dancing?* What the fuck I want with *dancing?*"

At that juncture, I went back to my second love, astronomy. I had been a celestial navigator along with my radar and physics and astronomy and all that crap. And I moved to Holland to study for my Ph.D. in astronomy.

On my way there, I had these films under my arm. I came here to New York to catch the boat because I couldn't afford a plane. Some guy took the films on rental and happened to show them in France.

And they said—"Jesus! This man's a genius! Where is he? He should be making films!"

"I think he's at the Cinémathèque!"

They didn't have Cinémathèques then like they do now. There was only one in France. The Cinémathèque wrote me a nice postcard, saying, *What are you doing? You should be making films!*

So I went to France. And they rolled out the red carpet. They took me to a screening room, showed my films. They came downstairs at the Champs Elysées. It was about nine o'clock at night. It was dark.

"It's wonderful! You're a genius!"

Everybody kissed me on both cheeks and drove off down the Champs Elysées. Left me with two cans of film, wet cheeks and not a fuckin' penny in my pocket.

DARIUS: And that's when you got a job translating *Mad* magazine into French.

MELVIN: I had to learn how to speak French first.

DARIUS: But, initially, weren't you writing in French?

MELVIN: Initially, I was begging.

I couldn't play an instrument so I got a kazoo. My big numbers were "La Bamba" and "Take Me, Tammy."

You know what's being said in the music magazines and all, this crap about how I invented rap? What happened was when I got back to the States, I was really taken by the fact that there were no protest songs by our folks. It was all Bob Dylan and Joan Baez.

DARIUS: There's Odetta . . .

MELVIN: They're singing the same songs but they weren't writing them the same way. There was Odetta and Richie Havens and so forth.

When I did it, what I wanted to say, the form didn't fit. So I said, "What the fuck, I'll do my own form."

At the time, people didn't know what to call it. "Well, it's spoken poetry." *No no no no no!*

In fact, there's a German term for it. It's called *sprachgesang.*[2] Each song I had done was a monologue and made up the play *Ain't Supposed To Die A Natural Death*–which did theatrically what *Sweetback* did cinematically. It broke a lot of barriers for us.

And also what happened was that the revolutionary message was pre-empted and became counter-revolutionary—subliminally counter-revolutionary—without people ever realizing. And it was still being hawked as a revolutionary message, i.e., *Shaft.*

Nothing like that had ever happened before *Sweetback.*

Being self-taught had its advantages. Since it was all new to me, I just did it the way I felt it should be done. Have you ever heard any of my early records?

DARIUS: Yeah. They used to play them on WYBC in New Haven on Sunday afternoons. As I thumb through your books, I realize that this kind of work isn't really being done anymore. It had real impact. It was extremely influential. There were a number of people, including yourself, who were working in this radical mode. And it seems to have disappeared.

MELVIN: That got pre-empted into the full politicism of current rap and the almost-retro eighties macho attitude that's now been taken and passed back to young people.

[2]Germany has a tradition of this, popularized by Brecht's *Threepenny Opera*, a gansta rap play based on the work of an eighteenth century Englishman.

DARIUS: In *Sweetback,* I thought what you were able to accomplish filmically was what The Last Poets were able to do orally. *Sweetback* is urban visual-poem.

MELVIN: That's why it's called *A Baadasssss Song.* My stuff predates The Last Poets. I did that. And I knew The Last Poets. They began to use that form and it was great. The music to *Ain't Suppose To Die . . .* pre-dated *Sweetback.*

You see, I was always good at guerrilla warfare. I did not have enough money to do theater. I did not have enough money to do a double album, so I talked people into letting me do one album. Through the album, I then sold it as a play. I just did it step by step. None of this was immediate.

That's the deal. Learn how to do that.

Now, of course, there's a price. You're talking about my books and all. I own those things, the copyrights, etc.

Most people don't even know I'm a writer. Most people think of me as a filmmaker. Some people think of me as something else, or theater people think of me as a theater man. But I'm primarily just a writer who got tired of getting dissed.

And *hmmmmm* . . . I figured there's got to be a way of figuring this thing out and I did. Step by step.

For example, it's when somebody says you can. Like when my first book was compared to a movie.

DARIUS: One of the things that impressed me about the *Sweetback* phenomenon was the fact that Huey Newton devoted an entire issue of the Black Panther Party's newspaper to it when it first came out.

MELVIN: When all the niggas was running for cover, behind walls an' shit, vis-à-vis the Panthers, I was saying the Panthers were great.

Melvin walks off and returns with an album. He points to a caption on the back. It reads, Free Huey.

MELVIN: My first album *Brer Soul.* This was long before *Sweetback.* All the lyrics are printed on the album. I got a phone call one day from a guy working at some bad boys schools here in New York.

He said, "We've been trying to teach kids to read, and with your album they're reading because they're interested in what the words say."

Melvin plays the album for me. Backed by minimalist Mingus–like music, it is "spoken-word" performance at its raw best. No detachable MTV-penis here. This is the real shit.

DARIUS: This is amazing. When *Brer Soul* came out with your Free Huey comment, what happened?

MELVIN: That was my thing. I didn't know of the Panthers or anything else. Everybody was ducking for cover. Those people who had a chance to say something weren't saying it. And I didn't give a shit.

They said I was going to lose sales but what's it all about, Alfie? You know what I mean? I'm saying what needs to be done. Later, I was able to get contracts but this was before *Sweetback*.

DARIUS: A recurring theme in this discussion is that you present a particular kind of message in your work that is constantly co-opted and switched. Do you want to talk about that?

MELVIN: I think it was great marketing strategy.

They said, "Oh no, we want to make money but we don't want this message. So how can we circumvent the message and still keep enough of this stuff on the level?"

I don't think much of this happens on a conscious level. And the golden rule is he who has the gold makes the rules.

When I had a three-picture deal with Columbia Pictures, after *Watermelon Man,* I wouldn't do it. I wanted to say what I wanted to say.

They wouldn't do *Sweetback* and I realized I needed a studio to produce this movie. So, one day, I looked in the mirror, shaving. And I said, "Melvin, this is your studio."

DARIUS: Over the years, how have you struggled with the problem of mainstreaming your work? Bleaching it out?

MELVIN: I don't have any problems with that. *I can't do it!*
Do you know my book *The True American*?

DARIUS: I've only come across it quite recently.

MELVIN: With *The True American,* for example, someone came to Paris and heard that there was this American working in the French newspapers.

Just to jump back for a second. What happened with me standing on the Champs Elysées with two wet cheeks, I just hustled my way around Paris. Begging.

And little by little, I began to know a few people. But I decided very early on that I wouldn't hang with Americans because Americans were the same as they were here. And I discovered there's a French law that says a French writer could have a temporary director's card.

So I made myself a French writer. I wrote a book. *A Bear for the FBI.* I had it translated into French and I was trying to get it published.

I was walking down the street one day and heard somebody say, "I don't think that's right . . ."

Who the hell is this? I thought.

I looked around and I was alone and I realized I had said it. I had read the headlines of a French newspaper. I didn't know I could read French. All of a sudden, I was reading the headlines.

It was about a murder. It sounded fishy to me. So I went and talked to the head of this magazine, sort of like a French *Newsweek,* to let me go and investigate.

And I went out and got a scoop!

Almost got murdered, found out this, that and the other thing. It was like a bad movie! Catching the train going out of the station and all that. A big investigation.

And before it could be covered up, I discovered it all. What I had discovered was so important it was used in the transcript of the trial.

After that, the people who had been throwing me out the door the day before began asking, "Didn't you have a book?"

So they took another look.

Then a guy came to me and asked me to write a book. He was interested in an American who wrote a book. He didn't know that I was Black. And he freaked.

He said, "Well, we should be able to do business. Write me a book. A Black book."

"So what's a Black book?"

"They're usually written in the third person."

Then he started to describe the killings of white Europeans, saying I needed to include a certain amount of rage.

So I wrote *The True American. And he got pissed off and wouldn't publish it.*

Consumed by Corporate America, and regurgitated by a world-wide fast-foot chain, Black private investigator John Shaft, munching a lettuce- and tomato-packed bun, returns to television in the bilious mold of a hamburger huckster. In the background, you can almost hear Isaac Hayes sing, *"He's a Whopper lovin' Black Dick no one understands because he likes his meat steam broiled . . . !"*

So, To Increase This Tome's Dubious Commercial Prospects For St. Martin's Marketing Wizards, I Offer A Trifle Entitled:

"SHAFT BITES THE WHOPPER!!!"

I don't wanna write about *Shaft*. Or its sequels.

Why? Simple. *I ain't got shit to say about da mutha-fucka!*

So, with the idea of discovering something unique to say about *Shaft*, I began by noodling over an essay concerning one of the few *Shaft* novels unlikely to ever appear on the miniscreen of your local shopping mall, the unreadable 1972 Dial publication—*Shaft Among The Jews*! (I realized I was wasting my time with this so-called "novel" when, after a group of Hasidim enters his badly decorated office, Shaft asks himself, *"Since when did cowboys start speaking Yiddish and wearing braids?*") My aborted essay included a treatment updating the novel for a contemporary reading audience, entitled—

Shaft Among
The Jews—*Again!*

While lounging on the roof of his West Village brownstone one night, with the head of a collagen-lipped blonde bobbing in the cleft of his burr-napped thighs, Black private investigator John Shaft absently stares up at the stars with a yawn. His eyes widen in disbelief.

Hovering eighty yards above his head was a silver, egg-shaped disk.

Emitting a succession of low-pitched beeps, the craft lands on the roof of the neighboring brownstone. Its doors open with an eerie electronic wheeze. Its metal staircase unfolds in a series of precise metallic clicks.

Encircled by a nimbus of magnetic blue light with his arms thrown open for embrace, Minister Louis Farrakhan steps through the disk's open portals, exclaiming, *"Shaft, my brother!"*

Farrakhan stands on the building's ledge, suddenly floating across the space separating the two dwellings; and—as the wrinkled elf's cap of Shaft's uncircumcised cock showers the blonde in a gob of thick grayish droplets—he orders the P.I. to give up eating pork and fucking whyte women.

Shaft breaks into a sweat, his eyes goggling with panic. He had *no* intention of abstaining from his two favorite varieties of whyte meat. As Farrakhan drifts down to the roof, he hands Shaft a briefcase full of money. The blonde vaporizes into a fine mist.

"Shaft, my brother! I have just returned from another of my many unearthly visitations with the Honorable Elijah Muhammad—*who,* as we all know, did not *die,* but *lives on* as a cosmic messenger of Allah, transversing the galaxies in the belly of a Great Wheel. Or what we on earth call a flying saucer!

"Standing inside the Great Wheel, I listened to the master's voice, learning many wise, wondrous things—*things* that will all be made clear to our people one day. But for now, I have been sent on a mission as his representative here on earth.

"It has a Black hero, but don't confuse that with a message— it's for fun!"
—*Shaft* press booklet

Shaft

(1971)
[On Video]
DIRECTOR: Gordon Parks; SCREENWRITERS: Ernest Tidyman, John D.F. Black; STORY: based on Ernest Tidyman's novel; MUSIC: Isaac Hayes.
CAST: Richard Roundtree (John Shaft); Moses Gunn (Bumpy Jonas); Christopher St. John (Ben Buford); Drew Bundini Brown (Willie); Arnold Johnson (Cul); and Antonio Fargas (Bunky).

Shaft was Gordon Parks's second feature after the beautifully shot but stiff *The Learning Tree,* based on his novel about his Kansas childhood. Parks is an accomplished human being—photographer, writer and composer. In 1942, he was named Julius Rosenwald fellow in photography. Later—after a documentary on the plight of farmers for the Farm Security Administration, working at the Office of War Information in W.W.II and a five-year stint at New Jersey's Standard Oil Company—he joined the staff of *Life* magazine as a photojournalist. One of his most famous photo-stories was on a young Brazilian named Flavio, who would be the subject of one of Parks's short films. His other shorts include *The Diary of a Harlem Family* and *The World of Piri Thomas,* the author of *Down These Mean Streets.*

But in spite of all that, I thought *Shaft* was actually pretty dull stuff for a Hollywood actioner—including the color scheme of the man's wardrobe, a drab beige (though master trumpeteer Flip Barnes argues, "It's an African thing! Earth tones an' shit!"). Ask me and I'll tell you the movie's over after Antonio Fargas does his Bunky the Junky "I don't know Ben Bufus" bit.

"The Honorable Elijah Muhammad said to me, 'Brother Louis! I *need* that Black Dick, the great John Shaft! Go out and find that bad mother (**"Shut-yo'-mouth, Mr. Muhammad!"** I interjected.)! Hire him to discreetly investigate the holdings of the JDL—*I need to know where them Jews be hidin' all they money!!!'*

"So, Brother Shaft, will you assist us? The future of our people depends on it!"

With a handshake and an embrace, Shaft accepts the assignment. Farrakhan begins to rise, his feet dangling awkwardly in the air.

As Farrakhan floats towards the craft, backstepping through the wall of the NOI mothership's metallic hull with the translucence of The Ghost of Christmas Past, he speaks his last words with a benevolent smile.

"Find the Jews' money," he said, "and you find the money that *rightfully* belongs in the coffers of our people's reparations account!!"

The NOI mothership disappears into a cluster of stars.

With Farrakhan lost in space, listening to Elijah Muhammad's disembodied voice as if he were Sun Ra interpreting the music of the spheres, Shaft finds himself caught in the crossfire of Fruit of Islam muscle-boys, JDL Kahane fanatics, Afrocentric space aliens and the umbrella-wielding, blue-haired old ladies of the Haddassah cabal (*"C'mon, girls! Time to kick some Schwvartze butt!!"*).

Then I gave some thought to the notion that Shaft was an "enpowering" descendant of Richard Wright's Bigger Thomas and realized that line of thinking was a crock of shit. Rudy Ray Moore's *Dolemite* had more in common with Bigger Thomas than *Shaft*. *Shaft* simply adhered to the cliché-ridden conventions of the hard-boiled whyte boys of pulp fiction.

I manufactured excuses aplenty to avoid a lengthy discussion of the character and the movies. I scowled, kicked and screamed but nothing I could say or do would overshadow the glare of publishing's bottom line: *$$$.*

And, just like you, I need it. Plenty of it.

As I'm considerably more than reluctant to expend my energies contriving some cockeyed gibberish on the popularity of *Shaft* (though some charge my "reluctance" is due to a lethargy rivaling the molasses-slow movements of Stepin Fetchit), this throws the legitimacy of anything I might have to say about blaxploitation into serious question[3]; but, if it isn't obvious by now, I should clarify, *I didn't write this book to position myself as an authority on the genre.* I wrote this to have fun. This book was never intended to be anything more than a satiric, trade-edition fanzine for the unacknowledged masses of Video-Dreads who like to drop acid and program home videofests on Friday nights.

Of course, there are plenty of others out there more than willing to wallow in the dung heaps of American pop culture analyzing the enigma of John Shaft. I'm just not one of them. The movies bore me senseless. Each time the heads of my VCR are sullied by cassettes of *Shaft, Shaft's Big Score* or *Shaft in Africa,* I fall into a deep, nearly narcotic sleep.

Yet, according to my editor, St. Martin's sales reps won't be able to move this baby unless it includes an essay on *Shaft* because that's the full extent of what they know about the genre (as if the sum total of the genre's meaning and importance is exemplified by this "savvy" Black dick); and that they were probably unaware of not only the other two films, but the short-lived CBS television series (eight installments) and the group of Ernest Tidyman novels (*Shaft, Shaft's Big Score, Shaft Has A Ball* and the aforementioned *Shaft Among The Jews*) the character is based on. If this book didn't include my opinion of John Shaft, I was told, the book buyer for your local bookstore would not stock *That's Blaxploitation!* on their shelves.

[3]After all, doesn't the exploitation of the Black ticket-buying public by a major Hollywood studio begin with the release of *Shaft?* Some might argue it began with *Sweetback* because of the publicity and money generated by its brilliant one-man marketing strategy. I would disagree. *Sweetback* is an independent, anti-Hollywood film. In all respects it is a subversive work of art. With *Sweetback,* Van Peebles formulated a highly individual cinematic vocabulary; so much so, its narrative seems almost secondary to its cacophonous poetic vision. Though the film established the market for Black moviegoers, and Van Peebles made money (in fact, according to the July 1994 issue of *Premiere* magazine, *Sweetback* grossed more money than *Shaft. Sweetback* sold 9,300,000 tickets to *Shaft's* 8,500,000), his artistic courage clearly demonstrates that his motives were not solely determined by financial greed. *Sweetback* only staked the territory. It was Hollywood that exploited it. For MGM, *Shaft* was a controlled risk. MGM didn't throw a lot of money at *Shaft* or Gordon "first black director hired by a major studio" Parks, Sr. The budget was $1,543,000—a "small" picture by Hollywood standards, even then. The result was a conventional action film for general audiences, enlivened by its Black cast members. In my view, the first true blaxploitation film was American International's *Slaughter,* which also bites.

PROFILE: RICHARD ROUNDTREE

Roundtree described himself as an introverted child with little faith in his ability to do anything.

"We often have that wall, that barrier which prevents us from believing in ourselves and our ability to do things. All of us suffered from what I call, for lack of a better phrase, a slave mentality."

Playing high school football changed all that.

". . . (It) meant something. People said nice things about me and that meant a lot. The whole thing of the newspapers, and the publicity, and feeling of self-worth felt good. The desire to keep that feeling alive is probably what caused me to start modeling and eventually acting."

It was while working as a salesman at the toney New York clothing store, Barney's, that he ventured into modeling. He was hired by the annual *Ebony* Fashion Fair, sponsored by Johnson publications (*Jet, Ebony*), touring seventy-nine cities in ninety days.

At the suggestion of Bill Cosby, Roundtree joined Robert Hooks's Negro Ensemble Company in New York. It was during a Philadelphia run of *The Great White Hope* that he was up for the role of *Shaft.* He had three callbacks. On the fourth he did a screen test.

Courtesy of Photofest.

Courtesy of the George Trow Estate.

Courtesy of the George Trow Estate.

Courtesy of the George Trow Estate.

Shaft Factoids

Shaft Factoid: Bumpy's bodyguard Willie was played by Drew Bundini Brown, Muhammad Ali's assistant trainer, who is credited with creating the line "Float like a butterfly, sting like a bee."

Shaft Factoid: Before his screen debut as John Shaft, Richard Roundtree had appeared in only one film—Alan "Candid Camera" Funt's *What Do You Say to a Naked Lady?* He was in it for one minute. He had no lines.

Shaft Factoid: Richard Roundtree once recorded an album of songs released under the title: *The Man Called Shaft.*

Frankly, as in most honkoid owned and operated companies profiting from the work of Black artists, the sales reps simply lack the vocabulary for selling "black" product, especially the kind of psychotic blather I write. It can find ways of marketing to an audience geeked out on *Gilligan's Island* and *The Brady Bunch* but a cult book for the sensibilities of Afro Acidheads?

Forget it!

Shaft and *Shaft's Big Score* are on video. You can rent them and form your own opinion. For all I care, you can use the cassettes as a convenient surface to chop a mound of cheap cocaine. What I think about *Shaft,* or any other film in this book for that matter, don't mean shit.

If, for instance, Siskel and Ebert gave *Shaft* a big thumbs down, and you happened to enjoy the film, as far as you're concerned, Siskel and Ebert can plug their thumbs up their hemorrhoid-knotted asses (I'd love to receive a note from Siskel and Ebert reading, "How dare you! Our rectums are unblemished pink puckers! *And here're the photos to prove it!*").

So, since sizable royalty checks are useful to perpetually penniless boholit types like myself, I've written—for the sole benefit of the St. Martin's "sales dept."—*Shaft Bites The Whopper.*

Now, St. Martin's sales force can goose step into your local bookstore, confidently stare the store's bookbuyer in the eye and say, "Dat's blaxploitation's be talkin' 'bout dat bad mutha shut yo' mouth—*John Shaft!*"

"One of the great disservices of western civilization that does us no favors at all," Michael O'Donoghue told me one Sunday afternoon as he sat curled on the sofa in the chandeliered living room of his Chelsea condo, sipping smoke from the gold-tipped filter of a Sobraine Black Russian cigarette, "is that mask you see in theater—the two Greek masks, comedy and tragedy—*as if there was any fuckin' difference between one and the other!*

"Things can be both funny and not-funny at the same time. You don't need to separate between the two. They're both basically the same thing."

As dawn broke on the morning of October 7, 1994, Michael O'Donoghue, two-time Emmy Award–winning *Saturday Night Live* writer, and originator of the darkly charming character "Mr. Mike," awoke with what he believed was simply another of the migraines that had tormented him throughout his life. He got out of bed, went to his bathroom and took some medication to relieve the pain.

Later, he awoke a second time exclaiming, *"Oh my God!!"*

His wife, Cheryl Hardwicke, in the bed beside him, reported that his eyes were the color of blood and that she could see bolts of "lightning flash behind his eyeballs." She immediately telephoned EMS.

In the ambulance on the way to St. Vincent's Hospital, Michael went into a convulsive seizure. Three hours later, a doctor informed Ms. Hardwicke that Michael had suffered a massive cerebral hemorrhage. He was now officially "brain dead." His body was put on life support, his organs donated to children.

Speaking of the dean of American satire, Michael O'Donoghue once wrote, "If there was a Mt. Rushmore of modern American humor, Terry Southern would be the mountain they carve it on." The same can certainly be said of Michael. Quite simply, Michael O'Donoghue was the single best satiric mind this country had to offer. His death was as shocking and bizarre as the art he devoted himself to in life. For all of us who loved and admired him, his death, like his humor, had turned our lives upside down. It was, as he once said in Mr. Mike persona to Garrett Morris's wizened Uncle Remus, *"There's no moral, Uncle Remus, just random acts of meaningless violence."*

Michael is best known for his work on *Saturday Night Live* (a show, he said of its recent years, that "couldn't suck more if it wore a pair of rubber lips") where he reinvented the nature and tenets of televised sketch-comedy with a courage, intelligence and integrity of comic vision painfully lacking in the medium in general, and *SNL* in particular, twenty-one years later.

After he left *SNL,* with two brief but financially lucrative returns (leaving on both occasions under a cloud of controversy because of two of his sketches: *The Last Days in Silverman's Bunker* (written with Nelson Lyons) and *The Good Excuse,* the latter set in a Nazi death camp (See: RED TAPE #7), he co-scripted a number of screenplays, among

Courtesy of the George Trow Estate.

Shaft's Big Score

(1972)
[On Video]
DIRECTOR: Gordon Parks; SCREENWRITER: Ernest Tidyman; MUSIC: Gordon Parks
CAST: Richard Roundtree (John Shaft); Moses Gunn (Bumpy Jonas); Drew Bundini Brown (Willy); Julius W. Harris (Capt. Bollin); and Gordon Parks (Croupier).

Not with me he didn't.

them *War of the Insect Gods* (a giant cockroach invasion film); *The Planet of the Cheap Special Effects; Biker Heaven* (a.k.a. *Easy Rider II* with Nelson Lyons and Terry Southern); and, with Mitch Glazer, the Bill Murray vehicle *Scrooged.*

With the unbridled wit and irreverence that typified all of his work, Michael established himself first as a star at *The National Lampoon.* At *The Lampoon,* in addition to writing numerous articles, short stories and comic strips, he co-wrote *The National Lampoon's Radio Dinner* album and produced *The National Lampoon's Radio Hour* radio show. He landed at *The Lampoon* after instigating a national obsession with Pet Rocks due to a slim volume he published entitled *The Story of the Rock.* At the time of the book's publication, Michael was the sardonic ringmaster of The Electric Circus' hashish-fueled happenings, and a contributing editor at *The Evergreen Review.* Under the editorship of Fred Jordan, *The Evergreen Review* gave Michael his first exposure in a national magazine. Among the things he wrote for its pages were *The Liberal Book* ("Liberals will actually pay money to hear Leroi Jones speak!"); *Cowgirls At War*; and the corpse-driven comic strip serial *The Adventures Of Phoebe Zeitgeist* (a character later resurrected by Werner Fassbinder in his play *Blood On A Cat's Neck*). Michael came to *The Evergreen Review* from San Francisco, where he wrote, edited and published a small literary journal called *Renascence,* publishing the likes of Charles Bukowski, and financed through the patronage of Bishop Pike. During the last year of his life, his work sparkled on the last page of *Spin* magazine in a column called *Not My Fault!*

It is to Bob Guccione, Jr.'s credit that he gave Michael's work a home when no one else would.

Michael once said he looked on life not with a jaundiced eye but a cancerous one. The first time Michael and I spoke was over a plate of clams casino fifteen years ago. He had just completed post-production on *Mr. Mike's Mondo Video.* It was during that talk he hinted at the origins of his "cancerous" vision. It lay in the childhood he spent in upstate Sauquoit, New York.

During his childhood, Michael confessed, he was unable to cry. The most automatic and natural thing in the world, but he couldn't do it; he had never figured out how. If he hurt himself, he would sit with the pain trapped inside, rocking back and forth with his hands clasped around his knees, frowning in anger at his own inability to let go and let the tears flow.

Finally, it was his mother who provided the perfect solution to his dilemma. She would sit, hold him and make him laugh.

"—*as if there was any fuckin' difference between one and the other!*"

"It's very easy to make people laugh," he said that same Sunday afternoon in his Chelsea living room, flicking the ash from the head of his Sobraine Black Russian. "That's not the point. It's very difficult to make people *think*. Art is the cake. Comedy is the frosting. The trick is to get them to eat the cake."

Original Shaft is one of the many sketches Michael wrote for *Saturday Night Live* that was never produced on the show. It was written for *SNL*'s first season with Chevy Chase in mind. This explains the absurdity of a button-down whyteman claiming he's Richard Roundtree—which seems like more than enough reason to check into the Betty Ford Clinic. Let a whyteman like that go too far, he'll start claiming, "Fred Williamson stole my dick!" and "I snorted a line of dried smegma scraped off of Richard Pryor's balls! What a *freeze! I couldn't feel my face for a month!*"

[Michael's handwritten note falls here. It reads: "DARIUS—THIS NEEDS EDITING—TIGHTENING. FUMETTI WOULD WORK AND I'D REWRITE FOR THAT FORM. BUT ANYWAY, THIS'LL GIVE YOU THE IDEA.—M.O'D.]

Courtesy of Photofest.

Shaft in Africa

(1973)
DIRECTOR: John Guillermin; SCREENWRITER: Stirling Silliphant; STORY: based on characters created by Ernest Tidyman.
CAST: Richard Roundtree (John Shaft) and Vonetta McGee (Aleme).

Last installment of the *Shaft* trilogy before it was launched as a short-lived CBS series. Same director and screenwriter who slapped together Dino De-Laurentiis's *King Kong* remake. Makes you wonder if Dino saw this on their résumés and thought they were the most qualified to redo the big monkey.

ORIGINAL SHAFT
(Coming Attraction)

FADE IN:

INT. OFFICE—DAY

We see Richard Roundtree standing in a late-60s office furnished with stylish modern furniture and a few black accessories such as African art.

CHEVY *(to Camera)* Hello, I'm Richard Roundtree. Perhaps you saw me in *Shaft,* the story of a black detective who goes up against the mob and shoots about five hundred white people in the face. But how many of you have seen the original *Shaft*, first made in 1934? Let's take a look at this classic of the black cinema . . .

FADE OUT:

(The original *Shaft*, although it has the look and style of an old movie trailer made in 1934, roughly parodies the black exploitation films of the late 60s/early 70s. It is in SEPIA. The Richard Roundtree top is in full, contemporary COLOR. The *Shaft* trailer might have a few scratches on FILM.)

MUSIC is dated, period orchestration and arrangement of the typical driving, black exploitation film background music. The Narrator should have that tough, cutting, black "Adolph Caesar" type of voice.

All action takes place in 1934, the year this trailer was made. Try to avoid cheap nostalgia like pixs of Roosevelt and NRA Eagles. Shaft works for the boss, a rich white man whose face is never seen. He owns a big fancy house where Shaft works and a big fancy limousine that Shaft drives.

FADE IN:

EXT. DRIVEWAY—DAY

We see Shaft, a black man dressed as period menial, is washing an expensive period limousine with a garden hose. Shaft talks with a slow, black accent.

NARRATOR (V.O.) Shaft is here!

SUPER "SHAFT" IN DATED LETTERING.
MUSIC STING.
LOSE SUPER.

NARRATOR (V.O.) He's out to wash your car!
CUT TO CLOSER SHOT of Shaft washing the hubcaps, smiling, he talks to OFF-CAMERA Boss.

SHAFT Ah kin see mah face in dem hubcaps, boss.

EXT. TRAIN STATION—DAY

Go to scene of Shaft trying to carry heavy old suitcases at a train station, perhaps along the platform with Pullman in background.

SFX: TRAIN STATION.

NARRATOR (V.O.) He's out to carry your bags!

SHAFT *(to OFF-CAMERA Boss)* You mus' be haulin' aroun' gold bars in dese-heah suitcases, boss.

EXT.—DAY

Shaft is shining Boss's shoes. All that can be seen of Boss is expensive pants leg and shoes.

NARRATOR (V.O.) He's out to shine your shoes!

SMILING, SHAFT TALKS TO OFF-CAMERA BOSS.

SHAFT Ah kin see mah face in dem shoes, boss.

EXT. STREETS—DAY

Go to SHOTS of limousine driven very fast, skidding around corners, just avoiding collisions with other old cars.

SFX: CAR SKIDDING.

NARRATOR (V.O.) Yes, Shaft is here!

SUPER: "SHAFT."
MUSIC: STING.
LOSE SUPER.

NARRATOR (V.O.) And he's out to please the man!

INT. CAR—DAY

CUT TO limousine interior where Shaft is driving car dressed in chauffeur's uniform. The Boss is sitting in the backseat. All that can be seen of him is his white hand with Harvard ring on back of seat. He talks with a Piping Rock accent.

BOSS (OFF-CAMERA) One more turn like that, Shaft, and you'll be back polishing the silverware.

DEATH IN THIS CASE IS A BLESSING NOT ONLY TO HIS WIFE BUT TO THE WHOLE COMMUNITY HE WAS ABSOLUTELY NO GOOD

HE OWED NOTHING BUT MONEY

Courtesy of Joy Glidden © 1995.

EXT. STREET—DAY
CUT TO the limo barely missing a collision with a trolley car.

SFX: CAR SKID.

INT. KITCHEN—DAY
Shaft is polishing silverware in large, old kitchen of mansion. Smiling, he talks to OFF-CAMERA Boss.

SHAFT Ah kin see mah face in dese-heah spoons, boss.

NARRATOR (V.O.) Sure, it's a dirty job but somebody has to do it!

EXT. LAWN—DAY
Go to scene of Shaft mowing lawn with old mower. White picket fence in background.

NARRATOR (V.O.) That's when they send for Shaft!

SUPER "SHAFT."
MUSIC: STING.
LOSE SUPER.

NARRATOR(V.O.) He's comin' down hard on your lawn!
CUT TO a TWO SHOT as DISHWAX, another Black man dressed as period menial, approaches Shaft who stops mowing and leans on the handle of his mower. Dishwax might smoke cigar.

DISHWAX Say, Shaft, ah seen a woman on de street de other day wid one side of her face entirely black.

SHAFT But, ahh, dat ain't possible, brother.

DISHWAX Sho it is, Shaft. 'Course, the other side was black, too! As Dishwax bursts into hearty laughter, CUT TO EXTREME CLOSE UP of Shaft crossing his eyes, totally nonplussed.

NARRATOR (V.O.) Shaft!

SUPER "SHAFT."
MUSIC: STING.
LOSE SUPER.

EXT. LAWN OF BIG HOUSE—DAY OR NIGHT

Go to a scene of Shaft, wearing a jockey's silks and carrying a large iron ring, tiptoeing across the lawn by an old sidewalk that leads to front door of the big house. Shaft suddenly spots someone OFF-CAMERA in the direction he is moving who frightens him.

NARRATOR (V.O.) He's caught between the mob! . . .
CUT TO P.O.V. Shaft SHOT of 3 or 4 tough period GANGSTERS pointing guns at him.

HEAD GANGSTER Freeze, nigger!
CUT TO Shaft rapidly tiptoeing across lawn in opposite direction, or backing up and then swinging around. In any case, he's surprised and frightened to spot someone OFF-CAMERA in that direction also.

NARRATOR (V.O.) . . . And the law!
CUT TO P.O.V. Shaft SHOT of 3 or 4 uniformed COPS pointing guns at him.

CHIEF COP Don't move, nigger!
CUT TO Shaft, holding ring up, frozen in position of lawn jockey by sidewalk as cops and gangsters have loud, smoky gun battle, shooting each other.

SFX: GUN SHOTS.

NARRATOR (V.O.) You'll meet his woman!

INT. KITCHEN—DAY

Go to a SHOT of fat, smiling black WOMAN dressed in 30s maid uniform and carrying a garnished ham on a tray. Takes place in kitchen.

FLOTILLA (TO CAMERA) Howdy, I'se Flotilla, the maid!

INT. SHAFT'S ROOM—DAY

Go to SHOT of Shaft in his room, a shabby servant quarters affair with faded peeling wallpaper, old radiator, whatever. Shaft, wearing only boxer shorts and a big grin, holds up his chauffeur's uniform on wire hanger with one hand, chauffeur's cap in other.

NARRATOR (V.O.) You'll see his wardrobe! (Pause a beat) You'll hear his music!

INT. BAR—NIGHT
CUT TO colorful jazzbo NEGRO playing banjo in Black bar.
MUSIC: "GOLDEN SLIPPERS"

BANJO PLAYER (singing) Oh, dem golden slippers, Oh, dem golden slippers . . .
CUT TO Shaft and Dishwax having a beer.

MUSIC: BANJO PLAYER CONTINUES TO SING AND PLAY IN BACK-GROUND.

DISHWAX Say, Shaft, do you know where de hair am curliest on women?

SHAFT Ahh, well, no, brother, where am de hair curliest on women?

DISHWAX In Africa!
As Dishwax breaks into hearty laughter, CUT TO EXTREME CLOSE UP of Shaft with eyes crossed, totally nonplussed.

NARRATOR (V.O.) Shaft!

SUPER "SHAFT."
MUSIC: STING.
LOSE SUPER.

NARRATOR (V.O.) Marks a whole new era in black awareness!

INT. CAR—DAY
Go to Shaft in uniform driving the big limo.

BOSS (OFF-CAMERA) The trouble with you jungle bunnies is—

SHAFT Ahh, boss, ahh, we doan' wanna be called "jungle bunnies" no moh.

Boss leans forward from back seat, putting hand with Harvard ring on back of Shaft's seat.

BOSS What *do* you want to be called, Shaft?

SHAFT Ahh, we wanna be called "jungle *rabbits!*"
Shaft flashes big grin to CAMERA.

NARRATOR(V.O.) Shaft!

SUPER "SHAFT."
MUSIC: STING.
LOSE SUPER.
Shaft turns back to road and spots big trouble coming up fast. He
hits the brakes.

SFX: CAR SKID.

EXT. CHICKEN COOP—DAY
CUT TO Limousine crashing right through a chicken coop, CHICK-
ENS flying everywhere. The coop EXPLODES in big multiple explo-
sions, the way every black exploitation movie trailer ends.

NARRATOR (V.O.) If you don't like what he does, don't tip him!
This is END of the '34 trailer. Use its ending MUSIC UNDER ART
CARD, however.
 CUT TO Distributor's Tag-on ART CARD, traditional lettering
against a bright background:

> WATCH FOR THE
> ORIGINAL *SHAFT*
> COMING HERE SOON!
> Distributed by Colortone Films

 SFX: Continue EXPLOSIONS under ART CARD. Should sound
like a munitions dump going up, plus a few CHICKEN SFX.

MUSIC UP AND OUT.
FADE OUT AFTER 4–5 SECONDS . . .

FRED "THE HAMMER" WILLIAMSON

....

I got the nickname because of a blow that I struck to my opponents perpendicular to the earth's latitude, trying to decapitate them and at the same time not injure myself. Thusly, and henceforth, I was named "The Hammer."

The Northwestern University Architectural Engineering graduate and former linebacker was watching *Julia* on the tube one night and noticed the title character had a new boyfriend each week.

"Shit," Fred said, "I can do that. They need somebody tall, dark and handsome like me."

So he shut down his Montreal-based architectural firm, loaded up a trailer hooked to the back of his Jag, and drove off "to Hollywood to become Diahann Carroll's boyfriend."

When he arrived, he made an appointment with Harold Kantor, a name he picked up from the show's credits; and convinced him "that I was a very talented young man and had done numerous plays in Montreal and New York . . . in reality, I didn't know shit."

Didn't matter. He appeared not only on *Julia* but on *Laugh-In* and an episode of *Star Trek*. His first feature film appearance was in Robert Altman's *M*A*S*H*. Altman needed a football player.

When it was time to shoot his scenes, and he saw that it was a crane shot, Williamson told Altman, "That's dumb. You can't film football that way. Get down. Put the camera two feet off the ground. Shoot down the line of scrimmage where you can see the guys spitting at each other and talking about each other's relatives."

So Altman let him direct the scene, though he received no on-screen credit.

His star debut was in *Hammer* followed by *The Legend of Nigger Charley* and its sequel, *The Soul of Nigger Charley*. His big hit was *Black Caesar* directed by Larry Cohen, whom he credits with teaching him how "to make movies down and dirty and fast with no money . . . I learned all these sneaky things from Larry Cohen."

Fred Williamson has either written, directed, starred in and/or produced fifty or more movies. As head of Po Boy Productions, he has this to say about his to date thirty-year career: ". . . my idea was to let Hollywood make me a marketable commodity, then to take that commodity away from them and continue it to my own benefit. So, the fact that the phone stopped ringing never really influenced me or slowed me down. By then, I had formed my own company, and had produced and directed two of my own films. Kelly, Brown and Roundtree, when the phone stopped ringing, became actors. Their superstar image was diminished to black actors, just actors. Once you do that, you're at the mercy of the dollar. You're at the mercy of the script."

Fred Williamson once owned one hundred and fifty pairs of custom-made white shoes.[4]

[4] The above quotes were taken from an excellent interview by Brett McCormick in *Psychotronic* #4.

Hammer

(1972)
PRODUCER: Al Adamson; DIRECTOR: Bruce Clark; SCREENWRITER: Charles Johnson; MUSIC: Solomon Burke.
CAST: Fred Williamson (B.J. Hammer); Bernie Hamilton (Davis); Vonetta McGee (Lois); Leon Isaac Kennedy (Bobby Williams); Mel Stewart (The Professor); D'Urville Martin (Sonny); and Al Richardson (Black Militant).

For the past twelve years, I've had this recurrent dream: upon entering the lobby of a fleapit 42nd Street multiplex with cum-stained carpets, I'm approached by two toothless dwarves bundled in fake-fur coats. They grin and ask if I want a blow job.

Standing at the concession counter, where the popcorn machine pops popcorn that smells like urine, I stare at the movie posters hanging on each of the doors along the hallway, trying to decide which film I want to see.

Most are lurid Italian shock-u-mentaries; but, among the many titles is Fred Williamson's dockworker-turned-prizefighter feature *Hammer*. And it's the door I dare not enter.

Black Caesar

(1973)
a.k.a. *The Godfather of Harlem* (British title)
[On Video]
PRODUCER/DIRECTOR/SCREENWRITER: Larry Cohen.
CAST: Fred Williamson (Tommy Gibbs); Phillip Roye (Joe Washington); Gloria Hendry (Helen); Julius W. Harris (Mr. Gibbs); Val Avery (Sal Cardoza); Minnie Gentry (Mama Gibbs); Art Lund (John McKinney); and D'Urville Martin (Reverend Rufus).

> "You tell 'em you want black actors, they send you black actors. Believe me, the door opens and they parade in. . . ."
> —Larry Cohen, *Re/Search* "Incredibly Strange Films"

According to Larry Cohen's interview in the "Incredibly Strange Films" issue of *Re/Search* magazine, *Black Caesar* was originally written for Sammy Davis, Jr. (probably as a vehicle for Sammy and his rat-pack cohorts à la *Robin and the Seven Hoods*—I can just imagine the marquee over 42nd Street: "Jerry Lewis's Black Caesar!!") but Cohen was stiffed out of a promised ten thousand dollars by Davis's manager.

But, luckily, after viewing *Bone*, Cohen's first film, American International Pics called Cohen, saying, *"You sure know how to direct those black actors!"*

Bone's one black face belonged to Yapphet Kotto.

In spite of the fact that A.I.P. head Sam Arkoff wrote in his bio, *Flying Through Hollywood by the Seat of My Pants*, that *Black Caesar* was "positioned to capitalize on the success of *The Godfather*," Cohen insists that his film is "not a black exploitation movie" (yeah, right, like A.I.P. produced anything else).

"Usually," Cohen explained, "the black guy beats up all the white people, gets the white girl, becomes successful, and it's kind of a victory of the black over the white society."

"But *Black Caesar* is a picture about a guy who tries," Cohen continues ". . . to be a white man and fails" (italics mine).

Can anyone seriously imagine Fred Williamson trying to motivate his character by muttering to himself: *"I'm a failed whyte man. I'm a failed whyte man . . . ?"*

I think not.

Even though I believe Larry Cohen should be walled up in a cell with Professor Leonard Jefferies for all eternity[S-1], and that Nicky Barnes deserves a fat check from Cohen as well as several filmmakers past and present for the rights to his life's story (the life of Harlem heroin king, Nicky Barnes, is the inspiration for many blaxploitation films), *Black Caesar* is street-swaggering entertainment concerning the rise, fall and later, in *Hell Up in Harlem*, mysterious resurrection of Tommy Gibbs with a great James Brown soundtrack.

[S-1] The title of this *No Exit*–like encounter would be *Leonard's New Girlfriend* with the tag line "When two men are walled together for life—Strange desires stir under the Kente cloth!"

Hell Up in Harlem

(1973)
[On Video]
DIRECTOR: Larry Cohen; SCREENWRITER: Larry Cohen; PRODUCER: Larry Cohen.
CAST: Fred Williamson; Gloria Hendry; Margaret Avery; Julius Harris; and D'Urville Martin.

For this, Larry Cohen should've caught hell up in Harlem.

The Legend of Nigger Charley

(1972)
DIRECTOR: Martin Goldman; STORY: James Warner Bellah; SCREENWRITERS: Larry Spangler (PRODUCER), Martin Goldman.
CAST: Fred Williamson (Nigger Charley); D'Urville Martin (Toby); and Don Pedro Colley (Joshua).

If John Brown had written *Uncle Tom's Cabin* instead of Harriet Beecher Stowe, this is the story he would have told: fugitive slaves buckwildin' in the Old West.

Soul of Nigger Charley

(1973)

PRODUCER/DIRECTOR/STORY: Larry Spangler; SCREENWRITER: Harold Stone; SONGS: Lou Rawls.

CAST: Fred Williamson (Nigger Charley); D'Urville Martin (Toby); and Nai Bonnet (Anita).

Buckwildin' action south of the border. Colonel Blanchard, and his crew of Confederates, just can't believe blacks are something more than livestock. So they hold seventy-one former slaves hostage in a Mexican labor camp. Nigger Charley got no choice but to get Nat Turner on they ass. *Star Trek*'s Lt. Uhura gives him some pussy.

Three Tough Guys

(1974)

DIRECTOR: Duccio Tessari; SCREENWRITERS: Luciano Vincenzoni, Nicola Badalucco; MUSIC: Isaac Hayes.

CAST: Lino Ventura (Father Charlie); Isaac Hayes (Lee Stevens); Fred Williamson (Joe Snake); and Paula Kelly (Fay Collins).

Hot-butter baldie, Isaac Hayes, teams with a priest to track down the clever Joe Snake, who pops a cap in Paula Kelly's shapely butt.

Boss Nigger

(1974)

a.k.a. *Boss and the Black Bounty Killer* (British title)

PRODUCER/SCREENWRITER: Fred Williamson; DIRECTOR: Jack Arnold.

CAST: Fred Williamson (Boss Nigger); D'Urville Martin (Amos); R. G. Armstrong (Mayor); William Smith (Jed Clayton); Carmen Hayworth (Clara Mae); Barbara Leigh (Miss Pruitt) and V. Phipps-Wilson (Bubbles).

An obvious rip-off of Ishmael Reed's 1969 novel *Yellow Back Radio Broke Down*.*

*Dear Mr. Williamson, this is a complicated in-joke. It is not a reflection of yr creative integrity. Please do not fly to New York and have yr lawyers beat me up.

Black Eye

(1974)

DIRECTOR: Jack Arnold; SCREENWRITERS: Mark Haggard, Jim Martin; STORY: based on the novel *Murder on the Wild Side* by Jeff Jacks; MUSIC: Mort Garson.

CAST: Fred Williamson (Shep Stone); Rosemary Forsyth (Miss Francis); Teresa Graves (Cynthia); and Floy Dean (Diane Davis).

The late Jack Arnold is best known for the 1950s sci-fi classics *It Came From Outer Space*, *The Creature From the Black Lagoon* and *The Incredible Shrinking Man*. Imagine what Arnold might have done with Fred Williamson in a black-cast remake titled *The Incredible Shrinking Negro?* It'd be kinda like watching *Welcome Home, Brother Charles* in reverse.

Bucktown

(1975)
[On Video]

EXECUTIVE PRODUCER: Ric R. Roman; PRODUCER: Bernard Schwartz; DIRECTOR: Arthur Marks; SCREENWRITER: Bob Ellison. CAST: Fred Williamson (Duke Johnson); Pam Grier (Aretha); Thalmus Rasulala (Roy); Tony King (T.J.); and Bernie Hamilton (Harley).

The United Catholic Conference condemned *Bucktown* as "vicious and mindless." *The New York Times*'s Vincent Canby called it "silly and vicious." Donald Bogle said it was "dreadful" (but this is the opinion of a man who got a bang out of *Buck Benny Rides Again*). I wondered if Fred had read Orwell's *Animal Farm*.

The corrupt law enforcers of a small, vice-ridden town are hammered out of existence by Fred and his gang of big-city-beat-'em-up-boys. The irony is that Fred's boys are more corrupt than the pigs they put out of power. *And Fred ain't havin' it!*

Adios Amigo

(1975)
[On Video]

PRODUCER-DIRECTOR-SCREENWRITER: Fred Williamson.

CAST: Fred Williamson (Big Ben); Richard Pryor (Sam Spade); Thalmus Rasulala (Noah Abraham Lincoln Brown); and James Brown.

While promoting *Adios Amigo* on the TV talk-show circuit, Richard Pryor would stare pathetically into the camera and say: *"I'm sorry. I needed the money."*

Mean Johnny Barrows

(1976)
[On Video]

PRODUCER/DIRECTOR: Fred Williamson; SCREENWRITERS: Charles Walker, Jolevett Cato.

CAST: Fred Williamson (Johnny Barrows); Roddy McDowall (Tony Da Vinci); Stuart Whitman (Mario Racconi); Elliott Gould (Theodore Rasputin Waterhouse); and Leon Isaac Kennedy (Private Pickens).

In Vietnam, silver-star soldier, 'Mean' Johnny Barrows, pops his commanding officer, and is dishonorably discharged from the army. With no training other than how to kill, he returns to your basic no-future existence in L.A., and gets tangled in the middle of a mob war. In the last reel, a double-dealin' dame does him in. It's a message movie, spelling it all out right there on screen— "... to the veteran who traded his place on the front lines for a place on the unemployment line. Peace is hell."

The Last Fight

(1983)
[On Video]

DIRECTOR/SCREENWRITER: Fred Williamson; PRODUCER/STORY: Jerry Masucci; MUSIC: Jay Chattaway; SONGS: Gary W. King, Ruben Blades, Tito Puente.

CAST: Willie Colón (Joaquin Vargas); Ruben Blades (Andy "Kid Clave" Perez); Fred Williamson (Jesse Crowder); Joe Spinelli (Angelo the Boss); José "Chequi" Torres (Ex-Champ); and Don King.

This and the piece o' shit *Badge 373* are the only films I found I might describe as "Puerto Rican Exploitation."

Of *The Last Fight*, Pablo Guzmán said it best in *The Village Voice*, "(It) swings wildly between moments of deluxe *teatro absurdo*/B movie/high trash and longer C-grade stretches of trash period."

Jim Brown satiates a dwarf.

Slaughter's Big Rip-Off

(1973)
[On Video]
DIRECTOR: Gordon Douglas; SCREENWRITER:
Charles Johnson; MUSIC: Jim Brown and
Fred Wesley.
CAST: Jim Brown (Slaughter); Ed McMahon (Duncan); Brock Peters (Reynolds);
Gloria Hendry (Marcia); and Scatman
Crothers (Cleveland).

"The mob put the finger on Slaughter
so he gave them the finger right
back—*curled around a trigger!*" Da
mob pops his boy and Slaughter ain't
sittin' for it. A pimp named Joe Creole
gives him a tip leading him to da killa,
but when he arrives, he finds da killa
dead. Anyway, P. I. Brock "I Am the
Link Between Man and Ape" Peters
talks him into breaking into the safe of
Crime Boss and Johnny Carson sidekick,
Ed McMahon. Now you know why he
can afford to give away a million dollars every year in the Publishers' Clearinghouse Sweepstakes, he's getting rich
selling your kids *crack!*

JIM BROWN

In the 1960s, one year after concluding a successful and legendary career as a running back for the Cleveland Browns, Jim Brown emerged at the box office as Hollywood's first black man of action; and appeared in such films as *Rio Conchos, The Dirty Dozen, Ice Station Zebra, Dark of the Sun, Riot* and *100 Rifles,* marking territory normally pissed on by one-lunged whyte boys like John Wayne.

In the 1970s, Beat 'Em Up Brown thrived as black action hero Cap'n *Slaughter* and pugged it out for the box-office jackpot with action stars Fred Williamson, Jim Kelly, Pam Grier and Tamara Dobson. Unfortunately, however, as a threatening celluloid symbol of black male virility, he slipped from boffing sex bombs like Raquel Welch in *100 Rifles* to humping dwarves of mongoloid aspect in *Slaughter's Big Rip-Off.*

Today, on the TV talk-show circuit, you can occasionally find Jim Brown, dressed in fashionable African attire, frightening whyte people with Black Nationalist rhetoric.

SLAUGHTER
(1972) [On Video]

DIRECTOR: Jack Starrett; **SCREENWRITER:** Mark Hanna; **PRODUCER:** Don Williams; **MUSIC:** Luchi De Jesus; **SONGS:** Billy Preston. **CAST:** Jim Brown (Slaughter); Stella Stevens (Ann Cooper); Rip Torn (Dominick Hoffo); and Cameron Mitchell (Inspector A. W. Price).

> **Jim Brown is 'Slaughter'!**
> *It's not only his* **name**
> it's his **business**
> *and sometimes—*
> his ***pleasure!***

A.I.P.'s "exploitation" media package presents the entire film in a set of seventy-six stills and a fourteen-page caption sheet with an orange 7" x 7" cardboard booklet providing production information and plot (reworded in my own degenerate fashion, which I must admit to avoid litigious action from Sam Arkoff's legal repesentatives) synopsis.

"Da mob blows up his mom and gangsta pops! And Beat 'Em Up Brown is hot! He grunts, tightens his anus and gnashes, *Whose ass am I gonna kick first?*

"Beat 'Em Up barges in on da babe his pops was ballin' on da sly. He wants some answers. But a mob-bullet blasts through the window, catching her in da heart. Her last words tell him what he needs to know. Da mob is flying da killer out dat night.

"He beats up a plane. And gets pulled into da pokey by da Feds. Dey make a deal. He flys south of da border and tangles with da mob and a cheesy blonde."

The Slams

(1973)
PRODUCER: Gene Corman; DIRECTOR: Jonathan Kaplan; SCREENWRITER: Richard L. Adams; ASSISTANT DIRECTORS: Thalmus Rasulala and Nate Long.
CAST: Jim Brown (Curtis Hook).

A jailhouse action drama that might cause the opium-eating playwright of *Short Eyes,* the late great poet Miguel Pinero, to say: "He threw away a suitcase full of *what?!!* *Shee-it!* That nigga *deserves* to be in jail!"

The Grasshopper

(1970)
a.k.a. *The Passing of Evil* and *Passions* [On Video]
DIRECTOR: Jerry Paris; SCREENWRITERS/PRODUCERS: Jerry Belson and Garry Marshall; based on Mark MacShane's novel, *The Passing of Evil.*
CAST: Jim Brown; Jacqueline Bisset; Joseph Cotton; Ed Flanders; and Corbett Monica.

Written by *Mork and Mindy* producer, Garry Marshall, and directed by Rob Petry's next-door neighbor. Jim Brown marries Jacqueline Bisset in Vegas. Gets a gap popped in his ass for his trouble. Supposed to be a satire though I don't know of what. Yawn.

(1972)
[On Video]
DIRECTOR: Robert Hartford-Davis; SCREEN-
WRITER: Franklin Davis; STORY: based on
an idea by Hartford-Davis and a
screenplay by Robert Shearer; MUSIC:
Tony Osborne.
CAST: Jim Brown (Gunn); Martin Landau
(Capelli); Brenda Sykes (Judith); Lu-
ciana Paluzzi (Toni); Vida Blue (Sam
Green); Stephen McNally (Laurento);
Keefe Brasselle (Winman); Timothy
Brown (Larry); William Campbell
(Rico); Bernie Casey (Seth); and Jeanne
Bell (Lisa).

In *Black Gunn*, Jim Brown plays a
nightclub owner whose brother, Seth, a
Vietnam-vet, rips off da mob and uses
the money to finance BAG, or the Black
Action Group, a unit of guerrilla soldiers
out to liberate the homefolk. And, oh
my God, why these idealistic, gun-totin'
knuckleheads wanna fuck up Green
Power! black bid'nis'man Gunn's do fo'
sef' capitalist dreamworld with some
crazy shit like that?

Along with *Trouble Man* and the obscure seventies underground comic
book *Super Soul Comic* by Richard
Green, *Black Gunn* also seems to be a
major source for Keenan Ivory Wayan's
lame blaxplo-parody, *I'm Gonna Get
You Sucka!*

... tick ... tick ...
tick ...

(1970)
[On Video]
DIRECTOR: Ralph Nelson; SCREENWRITER:
James Lee Barret.
CAST: Jim Brown (Sheriff Jimmy Price);
George Kennedy (John Little); and
Bernie Casey (George Harley).

Sheriff Jim Brown in a town full of
hooded Mississippi crackers ... *tick* ...
tick ... *tick* ... !

Shot in Mexico on a $750,000 budget, *Slaughter* qualifies as the world's first authentic blaxploitation movie.

As Arkoff points out in his bio, the film was clearly designed to exploit the trend among Black moviegoers initiated by *Sweetback*, diluted by *Shaft*, and what results is a production with the look, feel and pyrotechnics of an economy-class James Bond; displaying no aspirations greater than duplicating the formula of its moneymaking predecessors.

JIM KELLY

Black Belt Jones

(1974)
[On Video]
PRODUCERS: Fred Weintraub (Story), Paul Heller; DIRECTOR: Robert Clouse; SCREEN-WRITER: Oscar Williams (Associate Producer); STORY: Alex Rose; MUSIC: Luchi De Jesus (Music Director); MUSIC THEME: Dennis Coffy (Arranger).
CAST: Jim Kelly (Black Belt Jones); Gloria Hendry (Sidney Byrd); and Scatman Crothers (Pop Byrd).

Heller and Weintraub experienced an unusual stroke of good fortune with their production of *Enter the Dragon*—the legendary Bruce Lee *died* before the film's release (which, obviously, was part of the same conspiracy that took out Jimi, Janis and Jim). And, as a result of the tons of free publicity garnered by his death, the two producers made almost enough money to buy all the tea in China. So, as their follow-up feature, they contracted black black-belt champ Jim Kelly as Lee's replacement, blended blaxploitation with Kung Fu, hired *Enter the Dragon* director Robert Clouse and gave us another hood-against-da-hoods scenario called *Black Belt Jones*—worth the rental to watch Scatman Crothers finally kick some honkie butt!

T ournament black-belt karate champ Jim Kelly's first film appearance was in something called *Gas World*. This was followed by *Melinda*, a film on which he also functioned as technical advisor for its karate sequences.

For the role of Williams in Bruce Lee's *Enter The Dragon*, a role that would establish his reputation as a martial arts star, Jim Kelly was not its producers' first choice. Rockne "Black Samson" Tarkington, who was also in *Melinda*, was originally cast but quit because, according to the director, Robert Clouse, in *The Making of "Enter the Dragon,"* he thought either:

1. They weren't paying him enough. Or
2. The script was a piece of shit laden with racial slurs.

Kelly was hired one day before principal cast and crew left for Hong Kong.

As a result of co-starring in the enormously successful *Enter The Dragon* (though, curiously, it didn't perform that well in the Asian market on its release) and the crossover in audiences for black action films and martial arts movies, Jim Kelly emerged as a major box office attraction in *Black Belt Jones* (a film I first saw in Bogotá, Colombia, with a gentleman who learned to speak English by watching American blaxploitation films).

Unfortunately, the remainder of Kelly's short film career in the seventies was left to the likes of Al Adamson, thus leaving a legacy of mostly unwatchable sleep-inducers. In spite of all that, Kelly more than likely continues as a martial arts instructor, a champion in the lives of those he guides; and certainly a champion in my eyes if for no better reason than his prominent sideburns.

Black Samurai

(1977)
(a.k.a. *Black Terminator*)
[On Video]
DIRECTOR: Al Adamson; SCREENWRITER: B. Radick; STORY: based on the novel by Marc Olden.
CAST: Jim Kelly (Robert Sand); Bill Roy (Janicot); Roberto Contreras (Victor Chavez); Marilyn Joi (Synne); Essie Lin Chia (Toki Konuma); Biff Yeager (Pines); and Charles Grant (Bones).

What a collection of names—Biff Yeager, Erurn Fuller, Jesus Thillit—and the names of the characters they play are even more ridiculous!

All the ingredients are here for a pop-a-forty-and-prop-your-feet-on-the-coffee-table night of brainless video entertainment. It's got martial arts, voodoo, ritual murder, drugs, hoze and *a strap-on jetpack!* Unfortunately, *Black Samurai* was mixed and served up by Al "Brain of Blood" Adamson himself (how did *he* get in on the seventies blaxploitation boom?). Originally, D'Urville Martin was to direct with Playboy Bunny Jeanne Bell as co-star. But, *nooooo*, Al Adamson had to drag his tired, no-talent honkie-ass into da shit, boasting he had Ron Van Clief in da bag. Fucked up everybody's fun.

Black Eliminator

(1978)

a.k.a. *Death Dimension* (original title and Canadian video title)

DIRECTOR: Al Adamson; SCREENWRITER/PRO-DUCER: Harry Hope.

CAST: Jim Kelly (Police Lieut. John Ash); Aldo Ray (Mr. Verdy); Harold Sakato (Santavacino); and Terry Moore (Marie [Joan Mason]).

The man with the porkchop sideburns, Jim Kelly, is on the trail of "the Pig" and his bodyguard, Goldfinger's "Odd-job," who seek possession of a "freeze bomb." With Mighty Joe Young's jungle-slummin' whyte girl, Terry Moore. Al Adamson wastes everyone's time in the director's chair.

Allied Artists Pictures Corporation.

Take a Hard Ride

(1975)

[On Video]

DIRECTOR: Anthony Dawson [Antonio Margheriti]; SCREENWRITERS: Eric Berco-vici, Jerry Ludwig; MUSIC: Jerry Gold-smith.

CAST: Jim Brown (Pike); Lee Van Cleef (Kiefer); Fred Williamson (Tyree); and Jim Kelly (Kashton).

The Canary Islands stand in for Mexico in this no-budget spaghetti western with Jim Brown delivering $86,000 to a dead cattleman's widow. Fred William-son is a card shark and Jim Kelly is mute.

Courtesy of Photofest.

Three the Hard Way

(1974)

[On Video]

DIRECTOR: Gordon Parks, Jr.; SCREENWRIT-ERS: Eric Bercovici, Jerry Ludwig.

CAST: Jim Brown (Jimmy Lait); Fred Williamson (Jagger Daniels); Jim Kelly (Mr. Keyes); Sheila Frazier (Wendy Kane); Charles McGregor (Charley); Corbin Bernsen (Boy); Jeanne Bell (Polly); and The Impressions.

Wealthy and (needless to say) *de-ranged* neo-Nazi hatches a plot to wipe out the entire Black population of the U.S. with a deadly serum with mysteri-ous Jim Crow properties. You think Jim "Slaughter" Brown 'n his boys Fred "The Hammer" Williamson 'n Jim "Black Belt Jones" Kelly gon' git wid dat? *Hah!*

Courtesy of Photofest.

Truck Turner

(1974)

[On Video]

DIRECTOR: Jonathan Kaplan; SCREENWRIT-ERS: Leigh Chapman, Oscar Williams, Michael Allin; STORY: Jerry Wilkins; MUSIC: Isaac Hayes.

CAST: Isaac Hayes (Matt "Truck" Turner); Yaphet Kotto (Harvard Blue); Annazette Chase (Annie); Scatman Crothers (Duke); Dick Miller (Fogarty); Stan Shaw (Fontana); and *the* Stymie Beard as Jail Guard.

Shaft Oscar-winner Isaac Hayes in his second Oscar-level performance in this skip-tracer actioner.

If not believable, Hayes is always amusing. Who can forget the depth and definition he gave to his character in *Escape from New York* by simply twitch-ing his eye? Or his impressive delivery to a man condemned to die in *Guilty as Charged:* "Tonight, we gonna have somethin' real special. A bucket of Ken-tucky Fried! The Colonel make *goooood* chicken."

Fine, fine actor. Sing his ass off, too.

Courtesy of Photofest.

Gordon's War

(1973)
[On Video]

DIRECTOR: Ossie Davis; SCREENWRITERS: Howard Friedlander, Ed Spielman; PRODUCER: Robert L. Schaffel.

CAST: Paul Winfield; Carl Lee; Tony King; David Downing; and Gilbert Lewis.

I thought this was some wrong shit. If these were some true revolutionary brothers, they would have re-educated the misguided souls defiling the community with prostitution and narcotics instead of this Charles Bronson *Death Wish* blow 'em away vigilante bullshit. Now, if the brothers resist re-education *then* blow 'em away!*

*Note: Young Grace Jones being molested in photo.

Courtesy of Photofest.

Book of Numbers

(1973)
[On Video]

PRODUCER: Raymond St. Jacques; DIRECTOR: Raymond St. Jacques; SCREENWRITER: Larry Spiegel; STORY: based on the novel *The Book of Numbers* by Robert Deane Pharr.

CAST: Raymond St. Jacques (Blueboy Harris); Freda Payne (Kelly Simms); Philip Michael Thomas (Dave Greene); Hope Clark (Pigmeat Goins); Willie Washington, Jr. (Makepeace Johnson); Doug Finell (Eggy); Sterling St. Jacques (Kid Flick); C. L. Williams (Blip); and D'Urville Martin (Billy Bowlegs).

In *The New York Times*, Roger Greenspun described Raymond St. Jacques's directing debut as "uncommonly well-balanced . . . intelligently directed and cleverly edited."

As I've not seen this film about the numbers game in 1930s Arkansas, I cannot vouch for Greenspun's evaluation (though if St. Jacques made a film in which watching a performance by Philip Michael Thomas is tolerable, it just might be worthwhile).

Courtesy of Photofest.

The Greatest

(1977)
[On Video]

DIRECTOR: Tom Gries; SCREENWRITER: Ring Lardner, Jr.; STORY: based on the book *The Greatest, My Own Story* by Muhammad Ali, Herbert Muhammed and Richard Durham; PRODUCER: John Marshall.

CAST: Muhammad Ali (himself); Paul Winfield; Lloyd Haynes; Ernest Borgnine; Annazette Chase; Robert Duvall; John Marley; Roger E. Mosley (Sonny Liston); Phillip MacAlister (Cassius Clay); Dina Merrill; Lucille Benson; and James Earl Jones (Malcolm X).

Miles didn't do an Ali album.

Courtesy of Photofest.

The Great White Hope

(1970)
[On Video]

DIRECTOR: Martin Ritt; SCREENWRITER: Howard Sackler, based on his play; PRODUCER: Lawrence Turman.

CAST: James Earl Jones (Jack Jefferson); Jane Alexander (Etta); with Beah Richards and Moses Gunn.

Actually, check out Miles Davis's score for *Jack Johnson*. Now *that* shit cooks.

Sweet Jesus, Preacherman

(1973)

DIRECTOR: Henning Schellerup; SCREENWRITERS: John Cerullo, M. Stuart Madden, Abbey Leitch.

CAST: Roger E. Mosley (Holmes/Lee); Damu King (Sweetstick); Marla Gibbs (Beverly Soloman); and Lee Frost (Policeman).

Mob action with Black hitman posing as a Baptist preacher who wants control of the drugs and prostitution plaguing his congregation. *Are you ready to shoot dope for Jesus, brothers and sisters?*

Courtesy of Photofest.

Buck and the Preacher

(1972)
[On Video]

DIRECTOR: Sidney Poitier; SCREENWRITER/STORY: Ernest Kinoy; STORY: Drake Walker; MUSIC: Benny Carter; SONGS: Sonny Terry and Brownie McGee.
CAST: Sidney Poitier (Buck); Harry Belafonte (Preacher [Rev. Willis Oakes Rutherford]); Ruby Dee (Ruth); and Clarence Muse (Cudjo).

Wagon master Poitier and jackleg preacher Belafonte ferry a load of freed slaves to a housing project of the Old West.

Courtesy of Photofest.

Mandingo

(1975)
[On Video]

PRODUCER: Dino de Laurentiis; DIRECTOR: Richard Fleischer; SCREENWRITER: Norman Wexler; STORY: based on Kyle Onstott novel and the play by James Kirkland.
CAST: Ken Norton; and Brenda "Honky" Sykes.

One of my all-time plantation favorites, with James Mason propping his feet up on the back of a peasy-scalped black child, talkin' 'bout how them little pickaninnies is almost as good as one o' them hairless Mexican dogs for drainin' off the rheumatize! And a pitchforked Ken Norton boiling away in a bubbling cauldron, screaming, *"I sorry massa! I fo' sho' didn't know dat wuz my dick in yo' wife! De sheets on de bed wuz so whyte, I didn't see her or de pussy!"*

Courtesy of Photofest.

Slaves

(1969)
[On Video]

DIRECTOR: Herbert J. Biberman; SCREENWRITER: John O. Killens, Alida Sherman.
CAST: Ossie Davis; Dionne Warwick; and Julius Harris.

———————

Courtesy of Photofest.

Soul Soldier

(1970)

DIRECTOR: John Cardos; SCREENWRITER: Marlene Weed.
CAST: Rafer Johnson; Lincoln Kilpatrick; and Robert DoQui.

Obviously, the only reason I've included these two entries was so that I might exploit the accompanying stills of naked Negro nipples.

PAM GRIER TALKS

Courtesy of Photofest.

The Big Doll House

(1971)
[On Video as *Women's Penitentiary I*]
EXECUTIVE PRODUCERS: Eddie Romero, John Ashley; DIRECTOR: Jack Hill; SCREENWRITER: Don Spencer; MUSIC: Hall Daniels.
CAST: Judy Brown (Collier); Roberta Collins (Alcott); Pam Grier (Grear); Brooke Mills (Harrad); Pat Woodell (Bodine); and Sid Haig (Harry).

Not only did Pam Grier get her "big break" as the jail-house "boll-dagga" Grear[S-2] in this women-in-prison genre pic, but according to *New York Daily News* columnist "The Phantom of the Movies" in his book *The Phantom's Ultimate Video Guide*, *The Big Doll House* established the genre conventions for the films produced after it. However, the reason why this low-budget money-maker "set forth many of the conventions still rigidly adhered to by (the) broads-behind-bars movies today" is simple: the films were shot from the *same* script!

According to an interview with Jack Hill in *Psychotronic #13*, the script for *The Big Doll House* was rewritten for three different movies.

[S-2]Previously, Ms. Grier appeared in only one motion picture—Russ Meyer's *Beyond the Valley of the Dolls* (1970) as a party scene extra. According to her, she just happened to be visiting a friend on the lot when this particular scene was being shot.

As Queen of 1970s blaxploitation, and one of the most wildly popular action stars of the period (at one time, along with Barbra Streisand and Liza Minnelli, she was one of the most "bankable" female stars in Hollywood), Pam Grier hacked off honkie weenie on the screens of inner-city movie houses and redneck-run drive-ins all across America a full two decades before Lorena Bobbitt signed on the dotted line of her green-card application *(picklin' em up and thrustin' em in the faces of their gelded owners' mistresses!)*; and reigned over the altars of adolescent onanism in a dangerous "double-D" cup as if the black-skinned Goddess Kali had been reborn in modern guise. Both an

The Big Bird Cage

(1972)
a.k.a. *Women's Penitentiary II*
[On Video]
PRODUCER: Jane Schaffer; DIRECTOR/
SCREENWRITER: Jack Hill; MUSIC: William A.
Castleman.
CAST: Pam Grier (Blossom); Anita Ford
(Terry Rich); Candice Roman (Carla);
Teda Bracci (Bull Jones); Carol Speed
(Mickie); Karen McKevic (Karen); and
Sid Haig (Django).

In this sequel to *The Big Doll House*,
Pam Grier liberates some oppressed
money in the Philippino nightclub she
sings in to finance her revolutionary
comrades in arms, some of whom end
up in a primitive tropical pokey with a
big bamboo sugar mill—the scene of
some deliciously sadistic action. So Pam
and her chrome-domed boyfriend, Sid
Haig, bust in and incite the inmates to a
bloody insurrection. I admit it. I liked it
because I am a very sick man.

object of male sexual adoration and a 1970s feminist model of the liberated woman, Pam appeared nude in *Playboy* pictorials (and a frequently recycled set of pics in *Players* mag) and was the subject of an August 1975 *Ms.* cover story called *The Mocha Mogul of Hollywood*, written by Jamaica Kincaid.

Pam Grier was unique on the icon-littered landscape of 1970s pop America. In movies, she was a genre unto herself. She had no equal (Tamara Dobson you say? *Hah!* Her clumsy hapkido expert Cleopatra Jones was no more than a clotheshorse who provided a role model for the young RuPaul). Unlike much of what passed for "black" film in the period (i.e., *Blackenstein, Black Gestapo, Dr. Black, Mr. Hyde*) Pam's films had no Caucasian equivalent (Stella Stevens's *Scorchy*? TV's *Honey West*? The Avengers' Emma Peel? I think not! The only other actress who even comes close to matching her fierce independence, quick-witted aggression and heart-stopping sexuality is Tura Satana, who herself is Cherokee and Japanese, in the must-see *Faster Pussycat, Kill! Kill!* [though I gots to give it up to Juliette Lewis in *Natural Born Killers*]). Not only did the revenge motifs of Pam's films quell the racial hostilities of inner-city audiences hungry to see the whyte man get his ass kicked, she also presented the perfect model of the woman beyond male control (if you was dealin' wif' Pam, a pimp trick was a sure way to get yo' ass kicked quick!)—a fact she confirmed not only in the brilliant comic-book portrayals she brought to her action-movie roles but in her personal life as well (evidenced in how she handled her relationships with two notorious wildmen, Richard Pryor and John Lennon).

Ms. Grier was born on May 26, 1949, in Winston-Salem, North Carolina; growing up with three siblings on overseas military bases and in the housing projects of Denver, Colorado. With hopes of studying medicine and becoming a doctor, Ms. Grier entered a local beauty contest in order to finance her education. As the only dark-skinned contestant, she beat out her paler opponents in the category of "singing and dancing."

Her first on-screen appearance was in Mam-Gland King Russ Meyer's cult fave *Beyond the Valley of the Dolls* (penned by the pudgy half of the movie reviewing team of Siskel and Ebert). Ms. Grier was employed as a switchboard operator at American International Pictures when she attracted the eye of its head, Sam Arkoff, who launched her career in the series of films for which she is best known: *Coffy*; *Foxy Brown*; *Sheba, Baby*; *Friday Foster*; and *Scream, Blacula, Scream.*

At the height of her popularity, Pam put a Popeye on *Gojira* author Marc Jacobson. At the time, Marc was writing a story on her for *New York* magazine. According to Marc, the two were standing on 42nd Street. He said she seemed baffled by the movie houses where her films were shown.

Looking her up and down, he remarked: "You don't look so tough."

And she replied, "Oh, yeah?" Then punched him. *In the balls.*

Ms. Grier has since returned to school, studied her craft and reemerged in regional theater, television and films like *Fort Apache: The Bronx*; *Something Wicked This Way Comes* and *Above the Law.* In the following interview, Ms. Grier demonstrates why Quentin Tarantino called her "the Queen of Women." Our discussion opened on screenwriting, story structure and the movie marketplace. And, consistent with her Geminian nature, she dictated the terms of discussion, saying whatever she chose.

> **PAM GRIER:** After awhile, if you've been making movies and reading scripts, you develop an instinct for defining your turning point, your first and second act.
>
> It's a formula they didn't have for a long time. I don't think formula films came out until the eighties, or late seventies. They told a story but it didn't necessarily have that first, second and third act formula they do today.

DARIUS: I don't know. I only know that the structure of *Chinatown* is the model of a "good" screenplay presented in Sidney Field's book.

MS. GRIER: *Chinatown,* that's a mystery. That has a different formula, doesn't it?

DARIUS: What I understand is this—the way the structure of that particular screenplay is analyzed, you end up constructing your screenplay along the lines of a puzzle-box. And because that puzzle-box structure doesn't conform to the current paradigm of a commercial screenplay, you couldn't sell it.

Courtesy of Photofest.

Hit Man

(1972)
[On Video]
PRODUCER: Gene Corman; DIRECTOR/ SCREENWRITER: George Armitage; STORY: based on Ted Lewis's novel *Jack's Return Home.*
CAST: Bernie Casey; Pam Grier; and Roger E. Mosley.

It's on video. *You* watch it.

Black Mama, White Mama

(1972)
a.k.a. Hot, Hard and Mean
(British title)
PRODUCERS: John Ashley; PRODUCER/DIREC-
TOR: Eddie Romero; STORY: Joseph Villa,
Jonathan Demme; SCREENWRITER H. R.
Christian; MUSIC: Harry Betts.
CAST: Pam Grier (Lee Daniels); Margaret
Markov (Karen Brent); and Sid Haig
(Ruben).

One night, Jonathan Demme sat down
in his West Hollywood apartment to
catch Some Like It Hot on the tube. He
dozed off for a minute or two. When he
opened his eyes, he thought he was
watching Tony Curtis in The Defiant
Ones. So, years before Michael Jackson
lost his mind, Demme asked himself:
"When did Sidney Poitier turn white
and start wearing a dress?"
    He was so obsessed by this thought,
he wrote it down and sold it to John
Ashley for five hundred bucks. Ashley
and Philippino producer/director Eddie
Romero threw out the cross-dressing
angle, turned the Poitier character into
a transsexual and cast Pam Grier.
    And thus Black Mama, White Mama
was born. . . .

MS. GRIER: In the 1-2-3 formula, you set up the character and turning points. In act two, you go to the resolution while reaching your turning points.

DARIUS: It seems absurd. You tell a story and that's it. Why fit it to a "formula"?

MS. GRIER: We've seen a lot of movies like that. I'll watch a movie and think, "If this movie has all this structure, where are the turning points the first act goes to? This is really a two-act. I see a two-act movie here. I'd like to see Sid Field analyze this one because it's a two-act. Act one is the first sixty pages, the last act is thirty, and you know it's short, right up to the resolution."
    You're right. I haven't seen a lot of structure in the movies that get made. I think subject matter and who you know is a lot more effective than the basic structure. I have a friend who's had great movies written and optioned to stay out of the market.

DARIUS: What does that mean?

MS. GRIER: Low-cost competition floods the market with the possibility of more. Not mainstream films, but the popularity of a minority film that's so popular, all of a sudden it starts booking into the mall theaters, taking up space from the others they're trying to sell and make money off of.
    You'd be surprised by the competitiveness in the marketplace. A lot of artists ask me if there's a conspiracy to keep minority projects out. I say, "No. I don't think there's a conspiracy. When you consider the marketplace, you think how many dollars are going to be divided? How many pieces of pie? How many times is the pie going to be divided?"
    I think that it basically comes down to economics—the politics of money, the widest profit margin, the bottom line. That's where I think it is. It has nothing to do with color. It has to do with dollars. The color factor is secondary. There's room enough for all the pie to be chocolate and vanilla.
    You know there are so many different types of people who want to relate to so many types of movies. There's a lot of people that want

to see people in love. I want to see caring. I want to see people savoring life. It's the film industry's option to do that or not do that.

As I see movies being made by the widest three hundred million profit, I say there's a place for the smaller ones. The ones that I'm going to make. The first one is going to be a love story within a love story. It's contemporary and it wasn't written for the box office.

DARIUS: The script you wrote yourself?

MS. GRIER: Yes.

DARIUS: What's it called?

MS. GRIER: *Red, Right and Blues.* It's about love, unconditional love, and how an elitist group, instead of turning its back, says they want to be part of a change. We're in a class system. It's not racism. It's archaic and primitive to nail that tag on it. It's the haves against the have-nots. The wealthy against the poor.

I walk around watching people, hearing stories, getting involved with all walks of life. I've been around a lot of wealthy people who are amazed at their wealth. Some because they were born poor and some who were born wealthy. You learn from that. And I don't see any movies on it. I see movies where they're saving whales. They'll save cats and dogs before they save human beings.

My movie is a feel-good movie. I want to see some real feel-good movies about real things. The stuff that's really going on. This film might be my first. It might be my last. But I doubt it; I'm tenacious as a pit bull.

We now have the Black Filmmakers Foundation, which was going to evolve anyway, it was just a matter of time. We now have our own film community. The Latinos have theirs. The Asians have theirs. The Norwegians have their Bergman. The Italians have Fellini. And we have Spike.

In a capitalistic society, we have the wonderful freedom to create our own fantasy films, our own horror films, our own political gangster films, our own political elitist films—from a *The Parallax View* to a *The Manchurian Candidate*. I'd love to see one of our own surviving a political agenda.

Courtesy of Photofest.

Coffy

(1973)
[On Video]
DIRECTOR/SCREENWRITER: Jack Hill; MUSIC/SONGS: Roy Ayers; SONGS: Carl Clay, Roselle Weaver.
CAST: Pam Grier (Coffy); Booker Bradshaw (Howard Brunswick); Robert DoQui (King George); William Elliott (Carter Brown); Allan Arbus (Arturo Vitroni); and Sid Haig (Omar).

Author-activist Sarah Schulman tells me every time The Lesbian Avengers[S-3] advertise a dance using *Coffy*'s clip-art—with Pam Grier in halter-top and tight-fitting capri pants, holding a sawed-off, double-barreled, 12-gauge shotgun—d'place be *packed!*

"Why is that?" I asked.

"What could be more appealing to a lesbian?" she answered.

[S-3]Thanks to the FBI and COINTELPRO, there haven't been many worthy models of how to organize for revolutionary change for young activists since The Black Panther Party. The Lesbian Avengers is one of them (with a flair for the theatric). Send money/write for *The Lesbian Avenger Handbook: A Handy Guide To Homemade Revolution*—The Lesbian Avengers c/o The Center, 208 W. 13th Street, New York, NY 10011.

Friday Foster

(1975)
[On Video]
PRODUCER/DIRECTOR: Arthur Marks; SCREEN-WRITER: Orville Hampton; COSTUMES: Izzy Berne.
CAST: Pam Grier (Friday Foster); Yaphet Kotto (Colt Hawkins); Godfrey Cambridge (Ford Malotte); Thalmus Rasulala (Blake Tarr); Eartha Kitt (Madame Rena); Jim Backus (Enos Griffith); Scatman Crothers (Rev. Noble Franklin); and Ted "Loveboat" Lange (Fancy Dexter).

Glance magazine photographer, Friday Foster, finds herself in the middle of an airport shoot-out as assassins attempt to take the life of Black billionaire Blake Tarr (*Blake Tarr?!*). The next day, Friday sees one of the would-be hitmen at a fashion show presented by the cat-growling Eartha Kitt, and points him out to her boyfriend, P.I. Yaphett Kotto. The code words "Black Widow," uttered from the mouth of a dying fashion model, lead Friday and her P.I. boyfriend on a trail straight to Washington, D.C., where they learn that the entire plot was dreamed up by a racist *Mr. Magoo!*

DARIUS: Apparently, there is one—a script by Kyle Baker commissioned by the Hudlin Brothers. Rumor has it that reactions to the script were that under no circumstances should this film be made; due, obviously, to the paranoia-inducing and volatile nature of the script.

MS. GRIER: Yet, a gangster rap movie can be made. It should be made. It would stimulate thinking. Eventually, the Hudlin Brothers will be in a position financially to make that film and have it distributed. They could take it door to door if they wanted.

But, then, you have that fear. They had to take out scenes in *The Manchurian Candidate* because they thought it would create political unrest.

I think everyone will get to that point in their career that they're able to make that one film that says something about fairness and freedom and the evolution of man. That one film that says, "Here we are. We survived ourselves in spite of ourselves. In spite of our knuckle heads. In spite of the elitist people we're being ruled by."

Hopefully, we'll see more. Films where you and I and groups of people can sit and discuss various aspects of a film. There's not many rap movies and gangster movie I've seen, and I've seen them all, that I can have a discussion about afterward.

It's—he was on the wrong turf, took the drugs and got killed. End of movie.

Maybe I'll hear a rap song that's a little more poignant. It's interesting. If they made more movies about the songs they write, they could be almost poetic.

I hope *Red, Right and Blues* turns out to be that particular film for me because I have been involved with these kids. These young people have taught me, not only taught me, but reminded me of what poverty does. I lived in the projects as a kid.

My dad worked for the Air Force Strategic Air Command. We had that political cold-war paranoia then. That fear the Russians—the Reds—were going to bomb us. We had these strategic command missile silos all over the world.

Your dad would be stationed there, and there weren't family facilities, so sometimes we had to go stay with our grandmom, or a cousin, or an aunt somewhere until we could live with him in a certain place.

Because of that paranoia, I learned about a lot of things. I ended up living in a project, a very poor environment; where even today, thirty years later, we're talking about kids growing up in an environment where they don't even have a phone.

They strive to have a telephone! Today, these kids are so poor, they see so much on television and in magazines—clothes, cellular phones, cars and all this stuff—they say, "Well, if we had this stuff, we would belong. Since we don't have it, we don't belong!"

What a horrible felling it is to wake up every day and you don't get breakfast! You don't get breakfast or sit with your dad and watch him read the paper, put on his tie and white shirt and go off with his briefcase; or put on his dungarees, take his tool case and go to his plumber's shop. They don't have that.

What they have is a welfare check. They go down to an office, sit all day in line, get their check and go back home. Lucky if they have a television set. Lucky if they get sugar sandwiches like I used to eat as a kid. They got to fight for their shoes. They got to fight day in and day out. That can be some serious negative conditioning to a three-year-old child.

It's not like white kids, or affluent black kids, who know what they're going to do when they're seven years old. I see kids of affluent black parents who know what they want to be at six years old. They know where they are going to go.

These kids can hardly form a sentence. They're three years old and hardly talk. We're talking about several generations of being poor. One teenager I've talked to, he said, "I just want to have a phone. I just want something normal."

A telephone! To be able to pay for a phone bill every month. That's what most people take for granted.

The father constantly going to a pay phone. They're living in a motel, struggling to make the room rent. There are six of them sleeping on the floor. What are we going to eat today? Cookies and milk. We got enough money for a quart of milk. Think we could get a box of wafers if we don't steal them? That can make a child real

Courtesy of Photofest.

Foxy Brown

(1974)
[On Video]
DIRECTOR/SCREENWRITER: Jack Hill; MUSIC: Willie Hutch.
CAST: Pam Grier (Foxy Brown); Antonio Fargas (Link Brown); Peter Brown (Steve Elias); Terry Carter (Michael Anderson [Dalton Ford]); Kathryn Loder (Katherine Wall); Harry Holcombe (Judge Fenton); and Sid Haig (Hays).

Foxy's shiftless, would-be hustler brother (played by the great Antonio Fargas) is being chased by some numbers-running hoods he owes *a lot* of money. To pay off his debt, he rats on the whereabouts of Foxy's narc-agent boyfriend, who has just undergone plastic surgery (the scene with Pam and her boyfriend in the hospital room is one I *still* beat off to). Anyway, after her boyfriend is bumped off, Foxy develops some *serious* PMS—drivin' a plane through a ranch full of gangsters and orderin' castration for the head honkie in charge! Movie entertainment at its finest.

Sheba, Baby

(1975)
[On Video]
DIRECTOR/SCREENWRITER: William Girdler;
STORY: David Sheldon; PRODUCER: William
Girdler.
CAST: Pam Grier (Sheba Shayne).

The Windy City's best P.I., Sheba Shayne, goes back to her folks in Louisville, Kentucky, to help out her pops who is having problems with racketeers trying to muscle in on his loan company. Her car gets blown up and her pops is killed. Teaming up with her pop's business partner, they discover Shark, an insurance wiz, who's at the bottom of all this trouble, at a party aboard his yacht. After some basic B-movie business, Sheba takes Shark out with a spear gun. Once you've seen A.I.P.'s ad campaign for *Sheba, Baby*, you'll know where Tarantino got his "Queen of Women" line 'cause, in *Sheba, Baby,* "Pam Grier is Queen of Private Eyes." From the director who gave us *Abby*.

angry. Then they see MTV, and all the other things, and that can really push a kid over the line.

"I'm gonna go sell me three rocks today and bring home three hundred dollars, feed the family. I know I'm not supposed to do it but I did it. I survived. Here's three hundred dollars."

I see that, and I see them now being in a position where they're going to jail, now they've committed a crime. When they come out, they go back to the same situation and they get caught.

See, the thing is not to get caught. That's the whole game. That's the empowerment and personality. I can say the most violent, hurtful things to you and I won't even flinch. I'll say things you won't even say. That's a sense of empowerment. To other people, it can be quite disturbing: why can't they just go out and get a job? Because they dropped out of school in the third grade. When you hear some of these kids at eighteen years old and they can't speak and they can't read or write, what does that tell you about society?

I would hold them back, and I'd say, "Do you know why? I want you to work. I want you to buy a car. Have an apartment and have clothes. Until you learn to read, and we try and make it interesting for you to learn, you will not have those things. You will go to jail and you will be unemployed. It'll be hard for employers to insure you because you have a felony criminal record. I'm not going to let that happen to you."

That's what society should be saying. That's what my thing is about. Someone going up against the grain.

DARIUS: So the focus of your work is urging people to get involved?

MS. GRIER: I hope my movie will. People get tired because their daily life is so hopeless. You have to put some sort of entertainment out there. Let them live through your triumph vicariously without hitting them over the head or being dictatorial.

I grew up with so many kids that are dead, or they're vegetables and they had such potential. There are so many young brilliant minds that just aren't allowed to live up to their potential.

Smoking cocaine in the eighties, free-basing, was a serious thing. People who were brilliant thought they could do it once. And all of a sudden they found themselves completely enslaved.

DARIUS: Which leads to your association with Richard Pryor.

MS. GRIER: When you have a relationship with someone who does drugs, [that] doesn't mean that you also do it. That's one thing I will always have—independence—which is what he loved and respected. Even in his work, he refers to me as one of the smartest women he knows.

You end up walking away from someone because they're so self-destructive. They ask you to help them. You do. And when they fall off, they put you in a position where it's one thing when you get very far in life, and you work very hard, you're not going to let anyone else take it away. I don't care if it's someone you're sleeping with. I loved that man to death. He knows it and he knows I fought for him. It's all coming out in my book, the dynamics of our relationship—how it evolved, the second act, the third act. It's still unresolved.

One of my ideas is to work with him again. I don't know if he'll be able to work in the acting capacity, but as a writer. When we were together, I was the one who sort of got him straightened out.

I said, "Look, you've been high since you were twelve years old. Let's see what it's like to be unhigh."

He wanted to be with me. Those were the terms. He went as long as seven months. Then he had to deal with certain friends who challenged his masculinity and challenged me. He was able to stand up against them when he was sober. When he began to drink, he couldn't stand up against them.

He found himself not being as creative. I said, "You know you haven't written in three years. There's a point when you hit bottom and you're not creating anymore. You need to stop and say, 'What's wrong?,' 'What's up?,' 'What's different?'"

You reach certain plateaus in life. One day you're a teenager. The next day you're a young adult. Then you reach a certain plateau and you have to stand back and assess your life. Where do I go from here? What can I learn from?

If you don't do that, you get caught in a time warp. And if you do drugs that keep you wired or blindfolded or in the dark about what you want or where you want to go or where you've been then you have a problem managing. If you're going to do drugs, manage it

Drum

(1976)
[On Video]
DIRECTOR: Steve Carver; SCREENWRITER: Norman Wexler; STORY: based on the novel by Kyle Onstott.
CAST: Ken Norton; Pam Grier; Paula Kelly; Brenda Sykes and Yaphet Kotto.

More lurid tales of the Old South. Great lunatic storytelling, filled with incest, castration, bed-hoppin' miscegenation from the slave shacks to the big house, Ken Norton and Pam Grier as a pair of *breeders* and plantation slave-revolts. As Spike Lee's little brother, Cinque, is all too fond of saying, *"Yackum Smackum!"*.

The Arena

(1973)
a.k.a. *Naked Warriors*
[On Video]
EXECUTIVE PRODUCER: Roger Corman; DIRECTOR: Steve Carver; SCREENWRITERS: John Corrington, Joyce Hooper Corrington. CAST: Pam Grier (Mamawi); and Margaret Markov (Bodicia).

In my talk with Ms. Grier, she said she and her lawyers couldn't keep track of how, when and under what title pirate copies of this foreign-lensed feature showed up on the vid-market.

The Nubian Mamawi and the Druidic Bodicia are captured by those orgy-lovin'-feed-them-Christians-to-the-lions Romans, and sold into slavery to satiate their need for decadent entertainment (like watching big-boobed babes beating the living shit out of each other). But Ancient Rome or not, Ms. Grier kicks her some honkie hiney and talks plenty o' pro-Black shit. And I must add Margaret Markov is *fine!*

well. If you are going to be addicted to bead work, manage it well. If you're going to make furniture, and you don't want to go to work, manage it so you can at least make a living at whatever your addiction or passion is. Manage it so you have a balance in life. That's all it is, management.

He used to think he wasn't funny when he was sober. I said, "When you're sober, you're in a forest. You see the trees. When you're high, you become anything you want to be in your fantasy life. But, when you step out, you can actually see where you've been and where you're going. You have that option or choice, but manage it. Manage it well, Richard." That's all I told him and that's why he thinks I'm smart.

DARIUS: It's an unfortunate delusion, the idea drugs make you creative.

MS. GRIER: I know. But that's what he thought. He didn't get a chance to think about it. How would he know he's got to be able to think about it? When he was sober for seven months, he did funny stuff. I did funny stuff. He laughed at my stuff. I thought we'd be good writers. He was writing again. He was having people over. He started creating again. That was when he started creating some really good stuff. *The Richard Pryor Show* should have continued. I loved his show.

DARIUS: It was a brilliant show. He broke a lot of people.

MS. GRIER: I loved that show. We had just broken up. We were forming and stuff like that. I gave him a lot of ideas and then we broke up. I just wasn't going to let him tear me down at my expense. Some people will stay and love that person no matter what. Not me. I had family that I was supporting and caring for. I'm not dependent on emotional or financial or fame or infamy or spotlight. I'm that independent. I just walked away from someone I cared for. There were moments of real connection that, thank God, you encounter once or a few times in your life. It's great because a lot of people settle for less in relationships. They just go for the money, or she's pregnant or he's nice. I won't settle for less. I know what that connection is. I had it with him. And I've had it with a few others. It's all relative as to how long it's got to last. I got enough out of it. What I was supposed to get. I don't know if we'll be friends. I don't know if we'll be working professionals.

DARIUS: Growing up, he was an important figure for me. He was a role model in some ways.

MS. GRIER: You look like his son.

DARIUS: People have said that. In high school, I was a big fan of his. And I hitchhiked from New Haven to Hartford to see his show, except I didn't have any money. I stood at the stage door and waited hours for him to show up. When he arrived, he asked me why I was standing there, why wasn't I inside? I told him I didn't have any money. So he brought me backstage to see the show as his guest. It was a great moment. I'll never forget that.

MS. GRIER: You should have run his company. He'd be a zillionaire today.

DARIUS: I understand you're pals with Roman Polanski.

MS. GRIER: We happened to know the same film distributor, who was our mutual friend. I was invited one night to have dinner with Roman Polanski. My friend, Sam, he's the film distributor, we all had dinner. It was Jack Nicholson, Angelica Huston, Roman Polanski, Sam and myself. I kind of sat back and watched these people. You know, watched these white folks do their thing. It was at this restaurant called the Bistro, a high-profile place. I felt just like a little country girl out of water, like I fell off the turnpike right in front of the Bistro, and I joined them there. It was just regular people in tuxes. He was there with a very young girl. I don't remember who. It wasn't Nastassja [Kinski] at the time.

I was a little closer to John Lennon than Roman. We met during the Oscars. I was a presenter. That's the night we ended up with all that racket at the Troubador. That's mainly how you meet these people.

We went to the Troubador right after rehearsal with Jack Halley,

the executive producer; and Peter Lawford, who was also a presenter in the show. I can't remember the other gentleman's name, but he was also a director; and Harry Nilsson, who was a friend of John's.

We all decided to go over to the Troubador because the Smothers Brothers were making their comeback appearance that night. This was in 1974. We all got in a car and went over. I was just hanging along, wondering where white people go. You know, I'm going to write this down one day. I wanted to see what they do. So, we go over. They start the show. It's a packed house. Agents, managers, stuff like that. We're waiting for them to go on. And John starts. He's sitting across from me and Harry. And John starts singing "I Can't Stand The Rain." I start singing it with him, harmonizing. My background is gospel.

Everyone turns around and sees John. All of a sudden, the whole audience starts singing along with him. We're all singing and harmonizing. It's a great way to wait for the Smothers Brothers. So they're running late. By then, John has tossed down quite a few with Harry Nilsson.

We're sitting up on this platform at the back. It's a higher elevation than the rest of the room. The Smothers Brothers come on and start their show. They're not as hip as I thought they'd be. I thought they would come out different. I had seen them, you know, on their television show.

It was almost like a time warp. Time stood still only they didn't know it. So John got really bored, and all of a sudden he started singing again—"Come on, Pamela!" Peter Lawford said, "Sssh, John! It's the middle of their act!"

And John says he'd quit when they start doing their show. So John starts singing again! We're all like, John's a little drunk. How do we get him out of here? All of a sudden, a big red guy came over and says, "You're being rude to them. You know we wouldn't do that to you at your concert."

Next thing you know, John says the wonderful "f" word. And that starts a riot. This guy pushes John. John starts going at it. John's drunk. Harry Nilsson is trying to defend John. So all of a sudden, these guys try to help the manager, Marilyn's husband. Harry Nilsson and Peter Lawford are trying to help John, because they don't want him scarred for the Oscars, right?

A table is thrown. I'm trying to get out of the way. I put up my hand to block it. Now, I had the nerve to have those extension nails put on. And I broke all the nails below the skin line. *Ouch!* They started bleeding. I'm thinking this table's a little harder than I thought. I just want to get out of the way of this sluggin' an' kickin'. It was a fracas.

We all got thrown out. I'm saying, "Wait! Now do I look like I'm with these people? I'm the only black chick in there! Do I look like I'm with these people? I'm from Colorado!" I never even knew these people. It was a trip!

John was duking it out, then we went outside. We started laughing and howling. John started talking to me and stuff. He wanted to call me and stuff.

I said, "Look, you know if we have things in common, we'll gravitate towards each other and talk. But I'm not here to be a tramp for you. You need to go back to your wife and talk about how much you missed her. You're just coming to terms because she's smart." She's independent, Yoko.

He told me he loved her that night. He wanted to go back to her. He was saying, "I need to go back to her. That's where I belong."

But that was before the marriage thing set in. He needed to get his whatever. Now, you're with a person day in and day out. Baby day in and day out. Meal day in and day out. School day in and day out. It's different being a single man with the groupies and the musicians all night and drugs and all the other stuff you do. It's different. Marriage. A family. It's that new plateau you have to go to. How do I adjust to that? He was going through a period of adjustment. He told me that at the table.

I said, "You need to go back. That's your foundation. You've done your play. You've done it. And if you don't go back and try it you won't know. I understand being outside of the forest to see the trees."

He said, "I had a nice talk with you. Let me have your number. Here's mine. I'm staying here at this hotel. Maybe we'll hang out."

I said, "You're going to have a lot of drugs around you. I don't want to be indicted for your bullshit. You'll get off. I'll take the urine test but it won't matter. My career will be over."

John was really a pretty passionate person. That's where his music came from. He was really tuned in to a lot of oppressive situations. One of the things he said about the Smothers Brothers was that they were not singing about anything. That's why he got bored. He was in a state where things hurt him. Sometimes, you have to live through hypocrisy. There are people suffering and hungry and you can't change it.

Doing work that really matters and makes a difference, that's what's important to me. I don't care about getting an Oscar. I got an Image Award for my first play *Fool For Love*. I got it from the NAACP Image Awards. That mattered. I want to matter and not just sing about it. I want to have something tangible.

Courtesy of Photofest.

Courtesy of Photofest.

Courtesy of Photofest.

Cleopatra Jones

(1973)
[On Video]
PRODUCER: William Tennant; CO-PRODUCER-SCREENWRITER-ASSISTANT DIRECTOR: Max Julien; DIRECTOR: Jack Starrett; MUSIC: J. J. Johnson (with Carl Brandt, Brad Shapiro, Joe Simon).
CAST: Tamara Dobson (Cleopatra Jones); Bernie Casey (Reuben Masters); Shelley Winters (Mommy); Brenda Sykes (Tiffany); and Antonio Fargas (Doodlebug).

After destroying an opium poppy field in Turkey, Cleopatra Jones, a six-foot-two-inch narcotics agent employed by the CIA dreamed up by Max "The Mack" Julien, returns to Los Angeles at the request of her boyfriend, who runs a halfway house for ex-junkies, and mixes it up with lesbian drug lord, Shelley Winters, in a catfight to the finish. Despite the clumsiest martial-arts action I've ever had to sit through, vigorous direction makes the routine formula of its comic book theatrics seem quite involving.

Cleopatra Jones and the Casino of Gold

(1975)
[On Video]
PRODUCER-SCREENWRITER: William Tennant; DIRECTOR: Chuck Bail.
CAST: Tamara Dobson (Cleopatra Jones); Stella Stevens (Bianca Jovan [The Dragon Lady]); Tanny (Mi Ling); Norman Fell (Stanley Nagel); and Albert Popwell (Matthew Johnson).

Dragon Lady Stella Stevens holds home-boys hostage in Hong Kong and, with the help of Mi Ling and her motorcycle-ridin' P.I.s, clumsy hapkido master and clotheshorse, Cleopatra Jones sets down in the real Chinatown to bust up Dragon Lady's shit. But the real spectacle in this Warner/Shaw Bros. China-lensed co-production is Ms. Dobson's rapid-fire wardrobe changes—which, *I'm convinced*, elevated her status in the Black pop pantheon to "Patron Saint of Harlem Drag Queens." When it comes time to launch RuPaul's movie career (and I don't know why Donald Bogle didn't think of this first), the point won't be lost on some enterprising young producer, who'll not only insure the Ru-Paul's *Cleopatra Jones and the Casino of Gold* remake is infused with all the campy gusto it deserves but will remember to cast Joan Rivers as a *tyrannical, crack-smoking drug lord!* [S-4]

[S-4]Some months after writing the above, my friend Steve Pink was called in to talk with a Disney executive about writing a treatment of exactly what I've just described. And not only was Disney, of all companies, actually interested in producing a movie about Cleopatra Jones's cross-dressing son, as of this writing, it's been shot and is in the can!

T.N.T. Jackson

(1974)
[On Video]
DIRECTOR: Cirio H. Santiago; SCREENWRITERS: Dick Miller, Ken Miller.
CAST: Jeanne Bell (T.N.T. Jackson); and Stan Shaw (Charlie).

Stunt-doubling for *Playboy* skin-girl Jeanne Bell in the movie's absurd martial arts sequences is an afro-wigged dwarf with hairy legs. The movie's one other highlight? A bare-busted Bell hops up and down in her underwear for no other reason than to, well, hop up and down in her underwear.

Thomasine & Bushrod

(1974)
DIRECTOR: Gordon Parks, Jr.; SCREENWRITER: Max Julien.
CAST: Max Julien (Bushrod); Vonetta McGee (Thomasine); Glynn Turman (Jomo); and Juanita Moore (Pecolia).

She's an ex-bounty hunter. He's an ex-outlaw. Together they blaze a trail across the Old West, liberatin' banks and redistributin' the wealth among Blacks, Native Americans, Mexicans and poor whytes.

Courtesy of Paramount Pictures.

Claudine

(1974)

DIRECTOR: John Berry; SCREENWRITERS: Tina and Lester Pine; PRODUCER: Hannah Weinstein.

CAST: Diahann Carroll; James Earl Jones; and Lawrence Hilton-Jacobs.

Diahann Carroll on welfare. *Right.*

"Think we can cop two jumbos if we sell the baby?"

Pipe Dreams

(1976)

[On Video]

DIRECTOR/SCREENWRITER/PRODUCER: Stephen Verona.

CAST: Gladys Knight; Barry Hankerson; and Altovise Davis.

Gladys Knight musta been on da pipe wid dis niggas in Alaska shit.

Courtesy of Photofest.

Lady Sings the Blues

(1972)

EXECUTIVE PRODUCER: Berry Gordy; DIRECTOR: Sidney J. Furie; SCREENWRITERS: Terence McCloy, Chris Clark, Suzanne de Passe; STORY: based on the book by Billie Holiday and William Dufty.

CAST: Diana Ross (Billie Holiday); Billy Dee Williams; Richard Pryor (Piano Man); Isabel Sanford; and Scatman Crothers.

Lady gave me the blues.

Mahogany

(1975)

[On Video]

DIRECTOR: Berry Gordy SCREENWRITER: John Byrum; COSTUMES: Diana Ross.

CAST: Diana Ross; Billy Dee Williams; Anthony Perkins; Beah Richards; Nina Foch; and Jean-Pierre Aumont.

In the *Ripley's Believe It or Not* file: Diana Ross received an Oscar nomination for costuming!

Courtesy of Photofest.

Sparkle

(1976)

[On Video]

DIRECTOR: Sam O'Steen; SCREENWRITER: Joel Schumacher; STORY: Joel Schumacher, Howard Rosenman (Producer); MUSIC: Curtis Mayfield.

CAST: Philip Michael Thomas (Stix); Irene Cara (Sparkle); and Lonette McKee.

Donald Bogle said *Sparkle* began its career as a box-office ugly duckling but blossomed into a swanlike *Rocky Horror* hit among black high schoolers in the late seventies and early eighties—precursing the Broadway hit *Dreamgirls*. It also inspired Aretha Franklin to record an album of its songs. It's easy to see why. The movie's music was composed by the way too cool Curtis Mayfield, who scored the first real cult film of 1970s Black America—*Superfly*.

As I've not seen *Sparkle*, hoping to avoid the headache I was sure to get if I had to suffer through Irene Cara's singing, I've not a single thought to contribute to the topic. Hell, Philip Michael Thomas's acting alone is more than enough excuse for not wandering over to my local video-rental store.

ANTONIO FARGAS

. . . .

Antonio Fargas, like Mickey Rourke, and Jerry Lewis before them both, has a broad and enthusiastic following in France. In his case it is for the role he is best remembered for in the United States: Huggy Bear on the television series *Starsky & Hutch.*

Whereas many of the best-known actors of the seventies' blaxploitation cycle have ended up as figments of Sinbad's comic imagination, Antonio Fargas has survived (and so has Huggy Bear, as a *doll,* at fifty bucks a pop!); beginning his career at the *dawn* of "black" film's modern era in the Shirley Clarke film *The Cool World* (1964). And not only has he worked consistently ever since (in such films as *Putney Swope; The*

The Cool World

(1963)
[On Video]
PRODUCER: Fred Wiseman; DIRECTOR/SCREEN-
WRITER: Shirley Clarke; STORY: based on
Warren Miller's 1959 novel *The Cool
World.*
CAST: Hampton Clanton [Rony Clanton]
(Richard "Duke" Custis); Yolanda Ro-
driguez (Lu-Anne); Bostic Felton (Rod);
Gary Bolling (Littleman); Carl Lee
(Priest); Gloria Foster (Mrs. Custis);
Georgia Burke (Grandma); Charles
Richardson (Beep Bop); and Clarence
Williams III (Blood).

Shirley Clarke's *The Cool World* is not an
exploitation film. Nor should it be confused with Ralph Bakshi's dimly-
conceived animation effort starring the
really talented Kim Basinger. What it is
is an art-house product. The film is included here because one, I consider it
the first modern "Black" film; and, two,
the film links the sixties with the seventies' Black film cycle, foreshadowing
the work of Melvin Van Peebles and
Spike Lee. It also provides an actual
physical connection to the seventies
blaxploitation era.
How? Duke (Rony Clanton [who
later starred in *The Education of Sonny
Carson*]) wants to buy a gun owned by
a junkie hustler named Priest. Priest is
portrayed by Carl Lee, son of actor
Canada Lee. Carl Lee also plays Ron
O'Neal's coke-dealing partner in *Superfly*. And Ron O'Neal's name in *Superfly*
is what? Youngblood *Priest.*

Gambler; *Next Stop, Greenwich Village*; *Pretty Baby*; *Firestarter*; and
Whore), his career highlights some of the most significant films of the
blaxploitation period: *Shaft*; *Across 110th Street*; *Cleopatra Jones*; *Foxy
Brown*; *Cornbread, Earl and Me*; and *Car Wash*.

So, contrary to the wrong-headed view of another St. Martin's publication, *Platforms,* he is *not,* as it was stated, "a model of over-the-top
campiness"; and is, instead, a serious and versatile actor of considerable
range—as formidable and elastic as his features. He has portrayed
everything from a Jelly Roll Morton–like piano man and headless alien
(with m'man Tommy Towles in John McNaughton's *The Borrower*) to a
transsexual and parody of the very figure of "campiness" to which the
aforementioned tome referred.

Antonio Fargas was born on August 14, 1946, in the Bronx and was
raised in Manhattan's Chelsea area with ten siblings by a West Indian
mom and a Puerto Rican dad.

DARIUS: What was your experience working with Shirley Clarke on
The Cool World?

FARGAS: My experience with Shirley was as a director. She was a
discoverer, in a sense, of my talent—because it was the first thing I
ever did.

I was known as the lawyer in my family. I'm one of eleven children. I guess they have a word for it today. I was an "adult child" because I could bring everybody together and figure out how to make
peace and all that. I was a peacemaker.

I was also the sensitive one. When I was an infant and I cried, my
mother said I had this great voice. It sounded like I was singing.

When I was thirteen years old, there was an ad in the newspaper.
They were looking for young men to play in a film about gangs
called *The Cool World*. They were going to all these different settle-
ment houses trying to cast newcomers, one, because it was low-
budget. Two, I think they didn't have that many of the types they
wanted in the Screen Actors Guild at that time because there was no
work for young blacks in the business, 1961 to 1962, when she was
casting. My mother saw the ad in *The Amsterdam News* and said,
"Why don't you go try out for this?" I wasn't that thrilled about it

but I didn't say no. So, (as he was underage) she consented and made an appointment. I went down and read for Shirley and Carl Lee, who was one of the stars and also a very close friend of Shirley's.

DARIUS: He was the son of . . . ?

FARGAS: Canada Lee. He had a great eye for talent. He was doing a lot of work in terms of introducing Shirley to this genre—the whole Harlem scene and the black experience, so to speak, in terms of the book *The Cool World* by Warren Miller; which was produced as a play on Broadway with Billy Dee Williams in the lead. Frederick Wiseman was the producer.

They liked the way I read. And I was up for one of the leads in the film. They took some test shots, some screen test kinda things. I didn't get the role I was up for but I did get some work in the film, in a very small, small role[5]; but that was my being-bit-by-the-bug experience.

As I came to know later, after the film, while working with Carl Lee on a couple of projects—we worked together on stage in *Ceremonies in Dark Old Men* off-Broadway and a Joseph Papp production of a play for the Shakespeare Festival called *Mod Hamlet*—I got to know Shirley as a well-respected video artist who was at the beginning cutting edge of the whole video scene out of her camp at the Chelsea Hotel.

DARIUS: Do you remember what that movement was called?

FARGAS: What the movement was called?

DARIUS: Yeah. She organized "happenings" and videotaped them. I want to know if the particular group of artists she was associated with at the Chelsea had a specific name for themselves.

FARGAS: I don't recall. I know there is a name, one or two names that sort of rattle in my head; but I don't recall.

DARIUS: Curiously, although I don't know if you gave it a definition at the time, given the projects you've worked on, you seem to come out of that particular movement.

[5]Glimpsed briefly seated on a bus.

One of this book's happy coincidences occurred while tracking down some titles I had presented to the staff of Brooklyn Heights Two Bridges Video a few days before. The store's manager, Dawn, asked if I knew of a film called *The Cool World.* I said that I did and had a copy in my collection in fact. Why?

Dawn explained that a woman had come in the day before, asking if she knew how to locate a copy. Dawn told the woman that she knew of someone working on a book and would ask, so she was asking.

It turned out the woman was Yolanda Gilliam, one of the film's young stars. I arranged for Ms. Gilliam to receive a copy of *The Cool World* in exchange for an interview. Though what follows is only a brief excerpt, Ms. Gilliam welcomed me into her home on two occasions, and we talked at length about many things. She is a warm, charming and intelligent woman. She, and her husband, Clyde, were very generous with both their time and hospitality. As the demands of both space and theme won't allow it, it is with regret that I cannot offer my readers the full extent of my discussion with Ms. Gilliam. She opens with how she prepared for her role in *The Cool World.*

Ms. Gilliam: I hung out on 145th Street learning how to be Black, and not Puerto Rican, because I had to be Black in this picture. I saw the violence. I saw the husband and wife fighting; the neighborhood getting involved; the man being pelted with garbage by other women. This was something that never happened in my little world. Sex was very open. It wasn't hidden behind closed doors. It was part of the pleasure of life. Arguing led to the pleasure.

When the movie came out in sixty-four, I was eight months pregnant. I was married to an Irishman. I had my child. My child was half Irish and half Puerto Rican. I moved into Manhattan. That was a short-lived situation. I was a single mother raising a child and then I met my husband, who is Black. I went from one extreme to the other. That's what my parents said. And I've been with my husband ever since.

Darius: Where did the movie premiere?

Ms. Gilliam: At Cinema II. It was a lot of fun. I didn't go inside to see the movie. Everyone else went. Shirley Clark, Carl Lee, Fred Wiseman. We had no say who was going to go to the movie. We were told who we could ask in terms of our parents and relatives. And I invited my mother. My father didn't want to see it. My mother went and my sister went.

Darius: Why didn't your father want to see it?

Ms. Gilliam: I don't know why he never wanted to go see it. He never really ever gave me a good reason. When my mother came out of the movie, my mother said she was glad he didn't see it because she said I showed a little too much of myself. The first thing she shouted was that I was naked, which wasn't true. I don't know why my father never wanted to see it. He has never seen it to this day, although he's collected all the little memories. He gave me an issue of *Ebony* magazine that appeared. He gave me a newspaper clipping announcing the opening. He gave that to my husband, in fact, when we got married.

But, to this day, he's never seen it. Not that he wasn't proud. He used to

FARGAS: That was a Warhol time. There was Larry Rivers—all those people were running around the Chelsea Hotel—Janis Joplin. It was a very, very rich, rich time. The whole Max's Kansas City scene. I used to go there and dance all the time. It was a veritable living artistic experience that was going on—from the music to the video to the film to the theater to the *scene,* to the *happening*—and the whole development of this new pop culture. I was sort of an observer/participant in all that as a young man trying to find my way in this "show business."

DARIUS: What were the off-stage experiences that formed the basis of some of your characterizations?

FARGAS: I've always considered myself a voyeur/participant to life. And I know that as an artist you must keep your eyes open and your options open and keep an open mind about things. It depends on what period you're talking about. I worked as an usher at CBS. I did plays. I sold cards for UNICEF. It was a whole time when the Vietnam experience was happening and there was concern about the draft. I was particularly, for myself, conscientiously opposed to war. And that was my stance during that time.

It was a very, very emotional time. People were experimenting with drugs. The whole drug scene was very strong. And, like everybody else, I participated in my own way. All of that was what was going on. You had to be touched by all these powerful, powerful *forces* that were out there—as well as make a living and develop as an artist.

I was very fortunate through those periods. As an artist, I'm continually working every time I step through the door and take my next breath. That is part of my experience. The actual times when we are working for money are special times and are a part of that tapestry. I was able to have that ongoing building of my foundation as a person and as an artist. I was also studying, too, at that time.

Right after I did *The Cool World,* I went uptown to a theater group on 113th Street, headed by Maxie Glanville in the James Weldon Johnson projects. From there, a group of people formed the nucleus of a drama department at the 135th Street Y and that was what was keeping the summers cool. They put money up in Harlem to keep summers cool and started this drama department. A few of the guys from *The Cool World* were used as sort of a nucleus—Ronnie Clanton, Gary Bowling, Bostick Felton. We started that and from there we studied with a variety of teachers. Some from The Actors Studio: one named Allen Miller, and another close friend of mine, Rick Edelsteen, were brought in as teachers so we had a varied experience in terms of the craft from a black point of view.

We were young black artists/actors just getting involved in what was going on downtown; because at the same time Robert Hooks was just starting his Group Theater Workshop, which he began in his Chelsea loft, near my mother. Shortly after that, the Negro Ensemble Company was started on Saint Mark's Place. Douglas Turner Ward, Lou Gossett and Billy Dee Williams, all these people were downtown doing things. I was also a part of that. We were the young turks involved in theater at that time. And these were the people who laid the groundwork for us. We were all over the place.

DARIUS: What year was the Negro Ensemble Company started?

FARGAS: I'm not good on dates.

DARIUS: I'm asking you this to get a feel for the social climate at the time.

FARGAS: It had to be sixty-*eight,* around there. Sixty-seven. Sixty-eight. No wait, I was in high school. It had to be sixty-five, sixty-seven.

DARIUS: Then that would be when the Black Arts Movement was just getting started.

FARGAS: Uh hmm. Robert Hooks was doing *The Dutchman* off-Broadway. When I first got in the business, and started studying theater with Robert, I think he was also doing *The Blacks* [by Jean Genet] at the time. *The Blacks* was sort of ending up its long, long run at the Saint Mark's Theater.

Al Freeman, Jr., and I did a double bill of *The Toilet* and *The Slave* by Amiri Baraka. That was my first play, *The Toilet* by Baraka, who was called Leroi Jones at that time.

tell me I could be anything I wanted to be. He never gave me a good reason.

After the movie, and I had my son, I went to The New School. I took an actor's workshop. They had me go to Luigi's dance class. I took up dancing. They had a teacher to teach me how to sing. She said I should take up speaking rather than singing. That meant that I was lousy.

Parts for Puerto Ricans and Blacks were not available. Months after the movie, I met some of the young guys. They said they had gotten agents and wanted to be in movies. They told me horror stories about the things these people wanted them to do. And they didn't care whether it was male or female. And I said I wasn't going to go through that. I wasn't going to be *poor!* I wasn't going to *starve!* I had a child to take care of and it would have been difficult for me.

I got back into shape. But there's just something about being Black or being Puerto Rican and trying to pursue an acting career that just didn't appeal to me. The movie was very hard to make.

Not having any training, it was very hard. Learning lines was very, very difficult. I was a straight-A student in school. Reading and memorizing had nothing to do with anything. It was just the conditions. The conditions were extremely hard.

I guess maybe if I had been introduced to an easier director . . . because I assumed that all directors were like Shirley Clarke. I wouldn't have been able to deal with the next director that was that hard.

Not all the people were bad. I liked the camera people. I met this woman,

Terri. She was my hairdresser. She was marvelous. I loved her. But I couldn't deal with the hardships of making a movie. *And I couldn't deal with Shirley Clarke.*

I listen to everything she said. I did everything she said. But nobody could make me like her as a person. I don't think she was a nice person. And I guess that's what turned me off.

Darius: What did she do beyond throw temper tantrums?

Ms. Gilliam: She didn't manhandle us. We wouldn't have stood for that. We were naive and sweet but we were dangerous. She knew her limitations. She could throw her little temper tantrums. She could cuss us out. She could make us work under terrible conditions because that was our job. She could change the script and make us learn it, but that was the extent of how far she went.

Carl Lee was interesting. Carl Lee said that I had something that if cultivated and trained it would have come out eventually. He said I was certainly exuberant and forward and strong enough.

It was an adventure. It was something I did at the time and I just did it. The movie I did, I did at the time because it was a lark. I never thought of it as a profession. And learning all the things that I did at the time I started doing the movie turned me off to it anyway.

Darius: Did you meet Fredrick Wiseman?

DARIUS: Were there specific political/cultural issues you were directly involved in, either in conjunction with or in conflict with the other actors and writers of that time?

FARGAS: I was a young, brash, seeking observer of the scene; but in terms of the politics of it—it was the breaking out of the Village and the whole scene down there in terms of just coming out of the civil rights movement and all the brothers going down-downtown and the white girls and all this stuff that was going on. So, from that political point of view, the mixing of cultures was really strong.

At the time, I was a participant as well as an observer; but the only reason the politics came in was because of the political climate in terms of the whole Vietnam thing which was brewing. Those things weren't a big concern to me except, again—the war. You *are* talking about the business in terms of show business and how it related politically to blacks?

DARIUS: Actually I'm more interested in the internal politics among the artists. For example, there was a magazine called *Umbra*. It started downtown around nineteen sixty. Some of the playwrights you've mentioned were published in it. It was a multicultural enterprise.

Because of a poem submitted to them after the JFK assassination, which satirized the Kennedy administration, the magazine split in two factions. One faction wanted to publish the poem. The other didn't. Eventually, the magazine folded.

The faction who didn't want to see the poem published moved their act uptown to Harlem and announced themselves as a part of The Black Arts Movement. The faction which supported the poem stayed downtown and got involved with *The East Village Other, The Evergreen Review* and *Fuck You: A Journal of the Arts.* That split formed the basis of an ongoing "nationalist/multicultural" debate. I ask the question because I'm trying to gain some additional insight into that situation and how it might have affected your outlook as an actor.

FARGAS: I don't think it affected me. I think, as you say, it affected the writers more than the actors. The actors were the vessels used to stage the words that were being written at the time. How it affected me, or how I saw it, I saw the beginnings of Leroi Jones becoming Amiri Baraka, moving uptown and eventually to Newark. That certainly influenced the work he produced.

Then there were plays like *In White America* which Gloria Foster starred in—racially charged, civil rights kinds of things which fueled how the scene was ethnically polarized; or, in a sense, *pop* culturally.

There was this sort of *shaking down* of how everybody was gonna play their roles for the next ten to twenty years. I witnessed that; but mostly in terms, as you stated, of people moving uptown.

People got into their dashiki, or pre-dashiki period, where people were more into their blackness, y'know? When we became not "Negroes" anymore but "blacks." Now we are African-Americans. So this was the "Negro" to "black" period which we're talking about here.

DARIUS: As a writer, it's important for me to know the roots of my traditions—to know the writers who've contributed to the literary tradition I've chosen. I know my lineage. I say all of this to ask what actors influenced you?

FARGAS: Certainly there were many from my early experiences but the ones who stand out, the ones who stood out for me, was working with James Earl Jones; watching him create the Jack Johnson character in Washington and then bringing it to Broadway. Being overwhelmed by the play and the players in *The Blacks*; seeing Robert Hooks doing the role James Earl Jones created. And watching Adolphe Caesar in one of the roles in *The Blacks*.

DARIUS: You cite James Earl Jones as an influence. Does that mean you see yourself as a descendant of Paul Robeson?

FARGAS: Yes. Everybody laid the groundwork for the next generation so to speak. I consider myself one of the young pioneers because of where I started in 1961 to 62, coming out of the civil rights movement. And the people who laid the groundwork for me are the people that I mentioned—the Sidneys who were in the Village, the Belafontes, the Robert Hooks, the Lou Gossets and my buddy Glynn

Courtesy of Photofest.

Ms. Gilliam: Never. We only got to meet the people we worked with. They didn't keep us all together. This is my perception, I don't think they wanted us to get all friendly and socialize. Because, after the movie, they had me on radio programs, and they had me appear at RKO theaters . . .

Darius: What was that like?

Ms. Gilliam: It was fun. But I got asked by the manager to leave, though.

Darius: Why?

Ms. Gilliam: I caused a riot.

Darius: *You caused a riot?*

Ms. Gilliam: Yeah. They figured if I could kiss Hampton Clanton on screen I could kiss any of them. They started getting a little rambunctious. So they asked me to leave.
   Nicely.

Putney Swope

(1969)
[On Video]
DIRECTOR/SCREENWRITER/PRODUCER: Robert
Downey, Sr.
CAST: Arnold Johnson; Antonio Fargas;
Laura Green; Buddy Butler; Allen
Garfield; and Pepi Hermine.

"I'm not going to rock the boat. *I'm
gonna sink it!*" announced the gravel-
voiced Putney Swope, the newly elected
CEO of a New York advertising firm. So,
as his first task as the firm's new head,
he fires all the whyte folks except one.
He then renames it "Truth and Soul"
with the decree they will no longer handle
accounts for war toys and cigarettes,
employing a number of oddballs, including Antonio Fargas as "The A-rab,"
to inflict his agenda on the world.

Even without a head full of pot
smoke clouding my brain, my condition
when I saw this film every other weekend in the local art house during high
school, this film still makes me laugh.

Turman, who worked with Sidney on Broadway as a youngster in *A Raisin in the Sun.* These are the people who laid the groundwork for me. And, hopefully, there will be young African-American artists who will be able to say that I did something similar for them.

Being this "Negro" boy watching television, and never seeing ourselves represented on there, never seeing myself, except in *Amos and Andy* situations; then going to the movies and watching the screen, and being fascinated by this whole medium, and to be cast in a film, *The Cool World.* Even though I had a small role in it, almost like a glorified extra, to think that I could go see myself upon the screen where I've seen all these other people, bigger than life, was very overwhelming. I'm still getting over it and accepting that. I'm still very fascinated by the fact that I do this and I do this for a living.

One of the things I saw in film was that I always tended to sympathize and wanted to be the leading man. Looking at myself, and I wasn't able to honestly look at myself, I was thrust into the fact that I had to be a character actor because I was not the leading man type. I was a skinny kid with interesting features who thought he could do the leading man stuff because that was the hero. But I was also always very fascinated by "the bad guy," by the guy who was supposed to be not so good, or the character players in the things that I watched. It was interesting that I was nudged in that direction by the roles I was given and the opportunities that were presented to me to play.

As a young artist running around this town, I always was into characters because I liked getting out of myself. That was the escapism of embracing this make-believe world that we could live in and make a living at. I used to run around with headbands and costumes on because it was fun to get out of one's self. By doing that, we could also do it on stage and in front of a camera. The whole character thing—a young character actor developing into an older character actor—I wouldn't want it any other way, today.

Certainly, I had misgivings which involved maybe I'd like doing something else. But this certainly is fun, just doing it is fun. I didn't think that much about the characters. I had a hunger to *do,* to try and perfect and mirror some of the things that I saw in life and put them into what I was trying to put on stage and predominantly in film.

When you play transsexuals, homosexuals, drug addicts or pimps—all the things that are the underbelly of society which is so fascinating, which support and make the other people look good—it becomes a real compulsion to try and get them right because each one has to be defined differently and uniquely.

Sometimes people come to me and say, "Aren't you tired of playing the same kinds of roles?" And I'd say, "I dunno. Did anybody ever accuse Jimmy Cagney, or these people who came before us, about playing gangster after gangster?" Anyone who is astute would know each one was an individual essay of a character. I'm sure we see followers everywhere. But each one you play as an actor has to be an individual. You're not looking at who I'm like but at a character founded on *choice*. Choice is what we see and what we take from. Art is choice. Character building has to be how we build ourselves as human beings by the choices we make and by the influences that make us.

DARIUS: I'm going to name some films and I want you to tell me what your experience was working on them. *Putney Swope*.

FARGAS: That was the culmination of that period we spoke of earlier. I was doing *The Great White Hope* at night on Broadway and I shot my parts of the film later in the evening. After the play, I would go to the set and I shot with Robert. That's how we saved money, by doing night shoots and using office buildings that weren't working during the evening. The meat of the film, the bulk of it, was shot at night, the stuff inside as well as some of the exteriors. That was the height.

Here I was playing a ninety-year-old some-odd ancient man on Broadway at nineteen or twenty and twenty-one; then playing the A-rab, creating this character for Downey.

And most of it—a lot of it—was just clicking and hitting it off. Understanding what each one valued. As far as I could go [with the character] was acceptable to him. That was very liberating. It took fine work to be able to do that. It was a really great experience to be on the cutting edge of what seemed like insanity. But with a purpose.

DARIUS: It seemed like much of it was improvised.

Courtesy of Photofest.

Across 110th Street

(1972)
[On Video]
EXECUTIVE PRODUCERS: Anthony Queen, Barry Shear (Director); SCREENWRITER: Luther Davis; STORY: based on the novel by Wally Ferris; MUSIC: J.J. Johnson; SONGS: Bobby Womack.
CAST: Anthony Quinn (Capt. Frank Mattelli); Yaphet Kotto (Det. Lieut. Wm. A. Pope); Anthony Franciosa (Nick D'Salvio); Paul Benjamin (Jim Harris); Ed Bernard (Joe Logart); Richard Ward (Doc Johnson); Norma Donaldson (Gloria Roberts); and Antonio Fargas (Henry Jackson).

Antonio Fargas is one of three small-time hoods who rob a Mafia-controlled numbers parlor in Harlem. He gets his dick cut off for his trouble. Yaphet Kotto investigates with an actor who portrayed Quasimodo in a 1950s remake of *The Hunchback of Notre Dame*. Director Barry Shear shot the pilot for the queercult TV series *Starsky & Hutch. Need I say more?*

The Education of Sonny Carson

(1974)
[On Video]
DIRECTOR: Michael Campus; SCREENWRITER: Fred Hudson.
CAST: Rony Clanton; Joyce Walker; Jerry Bell; Paul Benjamin; Mary Alice; Don Gordon; Linda Hopkins; and Thomas Hicks

What I want to see is *The Re-education of Sonny Carson*—A Spike Lee Spliff.

FARGAS: It was like sketching. We had a skeleton of what this thing was about. But I think how he directed was in parts, then he put it together. Again, as a character actor, a lot of times, I would pull out the rest of the pages in the script because I didn't want to be influenced by what went on before or after what I did in the film. I considered myself a cameo artist who came in to do a specific job on a film. I just wasn't interested in what went on before. It was almost the same with this film. I was specifically interested in what I was doing at the moment in the scenes that I was involved in and filling out as much of this character as I could; giving the information he wanted me to convey and run with it. Creating it as it went. It was my duty after we locked in on something, when we had to do take after take, to keep it in the same ballpark so we didn't stray too much and start creating another movie. We worked well together.

DARIUS: How were you able to enter into the mindset of the A-rab immediately after your nightly performances in *The Great White Hope*?

FARGAS: It was real easy. First of all, I created the role in Washington, D.C., and then moved it up here. Once you get your chops down, it's very liberating. I've always said if you gave me a script in the morning of what I was going to do and what I was going to say, because I live in that world, I'd take to that world very easily, rather than the uncertainty of spontaneity that life has. I know that when I go to the theater I'm going to immerse myself in a world where I pretty much know what's going to happen and all I have to do is show up. That's very *freeing* for me, not confining. So that was fun. To come out and come down after doing a show, I need time to readjust. But to readjust into another world—which is a film—and that was also my second film, was very fresh for me.

DARIUS: Now, you did an anti-drug film between *The Cool World* and *Putney Swope*.

FARGAS: You know everything. (Laughter).

DARIUS: No. I just read your filmography.

FARGAS: I think I did three before I did *Putney Swope*. As I said before, I'm not good with dates. It was either my second or third film. But to go into the world of movie-making again, after my little experience in *The Cool World*, was very exciting. I had lots of energy and the character had to have that anyway, so it was exciting to come from the Broadway stage and stay up doing a film at night. It was very nice.

DARIUS: After *Putney*, you did *Pound* followed by *Shaft*.

FARGAS: Looking back, I now see what Downey was trying to do. From *Greaser's Palace* on, he was trying to form an ensemble or a group of people who understood the way he worked and could execute his vision on a continuing basis. I was very proud that I was asked to play the role of the greyhound in this film, I guess, that was a little too over the top for the establishment so it didn't get the kind of airing or reception that *Putney Swope* did. All in all, *Pound* was one of those pleasant nightmares and another chance to work with somebody I thought deserved to have the kick of so many artists who could do what he wanted to do.

    Shaft was my introduction to big Hollywood to a certain degree, low-budget by Hollywood standards because it was dealing with a black subject and a black hero. Again, looking back, I'm really proud I was able to be in projects that were the vanguard for opening acts for a lot of things that happened after that. *Shaft* was certainly one of those. It was again, in that film, my cameo situation. I came in and did one scene.

DARIUS: It's the one scene I remember most from *Shaft*.

FARGAS: What I try to bring is a sense of commitment to the character, and to the reality and beyond. Things that are intangible and that an artist doesn't know even that he is doing. It's like someone improvising, or when a jazz musician plays. You don't know what you're doing. And this is one of those moments in a visual sense when you don't know what you're doing. You're just there and you're being and you're naked. And that was one of those naked moments that I'm proud I showed up for.

Courtesy of Photofest.

Cornbread, Earl and Me

(1975)
[On Video]
PRODUCER/DIRECTOR: Joe Manduke; EXECU-
TIVE PRODUCER/SCREENWRITER: Leonard
Lamensdorf; STORY: based on Ronald
Fair's novel *Hog Butcher*; MUSIC: Donald
Byrd.
CAST: Moses Gunn (Ben Blackwell); Ros-
alind Cash (Sarah Robinson); Bernie
Casey (Atkins); Madge Sinclair (Leona);
Keith Wilkes (Cornbread); Tierre Turner
(Earl); Antonio Fargas (One-Eye); and
Larry Fishburne III (Wilford).

Prequel to the upcoming Rodney King
TV movie.

DARIUS: How do you relate your acting technique to jazz?

FARGAS: I didn't see it at first, because my life, in a sense, is a jazz piece. I'm really into the improvisation of life. And life is a big improv. Jazz musicians go free, spontaneous, moment to moment. That's how I live. That's how I was able to fashion a craft out of that. Sun Ra had this loft in the Village and he would invite people to come in and bang on a pot or somethin'. And I went. I remember being in his presence. He was the kind of guy who could find the music without the music. Not knowing anything about music but having feelings, I felt like I was really playing when I was giving to that group. Maybe this was the world I was looking for—the whole idea of an *eclectic* life, I think, is where an artist has to stay. Years ago, you couldn't ask me to explain how I worked a scene or how I created something because it was just an improv in my head; but because I've played this improv many times, I'm able to talk about what my technique is and what complication is involved in my technique. I relate very much to jazz. In fact, I had an aversion to jazz at first because it was so much like me. It was really interesting. Until I became a jazz person myself and I realized what that guy was doing that was so personal that he blocked out everything and just was *into* it. I said, "How can this guy be so selfish?" But you have to be that selfish as an artist.

I'm yo' mamma, I'm yo' daddy,
I'm that nigga in the alley, I'm yo'—

Pusherman!!

You know what's wrong with you so-called twentynothing, generation X kidz today? You goddamned ball-capped, plaid-flannel-shirt-wearin', Doug Coupland readin', Kurt Cobain mournin', MTV brain-controlled *fools* don't know how to get *high!* It ain't like when I was a boy! We knew how to get *fucked up* back in the seventies!

Drop too much acid? *No problem!*

A frizzy-haired, big-bosomed Earthbabe in a peasant skirt handed you a glass of orange juice and said, *"Relax. Be mellow. It's just a drug in your body. Breath deeply and go with the cosmic flow of the universe. Experience the vibe through your third eye. Remember; Timothy Leary says, 'When driving a Pontiac—be the Pontiac!' "*

And just as soon as we puked up the box of *Screaming Yellow Zonkers* popcorn we had gobbled waiting for the acid to hit, we was straight like a muthafucka—especially if Earthbabe was about to try that flesh-twistin', fingernail-scrapin' Reikian massage shit, talkin' 'bout rearrangin' *chakras!*

But you vegetable-n-tofu eatin', black-sneakered, would-be junk fiends? *Shee-it!*

Shoot too much dope? *Easy!* Roll 'em out on the sidewalk *and let EMS pick 'em up!*

And, while I'm on it, we was *fuckin'* in the seventies, too—none of this wetsuit and flippers and hammerin' nails through y' dick nonsense! Studs an' shit hangin' all off the pussy! If you wanna give head to a box of carpet tacks, *go to a hardware store . . . !*

(Actually, a really great interview with an *actual* drug dealer was supposed to go here. Unfortunately, the tape snapped in my cassette, and this manuscript is due early tomorrow morning. Or I'd spend the time repairing it and share this really great interview with you. I called the drug dealer the Singing Burgler because he was a burgler before he be-

Courtesy of Photofest.

Together Brothers

(1974)
DIRECTOR: William A. Graham; SCREENWRITERS: Jack De Witt (Story), Joe Green; MUSIC: Barry White.
CAST: Ahmad Nurradin (H.J.); Anthony Wilson (Tommy); Nelson Sims (A.P.); Kenneth Bell (Mau Mau); Owen Page (Monk); Kim Dorsey (Gri Gri); Ed Bernard (Mr. Kool); Lincoln Kilpatrick (Billy Most); and Glynn Turman (Dr. Johnson).

Hardy Boys' mystery on d'ghetto tip.

PROFILE: RON O'NEAL

The directionless, Cleveland native Ron O'Neal said he "just played bridge" when attending Ohio State but, on seeing a production of *Finian's Rainbow*, his life changed. Thereafter, for eight years, he trained in a ghetto-storefront theater called "Karamu" (a Swahili word meaning place of enjoyment), founded by Russell and Rowena Jeliffe in 1913. His first real break came when he was chosen to appear in the Broadway production *Ceremonies in Dark Old Men*, earning real attention after winning an Obie and Drama Desk Award as the lead in Charles Gordone's Pulitzer Prize–winning play, *No Place To Be Somebody*. O'Neal was brought into the *Superfly* project as a result of his friendship with Cleveland homie, Philip Fenty.

came a merchant of marijuana. He told really great stories like how to break into apartments with an eighteen-inch screwdriver. He was really, really good at it, too! He robbed Jean Shepard *twice!* He also said that the heroin on the street nowadays is real shit. He says it makes you really paranoid and anxious. It's not like the heroin they shot back in the sixties. "Now that was *real* dope!" he said. And he went on to describe the difference between that dope and the dope out on the street today. It would have been real helpful, especially if you ever shoot some dope and need to know if you're getting the real stuff or not.

It was a really, really great interview. I'm sorry I can't share it with you.)

SUPERFLY
('72)

PRODUCER: Sig Shore; **DIRECTOR:** Gordon Parks; **SCREENWRITER:** Phillip Fenty; **COSTUMES:** Nate Adams; **MUSIC:** Curtis Mayfield. **CAST:** Ron O'Neal (Youngblood Priest); Carl Lee (Eddie); Sheila Frazier (Georgia); Julius W. Harris (Scatter); Charles McGregor (Fat Freddy); and the Curtis Mayfield Experience (Themselves).

Aerial view. Harlem, U.S.A.
Two junkies shiver in sickness.
> *Did you get the money?*
> *I ain't got nothin'. She wouldn't give it to me.*

With his knotted hair swollen under a knit cap, a sallow-skinned junkie punches his partner in the arm with disgust.
> *Wastin' all this goddamned time. We do it my way.*

The two junkies walk Harlem's bustling sidewalks with uneven focus. Knit cap outlines his plan, bumming change from a passerby.

The *Ebony* mag–reading black bourgeoisie condemned *Superfly* as a glorification of the drug-dealer; though, ironically, the film is an attack on the very values cherished by that community—ostentatious materialism and Christianity. Both live on the backs of the poor. The only difference is one of means.

"You gon' give all this up? An eight-track stereo, a color TV in every room an' snortin' half a piece of dope every day. That's the American Dream, nigga!"

West Village. Bedroom.

His face is one of fierce, Christ-like beauty. A coke-spoon crucifix lies in his bed of chest hairs. A woman of *Playboy*-centerfold statistics rests by his side, her white rump prominently displayed. They bask in the after-glow of narcotized sex.

Spooning powder from a vial taken from the bed's backboard, he snorts. Each nostril. The freeze fans through his face. The woman caresses his shoulder. He turns to her.

You wanna blow?

You gonna leave?

Yep. I gotta make a pickup.

Then I don't want any. Some things go better with coke.

He fingers his BVDs. His face indicates he could care less if she did or didn't suck his dick. He gets out of bed.

As he pulls his pants on, the camera lingers on his crotch's bulging outlines. The naked whyte woman stares in the background, thinking, *Dat nigga fly. Superfly.*

His name is Youngblood Priest, the pusherman-redeemer who—*for a price*—offers the crystalized flesh of Christ in the bowl of a silver coke-spoon.

Priest enters a building in Harlem. And the two junkies try and take him off for his shit. They fuck up. Knit cap takes off.

Priest is on his ass. Down city blocks. Through alleyways. Across lots. Up a fire escape.

He corners the junkie in a cell of hellish poverty, occupied by a mother and her wailing child. As he stomps the junkie, who pukes a mouthful of oatmeal, Priest begins to sense his own implication in the construction of this hell, and it is here he begins to experience an attack of conscience.

He wants out of the coke-dealin' game and concocts a scheme to score thirty keys of coke, unloading the shit for one million dollars. In the end, he puts a contract out on the deputy commissioner's life, plays the mob whyte boys for fools and makes off with the cash.

And make off he did. *Superfly* not only grossed $6,400,000 at the

Courtesy of the George Trow Estate.

Superfly T.N.T.

(1973)
[On Video]

PRODUCER: Sig Shore (Story); DIRECTOR: Ron O'Neal (Story); SCREENWRITER: Alex Haley; MUSIC: Osibisa.

CAST: Ron O'Neal (Youngblood Priest); Roscoe Lee Browne (Dr. Lamine Sonko); Sheila Frazier (Georgia); and Robert Guillaume (Jordan Gaines).

In this sequel to *Superfly*, I'm really amazed by the fact that Youngblood's nose wasn't replaced by two scabby blowholes in the middle of his face!

PROFILE: MAX JULIAN

Max Julian studied at Carnegie Hall's Dramatic Workshop, making his professional debut in Joseph Papp's New York Shakespeare Festival; and, like many crafted New York actors of the seventies black-film cycle, he also appeared in Genet's *The Blacks*.

His first major film role was in Jules Dassin's *Up Tight* as Johnny, a Black radical activist turned over to the pigs. He also played a San Francisco hippie in a psychedelic Dick Clark production called *Psych-Out* with a demented Bruce Dern. He achieved national stardom with *The Mack*.

He went on to create *Cleopatra Jones*. He and ex-squeeze Vonetta McGee (with whom he appeared on the cover of *Jet*) starred in the late Gordon Parks, Jr.'s *Thomasine & Bushrod*.

Max Julian was last seen in a rap video.

Willie Dynamite

(1974)

DIRECTOR: Gilbert Moses III; SCREENPLAY: Ron Cutler; STORY: Joe Keyes, Ron Cutler; COSTUMES: Bernard Johnson; MUSIC: J. J. Johnson.
CAST: Roscoe Orman (Willie Dynamite); Diana Sands (Cora); Thalmus Rasulala (Robert Daniels); Juanita Brown (Sola); and Mary Wilcox (Scatback).

New York's number 1 pimp, Willie "Dynamite" Short don't be playin' dat "Lemme take m'hoze on a field trip to the Planetarium" West Coast hippie-pimp shit like Goldie be doin' in *The Mack*. He a cold-blooded, bidnisminded mack who pop a ho' in da mouf' inna minnit if she ain't right wid dat money. Willie a capitalist-practicin' free enterpriser.

box office, but the film's real star—its *soundtrack*—was on the charts for forty-six weeks. It stayed at number 1 for five weeks and sold over two million copies. The album's two singles *Superfly* and *Freddie's Dead* sold one million copies each.

As its production notes indicate, *Superfly* was a "miracle" with everything against it. It was shot in the dead of winter with half of its location shots outdoors. Power sources were drawn from nearby light poles. On at least two occasions, producer Sig Shore was forced to shut down production for four-day stretches because he simply couldn't afford raw film stock. He even had to negotiate with a Lower East Side gangleader to shoot on his turf by casting him as a junkie in the film. Gordon Parks, Jr., had never directed a feature so the studio suits wanted to see rushes before putting up the completion money and Sig Shore refused. He turned to an assortment of black businesspersons to raise the needed capital, including "pimps, madams and drug dealers"; one of the least publicized facts of seventies' drug culture—successful dealers often recycled their wealth to support art and artists, everything from painting and publishing to financing independent films and experiments in anarchistic living (which will become evident when someone gets around to writing the definitive Tom Forcade biography). Adman Philip Fenty, who had originally written *Superfly* for the stage, had never written a screenplay so the actors improvised large chunks of their scenes, which, later, as it turned out, had to be lip-synched (read: redubbed) in a sound studio. Still, the results are quite remarkable. It rises above its mythic reputation by remaining a true and artful portrait of a successful drug dealer fighting for his own redemption.

THE MACK
('78) [On Video]

DIRECTOR: Michael Campus; SCREENWRITER: Robert J. Poole; COSTUMES: Mr. Marcus and June; MUSIC: Willie Hutch; TECHNICAL ADVISORS: Ward Brothers, Roosevelt Taylor, Jan Payton, Don Barksdale. CAST: Max Julien (John "Goldie" Mickens); Don Gordon (Hank); Richard Pryor (Slim); Carol Speed (Lulu); Roger Mosley (Olinga); Dick

Anthony Williams (Pretty Tony); and Andrew Ward, Frank D. Ward, Ted Ward, Willie Ward.

How's this for teen-boy fantasy—

"Make way for The Mack! He attracts the sexiest girls, rides the biggest cars and wears the best clothes in town!"

The two defining films of the 1970s blaxploitation cycle are *Superfly* and *The Mack*. These are the two films mentioned most frequently when I've discussed this project with other blacks (and, not surprisingly, the anti-imperialist *Chinese Connection* often comes up. And why not? Bruce Lee was also pissed off at racism in America and young black audiences identified his rage at colonial oppression as their own— remember, Bruce Lee began his study of martial arts because he was tired of getting his ass kicked by Brit whyte boys every day). *The Mack* captures some of the ideological confusion of young black males in the 1970s by positing the ideals of the black revolutionary against the capitalist mentality of the pimp.

Set in Oakland, the birthplace of the Black Panther Party for Self-Defense, the film outlines the philosophy of the players' community as typified by the speech of an older pimp to the young, recently out of prison Goldie (Max Julian) (the raspiness of the older pimp's voice is a dead giveaway that the character is modeled after the legendary Iceberg Slim): "... a pimp is only as good as his product and his product is women ... anybody can control a woman's body, but, see, the thing is to control her mind. Pimping is big business and it's been going since the beginning of time...."

With the assistance of the Ward Brothers, one of whom died during the production of this film, some of its scenes were shot at the annual Players Ball in Oakland, which is considered the Academy Awards of Mackdom. According to the production notes, "The Players Ball is the social highlight for the Bay Area's macks and their women. The ladies in sequined hot pants, gowns with feather boas, elaborate wigs and jewelry are almost outdone by their macks in brocaded suits, silks, furs and ivory-topped canes. On this particular occasion the ladies treat their macks for the evening, and awards are given for 'the biggest and the best' macks."

In the movie, Willie got a new ho' named Passion. She a fine, young, fox with fashion-model aspirations. She gets busted and an ex-ho' turned social worker plays square-world games on her brain. Fuckin' wid Willie's head is a rival pimp named "Bell," who wants to cop Willie's stable under the pretext of startin' up a "Pimp Union"; two vice cops (one of whom indicates he's a Black Muslim); an assistant D.A., and the guilt trips of Willie's mom. When Willie's new ho' gets thrown in jail, some old hoze slash her face and she is forced to reconsider her flat-backin' ways. Meanwhile, the IRS freezes Willie's bank account, Bell's "Pimp Union" kicks his ass, his purple El D gets stripped and his mom dies. So, in an effort to save his ride, his hoze and closet full of clothes, Willie cracks under pressure and goes out his mind. It's some funny shit.

In my book (and this is *my* book), *Willie Dynamite* is the hands-down winner of the all-out best blaxploitation movie of the seventies. With a metaphor not unlike the one found in Barry Michael Cooper's script for *New Jack City,* *Willie Dynamite* is a sly satire told in the toast mode on the impulses that drive corporate America. As the rival pimp out to cop Willie's stable, Roger Robinson deserves The Players' Ball Award for "Best Movie Mack of All Time" for his highly stylized, over-the-top performance: its a hysterical mix of Count Blacula and Liberace. Most marvelous of all is Willy's outrageous sense of fashion. The trendoid, cyber-wizard nineties has yet to come up with anything that compares with Willie's wardrobe.

Sesame Street producer and *Willie Dynamite* star, Rosco Orman, was seen recently on the New York Stage in the role of Stepin Fetchit.

Courtesy of the George Trow Estate.

The Candy Tangerine Man

(1975)
PRODUCER/DIRECTOR: Matt Cimber; SCREEN-
WRITER: George Theakos; WARDROBE: Caro-
line Davis; MUSIC: Smoke.
CAST: John Daniels (Black Baron/Ron).

A pillar of boojie L.A. by day, but by
night, like Clarence Reid donning
"Blowfly" bodystocking, Ron becomes
the "Black Baron"—a vanilla ice-
cream suited Super Pimp riding a yellow and red Rolls-Royce on Hollywood's
Sunset Strip! Chocked full of the kind of
sleazy, surreal bits in the unflinching
Mondo Cane style that's made pimping
mighty unpopular with feminists the
world over.

Olinga, Goldie's brother, grounds the film in the reality of black oppression. He is a revolutionary activist who conducts political education
workshops in the community, and wants to clean up the 'hood even if it
means sacrificing his brother in the process.

Richard Pryor's presence in the film is significant, even if he behaves
as if he's hanging out with Gene Wilder instead of a pimp. According to
David Henderson, author of the Hendrix bio, *'Scuse Me While I Kiss The
Sky,* Pryor tired of the Cosby-like routines he'd been performing, left
the Hollywood/Vegas scene and came to the Bay Area to get his head together, where he befriended Cecil Brown, the author of *The Life And
Loves Of Mr. Jive-Ass Nigger,* and screenwriter for *Which Way Is Up?*.

Pryor swung back and forth between the writer/poet scene in Berke-
ley, which had become the western, Black bohemian wing of *Umbra,* to
the players' scene in Oakland. And because of the influences of both,
Pryor was able to find his voice as the comedian we've all grown to love.

In my talk with David, he didn't know if cha-cha champ Bruce Lee
had ever attended a dance in Seattle with music provided by a band
that included Jimi Hendrix on guitar.

WITH THE
FLAVORFUL FAB
FIVE FREDDY

While I was struggling with the early stages of this book, in the late months of 1992, poet Bob Holman telephoned one afternoon, and invited me to read that Tuesday night for "The Ayatollah's Granola: Rap Meets Poetry" series he organized with my friend and comrade-in-struggle, music publicist Bill Adler, at The Fez, Time Cafe's sub-basement cabaret on Lafayette and Great Jones Street in Manhattan.

With some reluctance, I agreed. And he scheduled my appearance for sometime between nine-thirty and ten. I showed up as promised—*and the joint was jammed!*

Journalists. A & R reps. MTV scouts. The East Third Street Stoop poet-posse. Uptown. Downtown. And the underground.

I slid through the crowd to the side of the room, and stood beside Tracie Morris with my back to the bar, exchanging affectionate barbs. Along with Dael Orlander-Smith, Dana Bryant, The Jones Twins, Jake-Ann Jones and Jennifer Jazz, Tracie is one of the few giving the New York–based "spoken-word performance poet" scene any of its distinctive flavor. They've defined its current state and set its standard. Largely (and this was the reason for my reluctance to appear), the scene is plagued by vampires obsessed with MTV's thirty seconds of fame. Tracie is a hop-scotch of jazz and hip-hop—throwing up real ideas and challenging word games, reading the "poetry" inside the poetry.

In his scrambled Dada style, Bob leapt onstage and introduced me in a jumble of surreal word-wit balloons. I faced the crowd and offered *The Blackman's Guide to Seducing White Women with the Amazing Power of Voodoo!*

The men in the room grew quiet with bewildered and defensive looks. But the women went pin-eyed *nuts*.

Hooting. Laughing. Cheering.

I was amazed. I felt like I'd flung my jockstrap into an audience of suburban housewives in a male strip joint.

As I left the stage and squeezed my way back to the bar, a hand reached up and grabbed my arm.

"Where can I buy that book?"

"Right here," I said, "ten dollars."

I reached into my bag and withdrew a copy of *Negrophobia*. I handed him the book. He stared at the cover with a puzzled expression.

"You wrote this?"

"Yeah. Ten dollars."

"About the pimps an' shit?"

"No. Whyte girl haunted by scary Negroes."

"*What?*"

"Check it out. Ten dollars."

He handed over a ten-dollar bill.

"Who do I sign it to?"

"Fab Five Freddy."

"You da muthafucka who be gettin' fucked up on TV wid Billy Dee?"
(I don't have cable.)

"Yeah."

Later, I'm home in bed. The telephone rips me out of sleep.

"Yo, money! Dis is da shit!"

"Who is this?"

It was two o'clock in the morning.

"Fab. *Did I wake you up?"*

And that's how I began my friendship with Fred Braithwaite, known to viewers of *Yo! MTV Raps* as Fab Five Freddy. He is not only a maxin' an' relaxin' TV host with a can of Colt 45 in hand, but an actor (*Wild Style*); producer (associate, *New Jack City*); and an award-winning video director with an emerging career directing feature film.

Courtesy of Joy Glidden © 1995.

Fab's roots into global Black culture extend deep. I'm consistently impressed by his intelligence, the encyclopedic reach of his knowledge and elegance of manner. Our personal discussions cover a range of topics, centering primarily on jazz and painting. Why? *'Cause Fab can paint his shiny black hiney off!*

Here he discusses the topic which first brought us together: pimps.

FAB: In the seventies, I was growing up in Bed Stuy, Brooklyn. I was still in high school. There was a cousin of mine. He left high school in his senior year because it looked like he was going to repeat that year over. So he left high school and left home. I wondered what he was up to. So I went and found out. My cousin had gone into the streets and become a pimp.

I had always been fascinated by all kinds of counterculture street life, especially what I had been exposed to growing up as a kid in Brooklyn. That included numbers bankers, stick-up kids, hustlers, gamblers and pimps. I wasn't exposed to a great deal of pimps. It was more like numbers bankers in my neighborhood so I was always curious about the pimping game. My cousin was curious too. He left home and went out into the Times Square area of Manhattan and got involved with it. One weekend, I left home to go hang out with him in Times Square. He was staying in a two-bit hotel somewhere off of Eighth Avenue in the forties. He was hustling in Times Square but he was actually living in Brooklyn. He had rented a real funky room in a brownstone, a few blocks away from where I grew up in Bed-Stuy.

While hanging out, we talked about the Life; about hustlers; about pimps; what it was like out there; the rules of the game. He pulled my coat to this whole structure and interesting thing going on with it. As we talked, he began to recite this long story that rhymed. They were known as toasts.

The toast flourished in shooting galleries, pool rooms, prisons, any kind of inner-city hangout spot where people got together and entertained each other. It was in jails where the writers really had time to focus, doing long stretches in state pens from coast to coast. They would sit and recite these things. Those who could recite them in an engaging style, recreating other voices and what have you, they were celebrated entertainers in the jailhouse. Cons would pay them with cigarettes to sit around and entertain them.

Now, the way my cousin recited it to me, he didn't tell me that he didn't write it. So at first, I was under the impression he did. Later, he told me it was in a book he had seen. It was called *Hustlers' Convention*. I don't know if it was first released as a record or written down in a book. It was originally written by a person named Lightnin' Rod, which was his a.k.a. I think his real name was Jalal (Nuriddin), one of The Last Poets. And it was his attempt to write the grandest toast of them all.

My cousin told me *Hustlers' Convention* was something that was known by several players. They would oftentimes recite it to hoze to impress them with the fact that this is a little something they wrote about their game, their life story and what have you. It went something like:

> *It was a full moon in the middle of June in the summer of fifty-nine. I was young and cool, shot a bad game of pool and hustled all the chumps I could find. They call me Sport. I push a ball short. And I love all the women to death. I partied hard and packed a mean rod. I can knock you out with a right or a left. I learned to shoot pool playin' hooky from school at the tender age of nine. By the time I was eleven, I could pad roll seven and down me a whole quart of wine. I*

made it a point to smoke me a joint at least once in the course of a day. And I was snortin' skag while other kids played tag and the elders went to church to pray. I was a down stud's dream, a hustler supreme, there was no game I couldn't play. If I caught a dude cheatin', I gave him a beatin'. I might even blow him away.

It would take you at least a good thirty minutes to recite the whole thing. It goes on from there to his main man comin' out the joint. He kind of lends his man some money. They both go into training to get their gambling skills together so they can go to this hustlers' convention—hustlers with big money would come from all over the country and gamble in every form and fashion; drink; hang out; party with girls. It was hustlers coming together.

The whole idea fascinated me. I went out, hunted it down in libraries and eventually found out it was also on a record. The record was done by CBS Records, I think, with people like Buddy Miles playing a little rhythm track behind Lightnin' Rod as he recited this thing. It was an album. Each section of the story had a seventies Soul R&B rhythm track behind it. But the rapping wasn't really performed to the beat. It was spoken and the music was just a backdrop to it. It was really exciting. It made me think about growing up in the Black community as a kid. There was always little nursery rhymes and things, little ways of talkin' about somebody's mother, sayin' shit like: *I hate to talk about your mother but she talked about mine. She got two-ton titties and a rubber behind. She got mulberry titties as big as a peach. She got more hair on her pussy make a dead man preach.* And: *Ain't your mamma pretty. She got meatballs on her titties. She got scrambled eggs between her legs—* There's a whole bunch of these little things which form, basically, what is the foundation of rap, as we know it, in nineteen ninety-four, going into the future.

I also remember, as a young kid, someone reciting *The Signifying Monkey* at camp. We were up one night, impressing each other with little stories, tales and rhymes of that nature. And somebody ran down *The Signifying Monkey,* which is a similar kind of story that rhymed. Real urban. Real ghetto. A lot of flavor.

Hustlers' Convention struck me as the most major thing of its kind I had ever heard. It was the equivalent of a two-volume set as far as the genre went. I remember finding the record, taking it home to Brooklyn and memorizing practically the whole thing. Then I would recite it for my homies around my way. And they were really impressed. I hipped them to it. Then they all learned it. So it was this big thing in the neighborhood.

Now this was like the early to mid-seventies. Around the same time hip-hop was brewing. It wasn't called hip-hop back then. We called them jams/discos. This was before disco became what it is known for and it was still an underground ghetto Black and Puerto Rican thing on the streets of New York. Rap at that point—at least the way I first heard it when I did first hear it by DJs that picked up on it in Brooklyn—it was no more than nursery rhymes. At a party with a hip-hop emcee, the emcee would talk to the crowd, get them to throw their hands in the air and get everybody to say, "Ho!" He'd talk about who the DJ was. He'd talk about who he was. Compare himself to all kinds of superheroes and comic book characters. And he'd say little rhymes like: *Me and Superman had a fight. I hit him in the head with some Kryptonite. I hit him so hard I broke his brain. And now I'm bustin' out Lois Lane.* That was the first stuff. It sounded incredible back then.

It wasn't until much later that I found out, after meeting some of the originators of the form called hip-hop—people like Grand Master Flash, Grand Wizard Theodore, rappers and DJs like Melle Mel, Kid Creole—that they, too, up in the Bronx, had access to *Hustlers' Convention.* In those early days of rap, it was an example of what it could be. A long, drawn out and advanced story with street flavor. It was kind of like a movie. It was kind of like you were recounting your life's story for a motion picture. That was the structure of *Hustlers' Convention* by Lightnin' Rod. That record gave the example of how the form could be much more than just nursery rhymes. It could be a much more advanced and complex form of storytelling. I guess that has a lot to do with where it's at now in terms of the foundation being built. Of course, there are all the obvious influences and inspirations for rap going all the way back to the days

Courtesy of Joy Glidden © 1995.

of the African Griot, advancing to the Black preacher and the Black recording artist. In a major way, rap has brought it back to the Griot tradition—the spoken word—the foundation of the form.

While hanging out with my cousin, and trying to develop an understanding of what this pimp game was about, a brother who had a lot of knowledge of the streets told me if I wanted to learn more about the pimp game, I should read Iceberg Slim's book, *Pimp: The Story of My Life.*

So I read his book. It was a page-turner. His whole grasp of black language; the whole flavor and tempo of the book; the whole person he was: not because he was a pimp but because he went deep into his own mind, analyzing why he did what he did. It was all really interesting to me. I later went on to read all of Iceberg Slim's works. He was definitely one of my favorite writers.

The essence of the pimp game is a mental game. It's a mental chess game not played against women but with women. Women are willing participants in the pimp game. A lot of people who have negative views on this lifestyle fail to realize that it is a chosen lifestyle. That's why it's called The Life: those who are in it choose to live that way. When a woman wants to be with a pimp, she has to choose him. And she has to choose him with a certain amount of money based on the status or level of the game that pimp plays at.

The essence of the true pimp—the true player—is a con game. It's not a looks competition. It's not a wardrobe contest. It's basically a con game. And a con game is a real strong mental chess game. It's cogent reasoning—a combination of con and the rules of logical reasoning applied to how you can convince a person.

One of the things that I found inspiring about pimps was that so many of the pimps that I knew were such intelligent young black men. I was in my teens and I was talking to brothers in their late twenties to mid thirties up to their early forties. There was one pimp I used to play chess with. He was just the most knowledgeable, worldly person I had probably met, next to people I knew around my house, friends of my dad's. I was just impressed by how smart and intelligent he was. It struck me as unfortunate that pimping was all he would ever get a chance to do. He also saw a great deal of intelligence in me and said I would go very far in the pimp game. It was obvious it wasn't a game he would have gone into if he had had other opportunities. It was something that inspired me to go beyond that.

You see, I wasn't completely into The Life to stay there. I was able to go home. But I definitely had one foot in the game for a minute. I hung out with real players, had a ho' or two. And I was able to get a close enough look at it.

Eventually, I faded out of that scene, and went on to other things.

After being involved with art and painting in the downtown art club scene in the eighties, I gravitated towards the hip-hop music scene and ultra-contemporary youth culture. I've watched contemporary Black culture expand and explode at a rapid rate from its epicenter. As host of *Yo! MTV Raps,* I began to see a lot of rappers refer to pimpin' terms, mackin' terms, players' terminology. And a lot of these rappers are a lot younger than me, and probably couldn't cross the streets by themselves when these films were coming out in the seventies. The pimp is not really a major force on the street anymore. You don't see that whole lifestyle. I was really curious why people like Big Daddy Kane, Too-Short and a lot of other rappers are always talking about pimpin'.

When the group Digital Underground came out led by Shock-G, (a.k.a. "Humpty Hump") and we flew out to the San Francisco Bay Area to interview them for *Yo! MTV Raps,* I had sensed a certain amount of player in Shock-G from seeing his videos.

So we were swappin' stories and I told him the effect Iceberg's books had had on me when I read them back in the seventies. I told him how you used to be able to find his books in practically any corner store in a Black neighborhood and how I couldn't find them anymore. He said, "Yo, we can go over to Oakland. I know this little bookstore that's got the whole selection!"

The next day he drove over, picked me up and we went over to this bookstore. We got there and I bought the whole collection.

I had all the books and I was laying in my hotel. I looked at all of Iceberg's books and thought, Damn. I've always wondered what he was like, how I wanted to meet him and talk to him, pick his brain.

I realized that prior to all the blaxploitation movies in the seventies, no one ever delved that deeply into the Black underworld, the Black criminal subcultures. Iceberg was the first who did it, in the form of a Damon Runyon–type character, and pulled the covers back in a major way.

So I said, "Fuck it, let me call up his publisher and try and meet him or somethin'." I called up his publisher and told him who I was. I didn't know if he was still alive. They said he was very sick. We'll call him up and see if he'll talk to you. Call us back in twenty minutes. I called back in twenty minutes. They said, "Yeah, he'll talk to you."

I called him up. I told him I would be in L.A. for a few days and I wanted to do an interview. I told him how I thought it was very important for people to know about his work because now that rap had become such a big part of culture in America, Black culture especially, it was important that people know because, in the form of his books, he was the rapper of his day.

Iceberg was very excited and thankful that I had come to him because I was the link to a younger world who didn't know much about him, who hadn't read his books as much as previous generations.

I went down there to meet with him. At that first meeting, I spent about three hours taping him. All in all, I'd say I must have over ten hours of taped conversation with him, done over the course of a year. We kept in pretty close touch. I called him every other week or so. He became an advisor and a spiritual inspiration to me. He was very sick at the time that I met him. He was living in practical squalor in a place off Crenshaw Boulevard in the South-Central area of Los Angeles. It was a one-room apartment with leaking water stains on the ceiling. His living conditions were not what a man of his stature deserved, not even what he did as a pimp but because of all the books he wrote, published and sold.

Unfortunately, he not only sold rights but he sold copyrights to his publisher. You see, after he came off the streets, living the majority of his adult life as a player, he didn't know how to work as a businessman.

Yet, he was provided with enough money to live a somewhat decent life; but with his hospital bills, and his inability to get out there to earn a living, he was in this situation. He once made quite a bit of money on the lecture circuit. And a film was made from one of his books, *Trick Baby*. He had a lot of scorn for men in business suits and saw them as tricks for his hoze to get money from. He was never able to deal with them. But he was really sharp in terms of his mental and philosophical outlook.

Mike Tyson also used to spend a lot of time with him. A friend would bring him over there to get marriage counseling when he was having trouble with Robin Givens. I thought that was brilliant. Who better would know the psychology of Mike Tyson? Although he was such a product of the streets, and had made astronomical amounts of money, he was still a young adult trying to sort it all out. Robin was a pretty sophisticated girl and there were a lot of dynamics going on there.

I plugged him into what was going on in youth culture. At the time, his landlord wouldn't put cable in the building. I made some phone calls and eventually his landlord put cable into his building.

One of the questions I had for him was what is the reason for this fascination with the pimp game, a fascination so pervasive you can even see it with this younger generation of rappers coming up who could not have had a close-up look at the game that I had in its last burst of its true form? How is it that they are able to pick up on the essence of this?

Basically, Iceberg explained it like this. He said the pimp game, in a sense, is about the battle of the sexes. One book he wanted to produce was *The Game for Squares*—pimp game codes and rules broken down and structured for the average man. It would deal with the basic structure we live in as Americans; which is a primarily European structure that Black Americans have been forced to adapt to over the course of a couple of hundred years, a situation that doesn't work as well for the Black man as it does for others. Iceberg saw some of the codes, rules and ethics of the game as something the average married man could use to maintain the balance of power in the home. For example, the way a wife will use sex as leverage against her husband. There was a lot of things he talked about he wanted to put into this book that could help the average married man in restructuring the codes of power in a typical marriage.

Also, pimping represented, in its simplest form, strength in a man. And strength in a man is perhaps the most powerful aphrodisiac for a woman. I remember Iceberg telling me the hardest thing he had to learn as a pimp was how to have seven to ten beautiful women under your complete control and be able to go to the bathroom and jerk off. This was because fucking is not what the pimp game is based on. Any man can rock a woman in bed but can he rock her in the head?

PIMP

Introduction

Study the definition offered below by *Funk & Wagnall's Standard Dictionary of the English Language International Edition* (1960) and note the fact it don't elucidate shit.

pimp (*pimp*) *n.* A pander. *v.i.* To act as a pimp. [Prob. *pim-pant* seductive, ppr. of *pimper* dress elegantly; ult. origin uncertain]

Now consider the illuminating little glossary I've constructed from *The Life: The Lore and Folk Poetry of the Black Hustler*; *Black Players: The Secret World of Black Pimps* and *Ripley's Believe It Or Not!*

pimp *v.* **1.** To succeed at some endeavor or encounter with Whitey which requires the guile of a gamester. **2.** To use human relationships to get money.

mack *n.* **1.** A skillful and clever operator of women. **2.** Pimp, esp. one who controls and organizes every aspect of the life of his stable (group of prostitutes working for a pimp) without soliciting for them.

The Book *n.* Oral tradition containing the rules and principles of the pimping game.

game *v.* To manipulate human emotions such as fear, greed, lust and love for monetary or personal gain.

player *n.* **1.** Skilled manipulator. **2.** A man who is able by charm, wit and game to move in rich strata, cross the color-line and extract money. **3.** Any man who wins wealth by wit and manipulative techniques.

Players *n.* **1.** The magazine for He Who Is. **2.** A periodical of sepia-toned tastes which, unbelievably, actually *published* the thoughts of Stanley Crouch![6]

[6] **Crouch, Stanley** *n.* [Black American, genius] **1.** Critic. **2.** Poet. Book/Record: *Ain't No Ambulances For Niggers Tonight*. Updated hip-hop version rumored circulating on bootleg. **3.** Source of amusement for the Lower East Side jazz community. **4.** Two-fisted intellectual and enemy of Public Enemy's "Media Assassin." **5.** Former trap-drummer for Butch Morris and Schrei-singer Diamanda Galas.

THE 1970s:
The Golden Age of the Pimp.

Nineteen-seventies' America was infected with pimp fever. Fuck *The Brady Bunch.* Everybody wanted to live "The Life." Pimp movies. Pimp books. Pimpmobiles. And pimp *socks.* Even Eve Plumb dropped her drawers and sold some pussy in *Dawn: Portrait of a Teenage Ho'.*

I didn't discover The Book until I was seventeen.

It was an actual book. *Pimp: The Story of My Life* by Iceberg Slim. My father gave it to me. Pops is hip like that.

I read it and shared it with my friends.

Iceberg became an important part of the pop pantheon in our pot-parlor discussions, along with luminaries Ho Chi Minh, Malcolm X, Bruce Lee, Huey Newton and Funkedelic's cartoonist Pedro Bell.

The pimp, like "the bad nigger" of folkloric tradition, "the backdoor man" of blues legend, or even Uncle Remus's Brer Rabbit, was a figure of mythic importance. He is, in many ways, like the loa Ghede who is, as described by Deren in *Divine Horseman,* "amused by the eternal persistence of the erotic and by man's eternally persistent pretense that it is something else." The pimp is the modern urban trickster.

As Roger Abrahams writes in *Afro-American Folktales,* "Trickster [has] the ability to dream up new and ever more clever and boundary-breaking schemes . . . He does not hesitate to steal, assault sexually, kill . . . from [his] perspective, actions are not judged in terms of their consequences so much as whether he succeeds in his ventures or not."

In the sanctuary of our basement pot-fests, the pimp was not a man of ignoble moral purpose, as defined by the whyteman's Funk & Wagnall. To use "pimp psychology" was to exercise "psychic ju-jitsu," to mentally *dominate*. To trick Chalk Charlie.

By our way of thinking, the whyte world created the language and the conditions the resourceful hustler was forced to exploit. The racism rooted in the whyte man's language was an ugliness we sought to appropriate, subvert and destroy through rhyme, wordplay and invention. The pimp was another yardstick, along with the drug dealer and the revolutionary, against whom we measured our manhood. We were under no obligation to respect a world that did not respect us. Our only obligation was not to get caught.

My father said we thought this way because—and I quote—"You young knottyheaded, reefa-smokin' hoodlums need to get *bar mitzvahed!*"

We saw movies like *The Mack and Willie Dynamite* not only as instructive entertainment but as art.

Just as the oils and pastels of Henri Toulouse-Lautrec had celebrated the prostitute, the blaxploitation film was a class of art with the pimp as subject. These films drew on and elevated the black underground's oral tradition of the trickster's tale and the hustler's toast, which we *all* performed with wine-intoxicated glee—long before Rudy Ray Moore released *Eat Out More Often* on the now defunct Kent label in 1970.

She moaned and farted and shit on the floor. The wind from her asshole blew the knob off the door. That's when Nell shit on the bed. And Willie copped a spoon and a loaf of bread.

> —from *The Ball of Freaks, The Life: Lore And Folk Poetry of the Black Hustler*

As we were far more obscessed with buying, selling and consuming drugs in unlimited "jus' say mo'" quantities, we had no serious inclination toward The Life, at least in the brutal, ho'-slappin' capacity laid down by Iceberg Slim.

We fantasized and talked about it. We emulated the pimp in appearance. But most of us weren't cut out for it. *Especially me.*

Besides the fact I was bookish and wholly boho, a product of bop, Beat and psychedelic Black-youth culture (and I still am), I didn't have the stomach for it.

And I'm lazy. Pimping requires stamina and effort.

To tell the truth, I've learned more about women by bar-hopping with lesbians in the East Village (some of whom, ironically, picked up licks reading Cecil Brown's *The Life And Loves of Mr. Jive-Ass Nigger*)

Brother—Do You Talk Black but Secretly Wish to Sleep White? Put Your Dick Where Your Mouth Is and Read . . .

The Blackman's Guide to Seducing White Women with the Amazing Power of Voodoo
Doctor Snakeskin
(Best-selling Author of *Young Girls and Where to Buy Them*)

INTRODUCTION

Back in the bubble-toed seventies, after Jimi choked on his vomit, but before Nixon faced the bull(shit) in the arena, my posse of platformed homeboys and I hid behind the hedges in the high-school parking lot, smoked toothpick-thin sticks of reefer rolled from shot-glass nickel bags, swigged chilled Strawberry Hill, and discussed the future following our impending graduation.

Sporting broad-brimmed *Mack* hats on the sides of our big, bushy, and bulbous Afros, we had nicknames like Shaft, Sweetback, Truck Turner, Superfly TNT, and Willie Dynamite.

My tag was Hell Up in Harlem. And, like my polyester party-pals, I wanted to be a pimp.

Why I thought I'd be more successful at pimping, instead of, say, *drug dealing,* is a question I'm baffled by to this day.

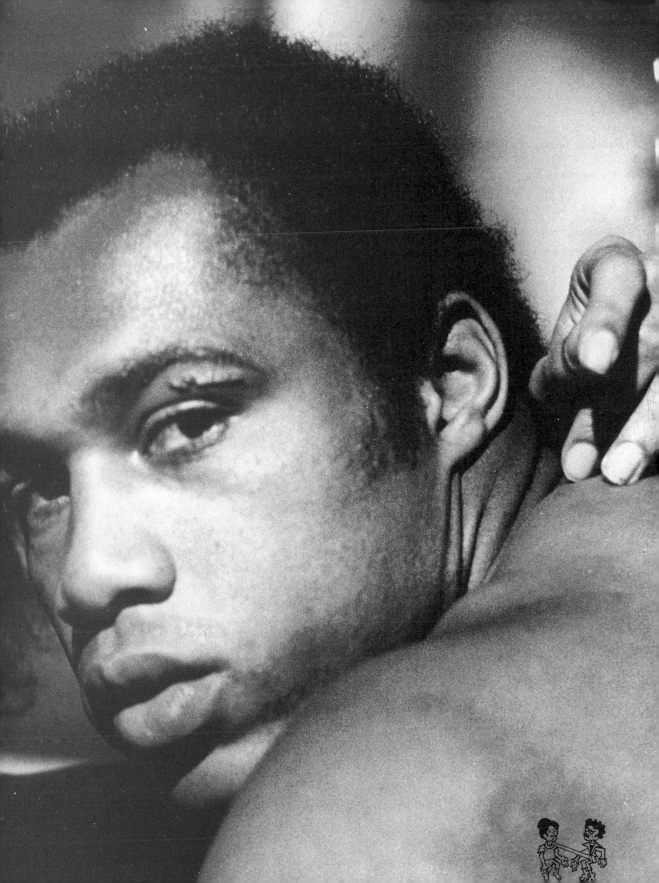

My entire range of sexual experience, at that point in my young life, consisted of one isolated incident with a fourteen-year-old pepper-faced blonde I dry-humped against a Coke machine in the New England boarding school I attended some years before.

My virginity notwithstanding, I was determined to be a pimp. Not a gorilla pimp like Iceberg Slim, but a *guerrrrilla* pimp who understood the world according to Fanon, and had the physical prowess of Bruce Lee, but dressed better than the average member of the Black Panther Party.

As I explained this to my pack of pot-puffing playmates, Sweetback looked up from his joint, coughing reefer smoke.

"Shit, nigga, is you trippin' out wid dem whyte boys on dat acid again or what?"

"Naw, brutha, I'm gonna be a pimp with a *revolutionary* agenda! My face is gonna be *stenciled* on walls throughout the third world, right alongside Che Guevara!"

"Sounds like somebody slipped som' Led Zeppelin in da sleeves o' yo' Funkadelic albums, nigga! You trippin'!"

"Naw, nigga, I *reads* my Uncle Ho! I gots the Cong down cold! My shit is *skulled!* Remember, the Panthers said: 'Political power begins at the lips of a pussy!'"

"Pimpin' be 'bout controllin' da bitches, not some Black Panther bullshit! When da bitch hol' out on yo' money, what you gon' do? *Quote Chairman Mao?*"

My comrades roared with laughter. Once the laughter subsided, I struggled against my feelings of embarrassment, and outlined my simple pimping plan.

than from any pimp book I ever read, but that's another story.

Iceberg's books were great, though, for their theory and history of street-hustling scams. In high school, I tried my hand at an ass-backwards gigolo scam I ran on the scatterbrained acid-queens I encountered in the glassed-in hallway leading to the gymnasium, outside the cafeteria.

This was the area in school where hippies, aspiring artists, druggies (and, inexplicably, depraved, sex-n-machinery obsessed "gearheads") met for "depthful" discussions of *Siddartha, The Hobbit* and the latest release by *Firesign Theater.* Its denizens were a bizarre, sandalwood-scented menagerie of wild-haired and wild-eyed eccentrics. The cynical called it "Doctor Leary's Cage o' Freaks" (**SEE!! THE SHOCKING RESULTS** of an experiment in the evolution of human intelligence gone *woefully awry!!!*).

The scam worked like this—

With a single-lense Reflex strapped around my neck, I'd focus the face of a vic (and/or potential futon-fuckmate) in the frame of my viewfinder, and snap her photograph.

She'd blush with a shy smile creeping on her lips.

Holding out my hand, I'd introduce myself. She'd ask what I was doing with the camera. I'd grin, my nicotine-stained teeth the color of a dried lemon rind.

"I'm doing a photo-essay illustrating the analogy between the contours of a woman's body and a chicken's egg."

Her mouth would spread into a broad smile. And she'd say something along the lines of, "I'm a dancer . . ." elongating the two syllables, "in the natural manner of Isadora Duncan."

(Of course, this meant she had no actual training, but spent her time flitting barefoot through the forest on a head full of acid, tossing colored scarves in the air.)

She'd stare for a moment, fixing me with her gaze.

"Would you like a model?" she'd ask. Again, elongating the last two syllables.

My mouth twitched into a slight smirk and I'd dispense with my previous pretense, making a direct proposition.

While pondering the possibility of presenting me with some pussy, she'd quickly cast my horoscope, deduce bad vibes in any future spent with my penis (based on a hard-square to my Venus), and hand me all her money.

(I rarely came close to any parts o' th' pussy but I *kepts* me a pocketful of loose change).[7]

The standard English (read: "eurocentric") definition of *pimp* refers to the dilettant disdained by successful players of the game, a currish fopling stage-whispering in a redlit alcove, "*Check it out! Check it out! I got it tight, white and alright!*" which insults the master Mack-Daddy's psychological sophistication by equating the skills of his trade with the bothersome, street-corner annoyances of the Rastafarian pot-slinger.

In high school, those of us who read Holloway House paperbacks like *Whoreson, Trick Baby, Street Players* and *AirTight Willie & Me,* knew that the true pimp didn't solicit. He counted his money.

The definition supplied by *Funk & Wagnall* applied to our high school's *popcorn* pimps. Popcorn pimps were not unlike gangster rap's bogus boojie-class nigras who exploit the structure of rap's form without the experiential substance that defines it.

Unlike my high school's authentic players, who turned out teachers who, in turn, turned out the football team's bubble-busted cheerleading squad by organizing suspicious, overnight slumber parties, our corridors clunked with husky, Dolemite–like characters in bulbous shoes with big square-block heels, discount-store felt fedoras and wide-lapel Edwardian longcoats, whose dreams of supreme Mack-*Daddy*dom were dashed by the obstreperous, middle-class daughters of *real* pimps (though our elders preferred to call them Reverend), who, while naively giggling, "*What's a trick?*" spent all the hard-earned Mickey D dollars these burger-bagging Mackmen could generate.

Unfortunately, none had been schooled in The Book.

Instead, each Friday night, clopping in droves to the local bijou, with a paper-bagged bottle of Boone's Farm apple wine, and a stingy stick of reefer, a vast sea of badly blocked hats convened in the darkened auditorium to applaud the exploits of that week's overdressed master of kung-fu schtick in platformed kicks.

---

[7] But when I did finally get some, I stayed all up *in* that muthafucka! Four or five days! That skinny, no tittie, flat-assed, diet-pill poppin' hippie-hamma's pussy was *good!* They don't even make pussy like that no more! She had that drug infested Hatha-Yoga *breath* pussy! It swolled all up like a balloon, turned purple and puckered like a pair of cartoon nigga lips!

I envisioned a bloodless coup. I was going to hypnotize the pale-haired daughters of the oppressor with the rhetoric of third-world liberation SLA General Field Marshal Cinque style, turn 'em out with some acid dipped on the tip of my black nigger dick, and then instruct my cadre of politically correct hoze to fuck the white man to death in the name of oppressed peoples everywhere.

I had no conception of how to initiate my plan until I enrolled in college a full five years later. It was the college the sixties wouldn't forget. Never mind the Sex Pistols. John Travolta didn't happen. The campus was located on fertile grounds near the Long Island Sound. God-eyes twirled in the doorways of candle-lit bedrooms perfumed with incense. Voices droned tunelessly over battered folk guitars in the hallway. Heavy-bosomed women in floral-patterned peasant skirts believed reading *The Hobbit* would somehow mend their drug-addled brains. It was John Lennon and Yoko Ono singing "All We Are Saying Is Give Peace a Chance" *twenty-four fucking hours a day!!*

Many went mad and hung themselves. Suicide by macramé.

The women outnumbered the men on campus but among the men there were two brothers—myself and a cat with a gigantic, wild-man Afro from rural Alabama who had a large library of Blowfly albums. I called him Alabama Blowfly.

Alabama insisted if you quoted Eldridge Cleaver's *Soul on Ice,* white girls magically dropped drawers and gave up the pussy. Obviously, he hadn't read Susan Brownmillor.

He was also a Muslim. I hadn't realized this until a buxom, grain-fed wondergirl of the midwestern heartland had grossly misinterpreted his intentions.

With salty tears balanced on the rims of his lower eyelids, Alabama fell to his knees, and in the name of universal love for all humankind, *begged* her for some pussy.

She said *no.*

The nigga went nuts!

Overnight, his jeans, the two ducks fucking on his "Fly United" T-shirt, and his Chuck Taylor Converse All-Stars were replaced by a white robe, a skull-cap, and a pair of cloth slippers.

Every morning at the crack of dawn, he knelt on his prayer mat, howling at Mecca, fervently begging Allah's forgiveness for being led astray by that "devil white girl" with the big *Playboy* titties.

I didn't have his problem.

I squandered my time on campus by guzzling cheap Californian jug wines, gobbling psychedelic fungi, and laying up with busty, big-nippled nymphs who stank of patchouli oil and stale reefer smoke—women of pure pagan *instinct.*

One woman had an affinity with night and taught me to traverse its blind darkness with surefootedness. Another communed with water and could divine the future by its rippling surface.

This water witch and I would make love on the shores of the Sound at night, our brains basting in savory psychedelic sauces; her sandy hips rolling beneath me, crashing like waves on the beach.

Most coeds, though, had no more doodled on the slates of their Etch-A-

With a tub of oily popcorn kernels clenched between the knees of their pink-pinstriped polyester pants, they would raucously exchange, in voices loud enough for all to hear, outlandish theories on the pimping game.

Heated arguments would erupt, punctuated by the swish of drawn straight razors slashed in the air, between peacock-clothed strangers at opposing sides of the theater.

"No, fool! I knows all 'bout turnin' out hoze! Put *red pepper* on y'dick, man! Pussy juice be flyin' all over d'muthafuckin' place! Splashin' all up at da ceilin'! Drippin' down da walls! *Red pepper* I'm tellin' ya! Da bitches love dat! Dey be sweatin' an' double-buckin' an' shit! It's like money in da bank!"

"Who schooled you on dat shit, nigga? *Ronald McDonald?* You ain't no player! You be turnin' tricks fo' *cheeseburgers,* nigga, suckin' d'*Hamburgler's* dick! Why you think they call it *Mack*-Donald's, nigga?"

"*Muthafuck you!* Check da *zircons* sparklin' on dese fingers! M'hoze *paid* fo' dis shit!"

"Sit yo' ass down, ya greasy french-fry baggin' ho', 'fo I shove dat cheap-ass glass up yo' fonky ass!"

Invariably, at movie's end, in the lobby's cold light, each of the dueling dandies failed to recognize the other. I knew one cat who wanted to be a player's player so bad, he went mad.

I met him at a party thrown by some hippies I knew on the second floor of a two-story house with a FUCK COMMUNISM!!! banner unfurled across its weathered facade, next door to the New Haven branch of the Black Panther Party.

When I arrived, and walked into the front room, a bare-bosomed Mexican girl with an egg-yolk yellow eye painted in the center of her forehead, transferred, from her mouth to my own, a square of golden acid, with a probing soul-kiss.

Behind her, thick clouds of pot smoke floated inside the cellophane shell of a geodesic dome. Multicolored oils swirled in a glass, water-filled bowl on an overhead projector and cast squirming, hologramlike shadows on the wall. Just above, movies of the NASA space walks flickered on the ceiling in Super 8.

On several speakers situated throughout the rooms, Yoko Ono screeched as if undergoing an unanesthetized hysterectomy. My face prickled. I saw dust balls of sound, tasted trails of light. The soles of my feet felt like sponges sopped in soap suds.

From blacklit cell to blacklit cell, scattered amidst clusters of naked, patchouli-oiled girls who brushed each others' skin with delicate fluorescent designs, the heads of long-haired boys bobbed in the laps of bearded, long-haired men.

Eventually, I wandered into the kitchen. I smelled a five-pepper pot of black bean chili bubbling on the stove.

Under the kitchen's pervasive black light, seated at a large butcher-block table heaped with two pounds of loose pot, his hair pressed in wavy marcel curls, was the would-be pimp named after a bottle of cheap Italian wine, Soave Bolla.

I was blinded by the ultraviolet vibrance of his clothes.

He was rolling joints, amassing a pile he planned to resell. An empty chili bowl sat at his elbow. A ring of dried black bean circled his mouth.

I stood at the stove, scooping chili into a porcelain bowl.

He stared through me with two hideous blood-red eyes.

I'm not sure he realized I was standing in the room. I doubt he was even aware of vocalizing his own thoughts.

He licked the gummed edge of a rolling paper, a corner of his upper lip aggravated by a spastic twitch.

"I'm gonna *hard* mack dat Mexican bitch!" he sneered. "Floppin' dem big pancake titties in my face, stickin' her tongue down my throat an' talkin' dat flighty hippie shit 'bout how she ain't gon' give *Soave* no pussy! *Shee-it!* She gon' give *Soave* pussy—*an' any otha muthafucka I tell her when I put m'brogans in her hippie ass!*"

As he catalogued the depraved indignities he planned to perpetrate against the nubile but wayward daughters of suburbia, who frolicked in decadent splendor in the next room, a curious thing happened.

The acute redness in his eyes suddenly disappeared—*his eyes were completely clear.*

A disconcerting but beatific smile upturned the black bean encrusted corners of his mouth. His eyes twinkled with elfin laugh lines.

"Wait-a-minnit! I c'n scoot-n-scam wif' dat *hippie pimp* flim-n-flam! Free love! Yeah! Dat's it! All I gots to do is lean in dem bitches' ears an' 'splain afta dey gives dey money to me, dey be givin' dey pussy away fo' *free!*"—his left eyeball bulged out of its socket and veered to the right—

Sketch brains than reggae lyrics and the outline of Bob Marley's cock. I'd approach a group of these young women squatting in a circle on the grass, strumming guitars and smoking pot, saying:

"If smoking dope doesn't damage your brain, why do so many Jamaicans believe a dead Ethiopian is god?"

Smoke would sputter from their mouths and their eyes would narrow into hateful slits.

Still, I got laid. *A lot.*

And by women with an amazing, tantriclike control of their pussy muscles. I don't mean bland, lackluster pussy with the consistency of wet Wonder bread. I'm talking about *trained* pussy. *Athletic* pussy. Pussy with a firm undulating grasp, clamped so tightly around the shaft of your cock, you don't cum unless it says so.

And when you do cum, the pussy snaps, barks, and farts in eruptive orgasm, sending bolts of heat spiraling through the barrel of your dick, and out your asshole, leaving a luminous blue ring revolving above your head.

Good, home-breakin' pussy.

Now I don't have any money, my breath stinks of beer and stale cigarette smoke, and my hair is a scraggly nest of unkempt pickaninny knots. So why did I get all that abundant white-girl pussy whereas Alabama Blowfly was left to beat his meat to the Koran?

I practice Voodoo—the *true* religion of the Amerikkan Blackman!

CHAPTER ONE: WHO SAID BLACK MEN DON'T EAT PUSSY?

Timing is the key factor in the practice of Voodoo and any other form of magick (Spellcasting, Witchcraft, Ceremonial, etc). As Crowley wrote in *Magick:*

In *Theory and Practice,* "the proper Force in the proper manner through the proper medium to the proper object" *at the proper time.* In order to do this, a good witch must know how to read the signs.

I learned to pay close attention to menstrual cycles. On campus, I observed that women who lived together menstruated almost simultaneously. One woman's menstruation, a dominant, initiates the cycle for the others. This situation frequently occurs among roommates, biker babes, and women in all-girl rock bands, especially if the band is on tour. (One New York band in the early eighties would only perform publicly "at that time of the month." Before mounting the stage, they would all ritually smear themselves with each other's blood. And the sound emitted by their amplifiers was so abrasive, it would turn Axl Rose's testicles ice cold.)

Why is this information you need to know?

Many women are very horny either before, after, or during their menstruation. And sex eases the pain of menstrual strain.

So prepare to chow down, brutha, *and earn those red wings!*

The height of menstrual activity on campus occurred when the moon was at its fullest. This is consistent with the nature of the Triple Goddess who symbolizes the moon in its three phases. The Goddess in her full-moon phase, her warrior aspect, represents the sexually active woman.

By keeping track of the phases of the moon, I could calculate who was bleeding and when. I became so proficient at this practice I actually developed a nose for detecting its warm, earthy aroma in the air.

"Wha' da' fuck was dat? *Da Tasmanian Devil?*" His ruminations resumed without pause.

"I c'n keep my honkie hippie-hoze in line by workin' dat guilt thang, tell 'em it's African tradition. A *real* black man mus' keep him a flock o' many wives! Say it from da Koran or som' shit. Da ho' stable be Allah's way . . ."

Suddenly, his eyes narrowed. His cheeks contracted, and his lips puckered into an O. He uttered two words.

"Red pepper."

He stood and walked stiffly from the table, his pantseat creased between his tensed butt-cheeks, his rectum inflamed by a stray fleck of undigested jalapeño.

He went into the bathroom and locked the door.

He grunted like Errol Garner over ivory eighty-eights. His bowels rumbled with the rolling thunderclap of a drunk tumbling headfirst down a flight of stairs.

He screamed, "DAT BITCH DONE PUT D'HOODOO IN MY DOO-DOO!" and fell silent.

Inside the bathroom, he must've sat on the toilet bowl seat, staring between his open thighs, down the shaft of his long limp cock, with that irksome pepper nipping his rectum's ring of raw flesh, watching a torrent of turd spin out of his gut in an animated whirl of wormy, multi-hued fluorescence.

After several moments, he spoke in a soft whisper. *"Huh? What you say?"*

More silence followed behind the door.

"Yeah!" he exclaimed finally, water splashing. "I likes dat! Dey gon' hafta rename da whole mack game afta me when I break out wif' dis otha kinda shit you done schooled me on!"

He whistled. More water splashed on the floor.

"Soave Bollin' da bitches!"

It became obvious, even to me, in my confused state of chemically induced schizophrenia, the man had engaged the contents of his bowels in conversation.

He was probably on his knees, staring at cylindrical clusters of putrefied chili-spiced beanpaste and blackened kernels of unpopped popcorn in the toilet bowl, anthropomorphized into chunky-cheeked, lazy-eyed faces, bored through with wiggling luminescent worms, cackling in tiny coke-hoarse voices.

"Da bitches gon' go crazy for dis! Yeah! Check dis' out! I'm gon' get in all da *fly* bitches' faces, talkin' my *sweetest* cat-daddy shit! *Damn!* Dere go *Taz* again!"

Water sloshed for several moments more. It spilled under the door and across the floor.

The bathroom door swung open. And a draft of stomach-turning pungency wafted into the kitchen. My nostril hairs withered.

He stepped out. *Grinning.* His face was hidden under a handmade prosthesis sculpted of soggy strips of toilet tissue and mucous-oozing lumps of wet shit. His eyes rolled wildly in his head.

He popped the palms of his hands together.

"I'm ready fo' dem hoze now, *Jack!*"

He cocked his head, tilted his hip to one side, and walked from the kitchen with a downward dip of his knee; repeatedly pushing a cupped, waist-level hand behind him. He paused in the doorway, turning to speak to me over his shoulder. He said, "A good pimp knows he's got to show his hoze he can always keep his *shit* together!"

As a clump of turd fell from his face, and plopped on the toe of his imitation-alligator shoe, his laughter preceded him into the adjacent room.

POSTSCRIPT

In the ensuing commotion, Soave disappeared. He slipped out the door, down the stairs and into the night. Needless to say, six hippies burst into the kitchen, lead by a bearded, beer-bellied hulk. He pointed his fat finger in my direction. This is what he said: "There he is! *Git 'im!*"

WARNING: MENSTRUATING WOMEN CAN BE UNUSUALLY AGGRESSIVE.

Living in a coed dorm with few men during a full moon is like being trapped in a den of cats in heat. I endured shrill whining, tits brushed "accidentally on purpose" against my arm, and, sometimes, I literally had asses pointed in my face.

YOU HAVE NO CHOICE, YOU MUST GIVE UP THE DICK. REPEAT. YOU MUST GIVE UP THE DICK. IF NOT, IT WILL BE RIPPED FROM ITS SOCKET, MOUNTED ON A STICK, AND USED IN SOME UNSPEAKABLE GIRL RITE UNDER THE FULL MOON.

Lastly, in the Hoodoo tradition, a mixture of African and Celtic folk magick, it is said that if a woman feeds a man her menstrual blood he will fall hopelessly and uncontrollably in love with her. So, if she invites you over for a home-cooked meal, I advise bringing along a dog, slipping the animal a portion from your plate. And if the dog humps your leg . . .

CHAPTER TWO: HOW NOXIOUS NEGRO ODORS CAN WET THE CRACKS OF THOSE YOUNG WHITE PUSSIES

Odor from a strong, foamy lather of underarm perspiration is a pretty effective people repellent—*but*—that social liability can be turned into a social asset.

Smells attract as easily as they repel. Animals are aroused by smell. People are too.

With the right combination of scented oils, you can enhance your natural body odor to arouse the sex urge in others. Mixed in balanced combination, those oils are:

Cinnamon, patchouli, almond, sandalwood, and *jasmine.*

Courtesy of Photofest.

Blended with your body's natural oils, the mixture enhances your animal sex appeal. One fourth of this mixture is cinnamon oil, an oil believed to exude the essence of Scorpio, the astrological sign ruling the sex organs.

This oil should be applied sparingly or poured into a bath. The cinnamon burns a bit, a sensation lasting under thirty seconds, so I don't advise rubbing it directly on your balls.

Don't overuse the oil. If you do, you'll end up smelling like some tie-dyed neo-hippie, killing the oil's overall effect by masking your real odor rather than enhancing it. Your natural odor is what draws a potentially compatible sex partner to you. The scent is subtle and detected subliminally. As she approaches, you will notice her nostrils flare with desire.

Once you've been sniffed out, and you have a potential bedmate standing before you, gaze into her eyes and begin to work your spell of *Fascination.*

CHAPTER THREE: HOW YOUR SIGNIFYING MONKEY-ASS CAN WIN FRIENDS, INFLUENCE PEOPLE, AND SCAM PLENTY O' WHYTE-GAL BOODY TO BOOT

According to *The Dictionary of Contemporary American Usage,* to fascinate is to hold by enchantment, *to charm.* This means your most important magickal weapon is your *personality* but you must follow these three basic rules:

1. Intent eye contact
2. Physical contact
3. Breath contact

One classic tactic of girl-hustling involves a basic element of Fascination—whispering in a woman's ear. It's intimate, erotic, and effective.

Slouch against a wall, standing so your mouth is level with her ear. Speak softly or mumble. She will automatically draw closer to you in order to hear what you have to say. Keep her pinned with your gaze, hold her there, and don't let your eyes wander.

As you speak, breathe on her neck and gently drape your arm around her shoulder. Be casual, but most important, be *empathetic.*

Watch and listen to the woman snuggled in the crook of your arm. You want her to understand that you are interested in *her* and not what unusual tricks she might know with your cock in her mouth.

Read her feelings, respond intuitively, and speak in a soothing tone of voice. It inspires confidence. The sound of your voice projects how you feel. How you express what you feel and what feelings you inspire is of primary importance. Words *stir* the emotions. Chose strong, evocative, and emotionally charged words.

"Verbal magic is a skillful combination of meaning and sound, effecting an almost alchemical change in the thinking of the listener."—Eric Maple, "Incantations and Words of Power"

In a state of heightened emotion one is susceptible to hypnotic suggestion. So don't waste time blathering about semiotics, deconstruction, postmodernism, or some other useless gibberish you might read about in the art & lit sections of certain New York weeklies. Use your words wisely and stir up a heady intoxicant. Your goal is to make her wet and tingly between the thighs. The ear is an erogenous zone. You can accomplish almost as much by whispering in her ear as you can by tongue-flicking her clit.

Practice the Taoist principle of Wei Wu Wei "to do without doing." Or, in other words, *seduce without seducing.*

With this attitude, you'll find that most women will do the work for you.

CHAPTER FOUR: SPELL-CASTING

Spell-casting is only necessary when all other means have failed. Why work your will over a lock of hair when a bouquet of roses and a book of poetry might accomplish your goal?

Often, love obtained by magick is unauthentic, short-lived, and delusional. It lasts only as long as it takes the moon to complete one full cycle. It is all you want and all you don't want. In the end, it proves insubstantial and has nasty side effects. *Disease. Impotence. Bankruptcy.* Venus can be a hellish bitch.

On the other hand, *sex* obtained by magick can be a *blast.*

The attraction spell I'm about to detail is a form of "lower" or "lesser" magick. Its use will not bind another's will to your own. The key is not to waste valuable psychic energies by projecting onto one desired person but rather to produce a scattershot effect and keep your options open.

By opening the sexual channels of your psyche through spell-work, you can activate the sexual energies in your

environment and attract the corresponding energies. In this way, you draw the right person(s) suited to your particular psychosexual needs. This method teaches you about your sexuality and sensitizes you to your preferred sex partner. (You may not want to fuck White-women at all, brutha. You could be just frontin' the shit off and might really want a young Whiteboy with a *ripe pink behind!*)

When practicing any form of magick, the first step is deciding what it is that you truly desire, and the next step is asking yourself what are the best circumstances under which you might achieve that goal.

Your goal must be realistic. No matter how expert your spell, the centerfold babe taped to your wall will not mysteriously come to life and materialize in your bed. You must have a clear and realizable magickal objective based, not on fantasy, but on real emotional need.

Clarify your intent in a journal. Ask yourself why you want what you desire. Try and understand the psychological needs associated with your desire. Describe your desire. What are its attributes? Its strengths? Its weaknesses? Reduce the information recorded in your journal into a few concise sentences, then visually codify these sentences into symbols for use in the ritual you will perform later. These are important steps in the spell-working process.

Next, select objects you associate with your desire, objects which appeal to your senses: music, scents, foods, textures, drawings, etc. These serve to intensify your emotions during the actual ritual. In fact, it's a good idea to actually draw pictures of what you desire or create images out of wax, clay, wood, etc.

This activity can be compared to programming a computer. You're etching a function on your psyche. Through these preparations, you are building up an energized emotional force you will later release in a focused and directed fashion during ritual.

In order for this force to travel, you must create a "magickal link." If this is not done, the force will either dissipate or strike you in the ass like a lightning bolt.

Hair, toenail clippings, soiled clothing, jewelry, etc. are normally used for this purpose.

As we are discussing creating a general auric field of seductive power, I suggest selecting objects dear to Venus as a "magickal link." It is Venus who has dominion over the kind of gifts you seek. Study Venus, try and understand who she is and what meaning she has for you. Offer her gifts with personal meanings you both share.

Venus, like the other deities, is not an external spiritual force. She is an aspect in all of our psyches, an archetype buried in our collective unconscious. Through ritual, the conscious is integrated with the forces of the unconscious. We invoke a God or Godette form by drawing it out of ourselves. It then becomes an operative force within our personalities.

CHAPTER FIVE: THE RITUAL: OR "THE MONEY-SHOT"

Seal your ritual area with a triangle of sea salt. The triangle should be vaginal in appearance. Some will suggest a circle. I prefer the triangle because of its associations with the womb and birth. The sea salt confines the psychic energies released during ritual to one area.

Set up your altar with the previously selected, emotion-evoking objects. Arrange your drawings and carved figures. As you want to appeal to Venus's lascivious side, drape women's lingerie, preferably stained with menstrual blood.

Now, back to your journal. Turn to the visually codified sentences. Symbols are the language the unconscious understands best. Consider the strange imagery and surreal situations of dreams. This is how your subconscious talks to you. One can use traditional symbols but I suggest creating your own. You are communicating with your own subconscious. It knows its own language. Let your subconscious tell you what that language is.

Once you've found your symbols, carve them on a red candle. Red is the traditional symbolic color of sex, lust, and passion. This is called "sigilization." It is the most simple form of ritual.

Anoint your carved candle with the previously described oils and armpit perspiration. Or use the sweat from the underside of your testicles (let's keep our eye on the old ball here: the point is to magickally energize the seductive power of your pheromone essence). Anoint the candle by stroking it upward three times from the middle and then stroke three times downward.

Set the candle on your altar and place the "magickal link" in front of it.

As stated before, timing is a key factor. You must decide when is the proper time to perform your ritual. The moon is a good and simple guide.

The new moon is the best time to initiate new projects. It is the time of planting and growth. The full moon is the time of harvest, when things have ripened to their fullest. The old moon is a time for dark deeds, hexing, for sweeping away the withered.

Never start a new love on an old moon. This ritual should be performed during a new moon or when Venus is in good aspect to the moon, Mars, and Mercury. Ultimately, you must deduce when conditions are most susceptible to your influence. The phases of the moon and the alignment of the planets are merely guides. In the end, you must objectively analyze the situation in order to know when to make your move.

Drink a glass or two of good Bordeaux. Undress. Enter the ritual area, burn incense, and light your candle. Enjoy the food you've laid out. Admire the drawings. Fondle the lingerie. Excite yourself into a heightened state of lust. Sit before your altar. Slick your hand with Vaseline. Are you ready? Good.

Now beat your meat. Hold your dick in a "Black Power" grip, visualizing fire-red sex energies swirling around you in an egg-shaped cocoon, shot through with needles of gold, and shake that muthafucka harder than a pair of dice. *Feel* the magnetic pull of hundreds of naked Whitewomen floating toward you, casting the cocoon of radiant red energies around the "magickal link."

Imagine yourself cradled between two strong thighs fanning open and closed with the grace of two palm fronds in a languid breeze, the pelvis rolling like a wave churning across the sea. A phantom cunt draws your cock deeper and deeper into its moistness with a gently flexing grip, its sweating walls rippling along the stem, kneading it like soft Plasticine.

A phantom sphincter tightens around your finger.

The cunt bubbles beneath you. It convulses with violence, and nibbles the bulb of your cock, snapping like a steel beartrap.

Cum spatters in your Vaselined hand.

On the altar, the candle's wick is a charred stump in a puddle of beaded red wax. Prick your finger, rolling the web of cum, the drops of blood, and blob of wax into a ball. Toss it into a live body of water under a new moon.

The ritual is over. The spell is done.

In the unlikely event my prescription fails you, walk the streets with your cock out. I guarantee—women will *stare.* And you'll get offers. Maybe only from scabby-legged bag women who neglected to take their Lithium. But, hey, *it's not called a "magic wand" for nothing.*

CHILLIN'
WITH ICEBERG SLIM

· ·

Iceberg Slim (a.k.a. Robert Beck), whose nickname was a result of the icy effect shooting cocaine had on his game, is the master pimp who, literally, wrote The Book, and became a best-selling author in the process, with an astonishing influence on both the nineteen seventies and the hip-hop young of now—causing my friend *Bring The Noise* co-author Michael Gonzales to say of this thirteenth generation, "They mo' *Mack*er than slacker!"

(Unless they're handling a stable of mangy crack-hoze, I've never seen no kinda Mack successfully work his game in a flannel shirt and baseball cap.)

Even Ice-T talks of how the work of Iceberg had such an impact on his thinking; he added Ice to his name in a spirit of tribute to the man's life (though, for the life of me, I can't make the leap from Ice-T and Ice Cube to Vanilla Ice's lacquered blond 'do).

Iceberg's books are *The Naked Soul of Iceberg Slim*; *Mama Black Widow*; *Trick Baby*; *Pimp: The Story Of My Life*; *The Long White Con*; *Death Wish*; and *AirTight Wille & Me*. His books have never gone out-of-print. The sales of his books are rivaled, perhaps, by Alex Haley.

In the summer of 1990, with the hope of one day directing the definitive cinematic biography of Iceberg Slim, Fab Five Freddy began a series of interviews, investigating the man and his life up until Iceberg's death in 1992. The following interview was done in Los Angeles, California, 1990. Opening with an explanation of the over-lay, the interview focuses on two points in his uncompleted manuscript, *The Game For Squares*. This is the interview's first appearance anywhere.

ICEBERG: To cover a particular mistake or sin you might commit in a relationship, you will talk at length.

For instance, if you are prone to gambling, and it's a secret from your mate, you will castigate in her presence anybody that gambles and tear them down, sayin', "How stupid can this muthafucka be? F'Christ's sakes, do you know what that nigga did? First, th' nigga had fifteen thousand dollars in the bank. Would you believe this dumb muthafucka blew all that money in Vegas th' otha mornin'?"

That's the over-lay.

Now, women use it a lot, which is why I'm explaining it. When women knock a particular female acquaintance about certain things, *look out*. She may be susceptible to the same flaw. But the average man, unless he's been a pimp, can't see that.

FAB: But a lot of times you can sense that in a woman, if it's actually an over-lay or if it's—

ICEBERG: —but you'll *know* if you've been in The Life!

If you can steep yourself in the principles of the game (not that you're ever gonna put anybody out in the fuckin' streets because your ambitions are higher than that), but purely as a pimpin' device. [Whispering conspiratorially] Because, look, nobody understands a

Courtesy of the George Trow Estate.

Trick Baby

(1973)
a.k.a. *Double Con*
DIRECTOR: Larry Yust; SCREENWRITERS: Larry Yust, T. Raewyn, A. Neuberg; STORY: based on the novel by Iceberg Slim [Robert Beck].
CAST: Kiel Martin (White Folks [Johnny O'Brien]); Mel Stewart (Blue Howard); and Ted Lange as Melvin The Pimp.

The only novel by best-selling author and master mack Iceberg Slim produced for the screen (which is still one more than Donald Goines). Iceberg writes that this story was first told to him by a cellmate in prison.

For a movie adaptation, *Trick Baby* is fairly faithful to the book. It's the story of two con men who run afoul of the mob. One is a Black man named Blue Howard and the other is White Folks—a "trick baby" born of a black hooker and a whyte trick. Blue schools White Folks on the psychology and tactics of "the con," who, in turn, uses his pale, washed-out complexion to scam *actual* whyte folks.

Though the movie is a worthwhile viewing experience, read the book. Iceberg's ear for the underworld makes writers like Jim Thompson read like Jacqueline Susann.

bitch better than a player. [The volume of his voice rises in right-eousness] If anybody stands up and tells me that he does, he's a *lyin' muthafucka!* Because the players have written it, *Jim!* His *survival* depends on it! Because if this muthafucka [the pimp] don't know, and he doesn't find out, he's in serious trouble!

Now this, in my opinion, is why these young rappers, and all the rest of them, have sensed that there is something valuable, and what they are doing is *calling out* all the negative aspects of the game, and incorporating it in their own psyches. They sense it's the great-est defensive tool, especially one that a *nigga* can use—because he's beset with a *problem!* [Laughs.]

FAB: That's the point that I'm feelin' and that needs to be fleshed out.

ICEBERG: [Fatherly.] Well, that's what I'm tryin' to do.

FAB: That's the point right here. It's the growing trend right now. It's a complex that's flirting with the romanticism; but, at its core level, it's kind of like the way you talk about looking in the mirror, knowing what you are looking at, that kind of strength.

ICEBERG: It's knowledge of the game that makes you impervious to marginal female attack.

If any professional Black man is under the impression he's not under attack from certain pernicious females, then th' nigga's *crazy!* [Again, whispering conspiratorially.] Any successful Black man that achieves success, monetary success in particular, he im-mediately becomes a target.

[Voice returns to its normal volume.] If he has managed to steep himself with some of the vital, significant and basic principles of the game, in effect he's as impervious to them and the bullshit as the player who's actually in the game; even though, for society, he's a clean-cut young successful man and it's his secret that he employs the techniques of the game in his relationship with the so-called square world.

Was that clear, what I'm trying to say?

FAB: Absolutely. One hundred percent. How would you carve out a blueprint? I wish there was some way—

ICEBERG: Well, for a number of years, at least three years, I had planned *The Game for Squares.*

FAB: Which was?

ICEBERG: The principles of what I just told you.

Iceberg and Fab share a laugh.

ICEBERG: But I've been beset with so many physical problems—

FAB: We all know that they're not going to last. We gotta get you back out there, man.

ICEBERG: I've explained the over-lay. Now here's what the prat-out is—

FAB: Oh, yeah, I wrote that down.

ICEBERG: The prat-out was taught to me by "Sweet" Jones [Iceberg's mentor in 1930s Chicago]. Here is a man with no college education. *No* education, in fact. I think he dropped out of grade school.

This is how it originally begins. Here's how he found out about the prat-out. He'd discovered that certain big-time whyte con mobs, back when he was a boy, utilized a technique on a victim. These white con men would show the victim the prospect of coming into a large fortune. Through various delaying tactics, they would deny his acquisition of the fortune so they could tap out his bank account. When the time came for him to call for his investment, he would jump at the opportunity.

The principle, at heart, is this (and it works with women better than it does with a sucker in the street): *pretend indifference to enhance desire.*

It works best on the prettiest bitches that walk, if any man can pretend to be indifferent to such a woman. Of course, you acquire degrees of skill with the prat-out. *Warm* indifference. Keep 'em comin' but prat 'em out. Keep them at bay until their desire is so titillated by your velvet-smooth rejection that their egos have to capture you for no other reason but to get revenge.

It works like a charm but it takes strength.

The key to everything for playing in general, and you can put this in stone, "Any individual, whether it's one of these young rappers like Ice-T and all the rest of them, if they were to really and truly reach perfection of this secret—and it has to be secret because no one must know—the outer world can't know that you have adapted all of the principles of such a low game that has been condemned by everybody in society. It's not written that you employ these techniques and these techniques must be secret to be effective. But you employ them and you live by them. You must learn *strength. Willpower!*"

You've got to learn to pass them up! If they've got their legs open, you've got to ask yourself the reason, "Why?"

And don't assume it's because you're so wonderful. Every female move is like a player. A player takes *nothing* for granted.

Be alert and strong. Don't let your ego give you any answers. It means to question any move any woman makes. *Question* it.

Use the prat-out. Develop enough strength to always use the prat-out. And be able to recognize the over-lay when you hear it. Be alert and strong. I can't stress that enough.

Be a top-flight player with a difference: *don't keep any hoze.*

RAPPIN' WITH THE RIB-TICKLIN' RALPH BAKSHI

Courtesy of Photofest.

Coonskin

(1975)

a.k.a. *Street Fight* [On Video]

DIRECTOR/SCREENWRITER: Ralph Bakshi; MUSIC: Chico Hamilton.

CAST: Barry White (Samson/Brother Bear); Charles Gordone (Preacher/Brother Fox); Scatman Crothers (Pappy/Old Man Bone); and Philip Michael Thomas (Randy/Brother Rabbit).

"Comix can't dance? Dig Cap'n Draw—*his comix even come with their own record album!*"—Tim Fielder, cartoonist.

Ralph Bakshi's combination live-action/animation feature, *Coonskin*, reads like an Uncle Remus folktale rewritten by Chester Himes with all the Yoruba-based surrealism of Nigerian-author Amos Tutuola.

Even before the film's credits roll, *Coonskin* challenges American culture with a pathetic, pot-bellied figure in overalls, who confronts the audience with a dismissive "Fuck You!" Suddenly, a second figure leaps out of the crumbling, rag-like shell of the first, uttering the word "Shee-It!" with a sneering grin.

Courtesy of Photofest.

I met with Ralph Bakshi back in the days of *The New Adventures of Mighty Mouse,* in the winter of 1989. Over the telephone, we arranged to meet on Broadway and 13th Street.

"I'll be driving a red Chevy," he said.

"I'm Black with blond dreads," I said.

On the corner, I spot the Chevy. It drives around the block three times. Finally, it parks in front of the old Cat Club.

Bakshi got out and walked up to me. He said: "Hi! I'm Ralph's friend. *Do you have any guns?*"

When Coonskin was shown at the Museum of Modern Art in 1975, and the above scene unspooled on screen, representatives from the Congress of Racial Equality (CORE) were outraged. There was a big commotion in the screening room. People shouted and marched up and down the aisle. After that, Paramount dropped the picture, and the film was handed to a small distributor who went bankrupt in two weeks.

Unfortunately, it was a false alarm. The scene was not the creation of a racist imagination. In fact, it's in the tradition: the figures are urban representations of the trickster-guardians of the crossroads, through whom all must pass to enter the realm of the invisibles.

In contrast, the character designs of Warner Brothers' 1930s and 1940s cartoons are true products of overtly racist imaginations, like Tex Avery's *All This and Rabbit Stew* with its pint-sized Stepin Fetchit and dice-tossing denouement. This cartoon, like several others of its type from the period, makes no attempt to challenge the racist thinking of the culture; but serves, instead, to reinforce it. This is the crucial difference between Bakshi's feature and the others: the racist eye versus the eye for racism.

Bakshi's character designs are only partially based on the coon icons common in this country between 1850 and the early 1900s. His designs are clearly rooted in African sculptural-motifs, which have images far more horrific than any conjured by a racist imagination. (See: *Flash of the Spirit* by Robert Farris Thompson.) My favorite designs are Bakshi's conception of how blacks

"You can't fool me! I'm in the know. I read the *Enquirer*. I know what you look like."

I thought he was joking. He wasn't.

"No. I'm Ralph's friend. He's had a lot of trouble because of this film. I gotta make sure you ain't gonna pull a gun and blow him away. Are you friend or foe?"

I could imagine the headlines of the next morning's *New York Post*:

Cartoon-porn Pioneer Gunned Down by Blond Rastafarian. Exclaimed: "Idi Amin is the True God!"

—Investigators say: "High on hip-hop"

So I read him an early draft of this article, the one that sat yellowing in a pile at the *Voice* for two years.

Needless to say, the man loved me.

"Y'know som'thin'," he said, "You look like Richard Pryor."

"I hear that a lot. Now people tell me I look like Whoopi Goldberg. And that started before I dreaded and she was still on the five-dollars-a-pop performance art circuit."

Bakshi laughed. It began as a titter and bloomed into a deep-lunged chuckle. He laughed a lot. We laughed a lot together. We was two laughin' fools.

"I've never met a reporter on the corner I didn't know before," he said. "I'm driving down here and suddenly I think, What's going on? A voice on the phone says I want to meet you! My age is showing. If I were a kid, I wouldn't have considered it for a second."

Coonskin had been opposed by the Congress of Racial Equality.

On the other hand, the NAACP had written a letter describing the film as a difficult satire, but supported it. CORE's protests led to the film's eventual disappearance.

"CORE created a big commotion at the Museum of Modern Art screening before anyone had seen it. They were geared to dislike it. They were booing at the *titles!*

"I guess it was an easy target. Or they were paid to do it. I don't know. It was very unusual. They were booing at something they hadn't even seen. This was interesting to me.

"The film was positive Black in a huge way. It shows what white people think of Blacks. I'm not a racist. I couldn't understand it and I still can't. If I were a racist for the Ku Klux Klan, I could understand it.

"But how could I understand the booing? Yes. There are certain images that upset Black people. But it depends on how those images are used and in what context. One of the interesting aspects of the film is it showed what white America was thinking about Black people at that point. The characters were acting in certain positive ways. In honest, Black ways.

"At the time, there were also these certain Black groups who were taking the money and splitting. That was driving me up the wall.

"The film was very popular with Black audiences. The trick was to get white audiences into the theater, not Black audiences. Let 'em laugh at what they always laugh at, then catch them off guard, which is what I do in all my films."

Interestingly, another of *Coonskin*'s supporters is Richard Pryor.

"Pryor loves it! He thinks it's great!"

Bakshi said he wanted to work with Pryor on a live-action feature with animation, coaxing him into doing the kind of material he performed in his early club days, like his classic Wino and the Junkie character sketch.

Bakshi began working in animation at the old Terry Toon studios at the age of nineteen. He didn't go to school but he did hang out in Washington Square Park.

Ten years later, he produced his first feature: *Fritz The Cat*.

He resides in upstate New York where he paints. He says he prefers the creative freedom of brush, paint and canvas to the restrictions of commercial film.

Bakshi was raised in the Brownsville section of Brooklyn, an experience, he says, that informs all of his work. He describes Brownsville as a "shtetl," Yiddish for ghetto.

"The only way you could get out of there was by subway. You couldn't walk anywhere. It's near Canarsie. It not near anywhere, really. It's deep in the heart of Brooklyn. It was basically a Black and Jewish, somewhat Italian neighborhood; but basically Black and Jewish."

perceive whytes—*as greasy burger bags from White Castle.*

In *Coonskin,* Bakshi pukes the iconographic bile of a racist culture back in its stupid, bloated face, wipes his chin and smiles Dirty-Harry style. *"Now deal with it . . ."* He subverts the context of Hollywood's entire catalogue of racist black iconography through a series of swift cross-edits of original and appropriated footage featuring a cackling, hanka-head Mammy doin' a de(re)constructionist flapjack dance on footage from *Birth Of A Nation* and a thick-lipped minstrel reciting blues lyrics to a star-spangled harlot named Miss America. He is lynched when the babe with the red, white and blue boobs coyly cries rape.

Coonskin, informed by African Art, African-American folklore, Thomas Edison's turn of the century minstrel films, the films of Oscar Micheaux, modern black literature, the Dozens and the jailhouse "toasts," also combines two uniquely American forms: comics and jazz. As in music and comedy, the animator's art is wholly dependent on timing. And *Coonskin* is the visual expression of Black music and humor, which has long been an important component of popular American cartoons.

Max Fleischer, to whom Bakshi owes a great deal, as both are urban-born and influenced animators, incorporated jazz into many of his animated shorts. In Fleischer's *Betty Boop Snow White,* a dancing Cab Calloway is rotoscoped for the sequence with Koko the Clown singing "Saint James Infirmary Blues." And in Bob Clampett's *Porky In Wackyland,* jazz was a direct influence in the visual shape of the cartoon.

Coonskin's comic pacing has a lot to do with the phrasings of Black music. Counter-point. Polyrythms. Mumblings corresponding to improvisations. This is especially evident when contrasted against the operatic surrealism of the film's "Godfather" sequences.

Bakshi's intent is clear—destroy racists with their own racism. In *Die, Nigger, Die!*, H. Rap Brown wrote, "What you don't control can be used as a weapon against you." Nowhere is it written Black people cannot take back the images of racism and use them as a weapon against those who oppress them. Racism is the madness of the Other and has nothing to do with how one chooses to define one's self. Racism is a form of the Evil Eye. And, according to occultist-science fiction author and Discordian prankster Robert Anton Wilson, the best protection from the "evil eye" is laughter. The fact that Bakshi is not Black is of no significance. The message is there.

The function of the satirist is magickal. To curse the enemy. The best satirists use the targets of satire as a weapon against itself. And the very best subvert the target while staying within the limits of its definition. Michael O'Donoghue is the unchallenged master of this technique.

There is an episode in *Coonskin* involving a corrupt, racist cop named Mannigan. Mannigan shows up at a Harlem club to wipe out Brer Rabbit, who has taken the racketeering payoffs intended for Mannigan. He sits at a table, waiting for Rabbit with a drink in his hand.

While he stares at the full, cocoa-hued breasts of a topless dancer, an LSD cube is dropped into his drink.

Because of the isolation of growing up in Brownsville, he feels he grew up with a strong sense of identity and freedom.

"You grow up so isolated, you end up making your own value calls. Racism was never an issue in Brownsville (I'm talking about the forties and the fifties). You end up being a very free person, I think in retrospect. The community was cool. You ended up making your own calls because you got no information from the outside world.

"Both my parents were from Russia. And they worked, so tradition was a rare commodity. They brought an Old World tradition and we basically hung around in the streets. We used to sit around in school yards drawing characters with chalk, the crudest means available. I was trying to do what I call "Ghetto Art." It wasn't "Graffiti Art." I called it "Ghetto Art." Graffiti wasn't a big deal when I was growing up. It wasn't a painter's medium at that point. And it was anti-Disney, which doesn't touch the subject of animation.

"It was a definite approach to the style of my earlier films. When I was designing *Coonskin,* and my earlier films *Fritz The Cat* and *Heavy Traffic,* there was a certain crudeness that I put into the films on purpose; *Heavy Traffic* and *Coonskin* especially.

"What I was trying to do was relate to the person in the street. I was looking for a sort of Graffiti Art feel—the colors, the structure, a certain crudeness of backgrounds. I even used grainy films at times. The important thing to me was to relate to a certain type of person that I grew up with. To do what I call an art of the street, a "Ghetto Art." It's my form of expression."

In *Coonskin,* there is a sequence of lyrical eloquence featuring figures modeled after the work of George Herriman, the creator of *Krazy Kat,* with a monologue that might have been written by Ntozake Shange.

I asked Bakshi about Herriman.

"The single greatest cartoonist that ever lived! George Herriman hid his blackness for years, though no one wants to admit it.

"He took a style called Krazy Kat, which was his strip. It was very much like an improvisational jazz piece. He did things in cartooning that have never been done to date.

"It was all done through feeling. You could sense a Black idiom throughout it: a Black sense of humor; a Black folktale; a Black history; a Black culture.

"Every thing that is in *Krazy Kat* is Black. And he sold it to white audiences by keeping his color a secret.

"*Krazy Kat* is reputed—and not just by myself—as one of the greatest comic strips ever done, if not the greatest. It's number one on most cartoonists' hit list.

"If there is a cartoonist's cartoonist, it's Herriman. Herriman surpassed cartooning—not that I'm saying it's important to surpass cartooning—but Herriman was a fine artist. He makes Basquiat look silly.

"Herriman was one hundred percent pure genius. The greatest cartoonist in America. And he was Black.

"There's a similarity, I find, between Herriman and Coltrane in their riffs, their improvisations. And there's a piano player, Erroll Garner. If you wanna do yourself a favor, read Herriman with a nineteen-fifties Erroll Garner record on. They play together like magic!"

Mannigan is led by the hand into a bedroom. A lounging gay hustler awaits him.

Mannigan is dicked and spiked with smack. He freaks. His face is blackened just like the National Guard General in *The Spook Who Sat by the Door.* Gremlins pluck at his eyes. Then he's dressed in full mammy drag complete with pickaninny sprouts and watermelon breasts.

Mannigan goes gun-blastin' beserk, and is taken down by the N.Y.P.D. His corpse cools to ice blue. His toes twitch with cartoon death spasms.

With *Coonskin,* Bakshi was mounted and became the voice of ancient African gods. WE ARE BACK. AND ON YOUR MOVIE AND TV SCREENS. DO NOT ADJUST THE HORIZONTAL. WE ARE THE VERTICAL . . .

Cotton Comes to Harlem

(1970)
[On Video]
DIRECTOR: Ossie Davis; SCREENWRITERS: Ossie Davis, Arnold Perl; STORY: based on Chester Himes's novel *Cotton Comes to Harlem*; MUSIC: Galt MacDermot; SONGS: Galt MacDermot with Joseph S. Lewis, Ossie Davis, William Dumaresq and *Paul Laurence Dunbar (!)*.
CAST: Raymond St. Jacques (Coffin Ed Johnson); Godfrey Cambridge (Grave Digger Jones); Calvin Lockhart (Rev. Deke O'Malley); Judy Pace (Iris); Redd Foxx (Uncle Bud); and Cleavon Little (Lo Boy).

After robbers stick-up Reverend Deke O'Malley's Back-to-Africa rally in Harlem for $87,000, Coffin Ed Johnson and Grave Digger Jones make the scene, and give chase to the getaway van. Both the van and Reverend Deke disappear. Looks like a setup to the cynical Grave Digger and Coffin Ed.

In hiding, Reverend Deke thinks he's been double-crossed by his partner. His partner believes the same about Reverend Deke. But, in fact, after all is said and done, the money was hidden inside a bale o' cotton found by junkman Redd Foxx who ends up a rich happy black man in Africa with many wives. Ossie Davis deserves kudos for creating a comedy that still resonates with audiences twenty-five years later.

Come Back, Charleston Blue

(1972)
DIRECTOR: Mark Warren; SCREENWRITER: Ernest Kinoy (under the *nom de cine* [which spells t-r-o-u-b-l-e] Bontche Schweig); STORY: based on Chester Himes's novel *The Heat's On*; MUSIC: Donny Hathaway (Music conductor); SONGS: Quincy Jones.
CAST: Godfrey Cambridge (Gravedigger Jones); Raymond St. Jacques (Coffin Ed Johnson); Maxwell Glanville (Caspar); Minnie Gentry (Her Majesty); and Tony Brealond (Drag Queen).

What this book should have, but doesn't, is a section on the late Chester Himes, his novels and how they've been translated to film. And I'll not begin a detailed discussion here. Suffice to say, I've always associated the narrative landscapes of Himes's slyly satirical, Harlem-based crime novels with the modernist gestures of jazz and abstract painting, and I've yet to see any of these qualities realized on film. The best notion came from Picasso, of course, Himes's drinking buddy in Paris, who thought Himes's novels would make great comic strips, which Picasso would then proceed to draw on cocktail napkins. (There is, in fact, a comic based on Himes's work in France— translated by Melvin Van Peebles.)

As for *Come Back, Charleston Blue*, I didn't see the film when it was first released and I haven't located it on video. I saw portions of an edited version one night on television, interrupted by a steady stream of commercials. So, although viewing conditions were less than adequate, I liked what I saw, especially its last moments.

Blazing Saddles

(1973)
[On Video]
DIRECTOR/SCREENWRITER: Mel Brooks; SCREENWRITERS: Mel Brooks, Richard Pryor.
CAST: Cleavon Little; Madeline Kahn; Gene Wilder; and Mel Brooks.

This is an obvious rip-off of Fred Williamson's *Boss Nigger* (1975). The fact that Fred's film came out *after Blazing Saddles* don't mean shit! Fred's a *Black man! In Hollywood!* And Mel Brooks—well, if we've read and understood our "*Secret Relationship . . . ,*" and learned from the logic of Professor Leonard Jefferies, we understand that Fred's predicament is simply another example of the Man's *blatant* trickology!*

*Dear Mr. Brooks, this is a complicated in-joke. It is not a reflection of yr creative integrity. Please do not fly to New York and beat me up.

Cooley High

(1975)
DIRECTOR: Michael Schultz; SCREENWRITER: Eric (Somebody tell me) "What's Happening" Monte.
CAST: Glynn Turman (Robert "Preach" Morris); Lawrence Hilton-Jacobs (Larry "Cochise" Jackson); Garrett Morris (Mr. Mason); Cynthia David (Brenda); Corin Rogers (Pooter); Maurice Leon Havis (Willie); and Joseph Carter Wilson (Tyrone).

One of the best films of the period, and certainly the best film in the whole of Michael Schultz's career, *Cooley High* mutated, unfortunately, into a brainless TV sitcom featuring three very fat performers (Mabel King, Shirley Hemphill and Fred Berry [who came to TV after a career performing a pre-breakdance variation on The Robot with a group called The Lockers]) who hung out in a *Happy Days*–style malted-milk shop in Compton where, amazingly, there wasn't a chopped barbecue, fried chicken or fish sam'mich in sight to explain the characters' high-cholesterol-intake physiques.

Courtesy of Photofest.

Uptown Saturday Night

(1974)
[On Video]

DIRECTOR: Sidney Poitier; SCREENWRITER: Richard Wesley.

CAST: Sidney Poitier (Steve Jackson); Bill Cosby (Wardell Franklin); Harry Belafonte (Geechie Dan Beauford); Flip Wilson (The Reverend); Richard Pryor (Sharp Eye Washington); Rosalind Cash (Sarah Jackson); Roscoe Lee Browne (Congressman Dudley Lincoln); Paula Kelly (Leggy Peggy); and Calvin Lockhart (Silky Slim).

Bill Cosby and Sidney Poitier, playing working-class stiffs, lose a winning lottery ticket during the holdup in an classy uptown after-hours joint. Then they lose an additional $200 to Richard Pryor as P.I. Sharp-Eyed Washington. Later, the two meet a midget who has their butts kicked. Then we're introduced to Harry Belafonte doing a wonderful turn as Harlem crime boss Geechie Dan (still, Harry, that doesn't excuse you for your participation in that *Planet of the Apes* remake, *White Man's Burden*). Overall, *Uptown Saturday Night* is pretty numbing in the laff dept.

Let's Do It Again

(1975)
[On Video]

DIRECTOR: Sidney Poitier; STORY: Timothy March; SCREENWRITER: Richard Wesley; MUSIC: Curtis Mayfield.

CAST: Sidney Poitier (Clyde Williams); Bill Cosby (Billy Foster); Calvin Lockhart (Biggie Smalls); Mel Stewart (Ellison); Julius Harris (Bubbletop Woodson); and Jimmy Walker (Bootney Farnsworth).

Please, let's not. I have a headache.

A Piece of the Action

(1977)
[On Video]

DIRECTOR: Sidney Poitier; SCREENWRITER: Charles Blackwell; STORY: Timothy March; MUSIC: Curtis Mayfield.

CAST: Sidney Poitier (Manny Durrell); Bill Cosby (Dave Anderson); James Earl Jones (Joshua Burke); Denise Nicholas (Lila French); and Ja'net DuBoise (Nellie Bond).

Let's see, *Uptown Saturday Night* was about a missing lottery ticket. Hmmm, Harry Belafonte was actually kind of amusing as Geechie Dan. *Let's Do It Again* was about an underweight boxer under hypnosis. Makes sense. Jimmy Walker sleepwalked through that one. And, well, wouldn't ya know it, I don't remember what the hell this one's about.

Courtesy of Photofest.

Car Wash

(1976)
[On Video]

DIRECTOR: Michael Schultz; SCREENWRITER: Joel Schumacher; PRODUCERS: Art Linson, Gary Stromberg.

CAST: Franklin Ajaye; Richard Pryor; Antonio Fargas; George Carlin; and The Pointer Sisters.

Apparently, a lot of you thought earning $4.25 an hour was *really* funny.

Courtesy of Photofest.

Courtesy of Photofest.

Courtesy of Photofest.

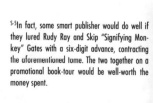

Which Way Is Up

(1977)
[On Video]
DIRECTOR: Michael Schultz; SCREENWRITERS:
Carl Gottlieb, Cecil Brown.
CAST: Richard Pryor; and Lonette McKee.

Every time Michael Schultz sets foot on a movie set, he's stymied by this very question!

Greased Lightning

(1977)
[On Video]
DIRECTOR: Michael Schultz; SCREENWRITERS:
Kenneth Vose, Lawrence DuKore,
Melvin Van Peebles, Leon Capetanos.
PRODUCER: Hannah Weinstein.
CAST: Richard Pryor; Pam Grier (Pryor's squeeze at the time); Cleavon Little; Richie Havens; Julian Bond; Minnie Gentry; Vincent Gardenia; and Beau Bridges.

To paraphrase Hermann Goering, whenever I see "Directed by Michael Schultz," I go for my gun.

The Wiz

(1978)
[On Video]
DIRECTOR: Sidney Lumet; SCREENWRITER:
Joel Schumacher; STORY: based on William Brown's Broadway play; SONGS: Charlie Smalls.
CAST: Diana Ross (Dorothy); Michael Jackson (Scarecrow); Ted Ross (the Cowardly Lion); Nipsey Russell (Tin Woodsman); Theresa Merritt (Aunti Em); Lena Horne (Good Witch Glinda); Mabel King (Evilene); and Richard Pryor (Wiz).

During the film's Cleveland run, a young Arsenio Hall scratched his head, rolled his eyes skyward and thought: "Flying monkeys, *hmmmm.*"

Dolemite II

(1976)
a.k.a. *The Human Tornado*
[On Video]
EXECUTIVE PRODUCER: Rudy Ray Moore;
DIRECTOR: Cliff Roquemore; SCREENWRITER:
Jerry Jones; SET DESIGNERS: Rudy Ray Moore, Jimmy Lynch; MUSIC: Arthur Wright.
CAST: Rudy Ray Moore (The Dolemite); Lady Reed (Queen Bee); Jimmy Lynch (Mr. Motion); Howard Jackson (Himself); Gloria de Lani (Hurricane Annie); Jerry Jones (Pete); and Java (Java).

Unlike most of the commercial cinema's Black-market movies, which rely on the story formulas of their honkoid counterparts, the movies of Rudy Ray Moore are rooted in the structure, imagery and motifs of a tradition of Black oral narrative known as "The Toast"; and deserve a booklength study of their own[S-5]. The popularity he's found in his varied career (from minister to "blue" comedian ["I'm a church-going religious man. I do this because I got to make a living."]) is due to "The Toast." And, to his credit, his films, whatever their budgetary shortcomings, have preserved that tradition.

[S-5]In fact, some smart publisher would do well if they lured Rudy Ray and Skip "Signifying Monkey" Gates with a six-digit advance, contracting the aforementioned tome. The two together on a promotional book-tour would be well-worth the money spent.

Of all his chitlin' circuit capers (which include *Disco Godfather* and *Rude*), my favorite is *Petey Wheatstraw: The Devil's Son-in-Law* with Wildman Steve Galon and the comedy team of Skillet-n-Leroy. The film's opening sequence illustrates more than any why Rudy Ray Moore was unique to the seventies blax-pac: his gangster-oriented sub-plots are wholly subordinated to the story patterns of Black folklore.

In a *Washington Post* article in July 1992, Moore explained to writer-archivist David Mills, "These rhymes and raps that I have were told fifty years ago by the beer-joint and liquor-store wise men (who) used to sit out in front of the store, drinking beer, lying and talking shit.

"What I did, I picked them up. I even gave older winos money to tell me these tales. And then I'd take them and freshen them up."

Rudy Ray Moore first heard *Dolemite* in 1970 from a wino who hung out at the Hollywood record store he worked in at the time:

Dolemite had an uncle they called Sudden Death who could kill a dozen muthafuckas with the smell of his breath!

Improvising on its basic story (which is what one is supposed to do with a toast—like Coltrane taking out "My Favorite Things"), Moore included it in his nightclub act. The bit evolved and he made it the centerpiece of his album *Eat Out More Often* (a title he found scribbled on the wall of a men's room in a Greyhound bus station). The recording made Billboard's Top 100 album chart.

In 1975, *Dolemite* found renewed life on the screen with a story concerning a pimp who regains control of his nightclub from da mob with the help of his stable of Kung-Fu hoze.

The Human Tornado is the same story except more so. Now if only someone would produce *Kung-Fu Hoze Go To College.*

(If you wish, you can send your money to Mr. Moore c/o P.O. Box 11591, Los Angeles, California 90011, and he'll send you cassettes of his albums [$7.98] or his movies [$27.50] prepaid.)

Disco Godfather

(1979)
a.k.a. *The Avenging Disco Godfather*
[On Video]
DIRECTOR: J. Robert Wagoner; STORY: Rudy Ray Moore, Theodore Toney; SCREENPLAY: Cliff Roquemore and J. Robert Wagoner.

CAST: Rudy Ray Moore (Tucker Moore); Carol Speed (Noel); Jimmy Lynch (Sweetmeat); Lady Reed (Mrs. Edwards); and Julius J. Carry III (Bucky).

If the NAACP had a *Reefer Madness* movie category for its annual Image Awards, and nominated Rudy Ray's disco-driven act of ghetto surrealism, it would lose out to Republican Tony Brown's *White Girl* and its green-eyed, biracial coke demoness (for underneath its "anti-drug" message, *White Girl* is a study of class-based, color-coded, intragroup racism within the Black community). A real shame, too, 'cause George Kirby's rendition of "King Heroin" is no competition for the snotty-nosed demons in *The Avenging Disco Godfather*'s hallucinatory sequence of an angel dust bug-out.

Monkey Hustle

(1977)
[On Video]
DIRECTOR/PRODUCER: Arthur Marks; SCREENWRITER: Charles Johnson; STORY: Odie Hawkins; MUSIC: Jack Conrad.

CAST: Yaphet Kotto (Daddy Fox); Rudy Ray Moore (Goldie); and Rosalind Cash (Mama).

Some lame nonsense about a Fagin-like con man played by Yaphet Kotto leading a gang of nascent hustlers. The film is not elevated by the all-too-brief presence of Rudy Ray Moore.

DA MINISTER OF CARTOON CULTURE: PEDRO BELL

· ·

Back before the spermjets of platform funk seeded the ovum of acidhead psychedelia, and the huckabuckin' JB was still xeroxin' the same dumb-ass beats 45 after 45, my nappy-headed homies and I hung out on the stoop of a city health inspector's nightmare with a bottle of Boone's Farm apple wine, gobbling salmonella sandwiches disguised as fried chicken chunks laid between two greasy, Tabasco sauce–soaked slices of Wonder Bread, waitin' for the genius to come along and put that freakish Hendrix spin on the James Brown funk.

So when Funkedelic hit with "If you suck my soul, I will lick your funky emotion," a whole culture of Black freakdom was born. And my platformed posse and I lost no time gettin' with the program. In black-lit basements papered with posters of Ho Chi Mihn, Angela Davis and the Kama Sutra Zodiac, we sprawled across dingy, mildewed mattresses with flecks of lint glowing in our phosphorescent 'fros, blowing shot-gunned streams of reefer smoke up each other's dried-snot encrusted nostrils, listening to Eddie Hazel's guitar shriek through a pair of junk-yard speakers duck-taped to the wall.

Once our eyes were sufficiently bloodshot, and our pupils significantly enlarged, we settled back with Funkedelic's album jacket opened on our laps, and argued the secret symbolism and hidden meanings of the album's liner notes bombast:

> "Fear manifests in the pale grey shadow of the ordinary person, whose fear clamps down on all his instincts and traps him in the narrow confines of the socially accepted norm. Afraid either to step down into the darkness of the lower self or to rise into the light of the higher self, he hangs suspended in between, stultified into an alien pattern of nothingness."
>
> —*Maggot Brain* liner notes

The liner notes of Funkedelic's first four albums consisted of text which originally appeared in a magazine published by the Process Church of Final Judgment, composed by its founder Robert De Grimston. The long-haired, black-robed Gnostics of the Process Church believed that God and the Devil had settled their cosmic squabble. Come the final bugle call of the Apocalypse, God would sit in judgment over a bunch of folks who looked like they had just shown up for an open cattle call of *Night of the Living Dead* movie extras; and, Satan, acting on the wisdom of God's orders, would cast the damned (and anyone who was ever involved with a 12-Step recovery program) into the dreaded Lake O' Fire.

If God and the Devil were runnin' pardners again, the Processians figured they better not take any chances so they worshipped them all—Jehovah, Christ, Lucifer, Satan—*the whole (un)holy lot!*

For the Processians, it appears "mass" and "black mass" were one and the same. The fact that the Process Church could reconcile the seemingly polar differences of "Christians" and "Satanists" tells us that

Welcome Home, Brother Charles

(1975)
a.k.a. *Soul Vengence*
[On Video]
PRODUCER/DIRECTOR/SCREENWRITER: Jamaa Fanaka.
CAST: Marlo Monte; Reathea Grey; Tiffany Peters; Ben Bigelow; Jackie Ziegler; and Mordo Dana.

You'll learn all you need or want to know about Fanaka's U.C.L.A. student film by rapidly thumbing the pages of this book and staring at the image in the corner.

Emma Mae

(1975)
a.k.a. *Black Sister's Revenge*
[On Video]
DIRECTOR-SCREENWRITER: Jamaa Fanaka.
CAST: Jerri Hayes (Emma Mae); Ernest Williams II (Jesse Amos); Charles David Brooks III (Zeke Johnson); Eddie Allen (James); Robert Slaughter (Devo); and Malik Carter (Big Daddy Johnson).

One year after his graduate film *Welcome Home, Brother Charles* (*Soul Vengeance*), the great Jamaa Fanaka shot *Emma Mae* (a.k.a. *Black Sister's Revenge*) to complete his master's thesis at U.C.L.A.

Arriving in Los Angeles from Mississippi, Emma Mae falls in love with Jesse, a local gangleader. He gets busted and thrown in jail. With the aid of his gang, Emma Mae tries to raise money for his legal defense by working at a car wash and fails. So she robs a bank and gets Jesse out of jail. To show his gratitude, he fucks another woman. And, well, watching Emma Mae kick the shit out Jesse in front of all their neighbors is certainly worth the cost of a one-night rental.

the PTL Club's Pat Robertson is really just the flipside of the Church of Satan's Anton LaVey.

Why these tracts were chosen for the albums' liner notes, and what, exactly, was Clinton's involvement with the Process, is, according to *UnCut Funk* publisher and Funkedelic's archivist, David Mills, "One of the great mysteries of Funkedelic fandom."

As to the band's relationship to the Process, bassist Bootsy Collins had this to say: "George Clinton was the one who was really involved in that. He was the one who was really involved and went to meetings. He was the one who studied and read. I think he was doin' it for his own satisfaction. Everybody else in the band was still freaked out on just bein' freaked out. We was just floatin' with it, goin' with whatever he was sayin'. Everybody else was kinda there but they wasn't really there."

In any case, the idea of a funk band playing acid-crazed jungle noise associated with a group of quasi-satanists represented by a proto-nazi swastika symbol immediately conjures up images of horned niggas runnin' rampant, swingin' dem tail-like wangs and eatin' up precious Caucasian babies (*Yum! Yum!*) in the minds of the nation's negrophobes. So by the time of *Maggot Brain*'s release, with De Grimston's "Fear" essay as its liner notes, the association between Manson and the Process Church had been discovered (in fact, Manson published an essay in the Death issue of the Process's magazine), Clinton realized it was time he best stop monkeying around with them devil-worshippin' hippie mofos, and come up with a new design scheme. *Fast.*

With Funkedelic's *Cosmic Slop* cover in '73, and its crawling ink splatter of zombified pinup pussy and turn-da-knob titties, Cap'n Draw careened into the scene with some serious necro-Negro doodles on the pads of his jizz-tipped markers—hijackin' all the shit into the ghettosphere of the Twilight Zone. And that's when we knew, in our Afrofied freakhood, that we was one up on the whyte boys.

Hippie whyteboys had S. Clay Wilson's corpse-felching vampires and R. Crumb's hard-nippled nymphets fellating their way through the pages of Zap Comix in a trail of ejaculatory penile foam. But our comix could dance and bump behinds. How? As cartoonist Tim "Rahsaan" Fielder observed, "They come with their own record albums!"

Check that!

When Pedro was beamed aboard the mothership, Funketeers awaited each new Funkedelic's release for its cartoon-based liner notes with as much anticipation as they did for the music. It was key to the experience. As cult-crit Michael Gonzales points out, "It was like Clinton was makin' music for Pedro's cartoons."

With an open disdain for the bourgeois and its "aesthetics," the results of Pedro's deliberately anti-classical and vibrantly hallucinatory line exploded in a juxtaposition of pop culture, politics, word play and, most importantly, ideas that achieves a mythological, ghettocentric universe as integrated, subversive and philosophically complex as the work of 1980s neo-expressionists Jean-Michel Basquiat, Keith Haring and Kenny Scharf. Through what he calls "concept-driven" packaging, Pedro Bell gave visual substance to the G.C. noise-clan's psychedelized funk, and conceived of a world operating under its own laws, logic and language—a hyperbolic burlesque of inventive liner-note prose combined with a deceptively "crude" cartooning style. Not only did his work broaden the vocabulary of street slang with the introduction of "Zeep-Speak" (a linguistic invention, according to distinguished pop-culture critic, Lou Stathis, which predates William Gibson's "cyberpunk" fiction by ten years); but, by incorporating the motifs of pulp science fiction (which, in the theme park that is Pedro's mind, is directly influenced by the cosmology of Sun Ra), propelled the traditional narrative patterns of the "Hustler's Toast" into a whole new sphere of satiric storytelling. Pedro's cartoons, like the music of P-Funk, are the clear products of black oral street culture.

Pedro Bell's liner-note "scartoons" (cartoons that result from scars) are scatological masterpieces of street-corner culture reconfigured into a ghastly science fiction universe. As key to the P-Funk mythos as Clinton and the music, Pedro's unique approach to graphic design and album packaging not only supplied the logos of the Funkedelic spirit, it also uncovered a growing "counterculture" within traditional Black communities across the country; who, in turn, viewed the work as emblematic of a particular breed of culture outlaw, investing it with talismanic meaning, and assumed it as a badge of their own rebellious creativity. His "scartoons" gave voice, vision and imagination to the angry, rebellious and cynically playful views of the post-sixties' generation of seventies black youth. In other words, the hallucinations rising out of the scars of his felt-tip markers matched our own.

Courtesy of Photofest.

Penitentiary

(1979)
[On Video]
DIRECTOR/SCREENWRITER/PRODUCER: Jamaa Fanaka
CAST: Leon Isaac Kennedy (Martel "Too Sweet" Gordone); Thommy Pollard (Eugene T. Lawson); Hazel Spears (Linda); Donovan Womack (Jesse Amos); Floyd Chatman (Hezzikia "Seldom Seen" Jackson); Wilbur "Hi Fi" White (Sweet Pea); and Badja Djola ("Half Dead" Johnson).

In the films of Jamaa Fanaka, Rudy Ray Moore collides with the work of Italian director Dario (Suspira) Argento. The surrealist improbability of his raw, street-level humor spins his simple prison-as-black-oppression-metaphor premise into worlds rarely seen outside of a Pedro Bell cartoon. To demonstrate this conceit, I've asked Montreal-based *genius*, Rick Trembles, who R. Crumb once described as more twisted than he, to render a fun house tour of the first of Fanaka's *Penitentiary* trilogy.

Pedro Bell is a card-carrying member of The Church of The SubGenius, a.k.a. Reverend Mayhem, born and raised on all sides of Chicago under the sign of Gemini.

PEDRO: Funkedelia on a two-dimensional surface is about chaos. There's either all yin or all yang. And no balance between the two. I figured that if the audience could get past some of these comix, maybe some of this stuff will start makin' sense, maybe it won't. I'll at least make it interestin'. Maybe they'll come back to it later and it'll give them some kind of information they won't get through traditional means. People thought Clinton and I worked in close cooperation in terms of putting the package together. That wasn't the case at all. He rarely saw any projects that were in progress and very few that were finished before they were already out. And none of my liner notes. He would have to wait until my liner notes came because I would do that last. I remote-controlled the situation through osmosis. Still, I was in a hell of a position. I was an artist and art director for an organization that was ultimately responsible to a record company. I didn't have to take orders, got paid and talked as much smack as I wanted.

Y'see, I had a degree in Funkology day one. I was just a cruise missle lookin' for a place to land. In the late sixties, I was goin' through the Black Power thing, the Black Panther thing, the drugs, the tart actions. On the music tip, I was seriously into Frank Zappa, Jimi Hendrix and Sun Ra (who all, by the way, were not particularly popular with blacks at that time). Blue Cheer was another group I was geared towards. I really had access to both sides of the radio channel. I know the words to "Beauty Is Only Skin Deep" as well as I know the lyrics to "409" by the Beach Boys. When all this music thing was goin' on, I said "Dag! There's somethin' that can be done

with this Hendrix thing. Blacks ain't up on that yet but there's goin' to be somethin' to it."

Then there was that Frank Zappa style of packaging, which is what I liked about him actually. His music was smokin'. It was just that there were no black folks doin' stuff like that. He had his own artists do his artwork and he wrote most of the liner notes himself. It was seriously sarcastic, tongue-in-cheek and sometimes blatant. As a matter of fact, I met Zappa once after a Mothers concert. I asked him what he thought was a serious car and he said a '29 Ford Woodie called "Ms. Carriage." I told him I liked the name of his fan club, *"The United Mutations of America,"* and how much I liked the way he was controlling his product. I told him that I was involved with a group and I was going to package the same way, except with a Black perspective.

With all of those elements happenin' on the music tip, and all those other elements on the external tip, the Funkedelic evolutionary thing was just somethin' that was going to happen.

I had gotten to the point that I was sayin' I ought to hook up with some musicians. So I started messin' around in a garage band but it was mostly "Top 40" stuff. I was the only one on the block who had a real live synthesizer. [Giggles.] So I got props!

We just did a few hole-in-the-wall clubs. I was the oldest one in the band. I came in as an advisor. Because I had the synthesizer, they drafted me! [Laughs.] I had to get together with dudes closer to my age.

Then I heard Funkedelic on the radio. The DJ was takin' a chance. She said this just came in the mail. She played it and it was *intercepted!* You know that first cut? "If you suck my soul, I will lick your funky emotion"? She came back on and said it was time to go to a commercial while she checked this thing out. She came back on and said, "Well, anyway, the name of the group is Funkedelic . . ."

I said, "Damn! That's the shit! Funkedelic? Pencil time! I gotta check these boys out!"

I figure I don't need to be wastin' my time tryin' to get some boys together when I can just hook up with somebody who sounds like this.

I finally found the record in a mom-an'-pop store. There wasn't that much information on the jacket but when I got far enough along, it didn't take five minutes to get an address on management.

Cosmic Slop was the first album that I was involved with but I was doin' stuff for them behind the scenes in between the first album and *Free Your Mind,* their second one. I did early promotion. I did flyers for a few shows. I did Clinton's makeup in the chittlin' circuit days. Jack-of-all-trades, so to speak.

DARIUS: I understand you began as a writer.

PEDRO: In the P-Funk realm?

DARIUS: No, before.

PEDRO: In terms of making money off you know what, I got my props first as a writer doing editorials and features. My old man got me and my other two brothers into the cartooning action at an early age. We was like micros. I was the oldest, six. But my mama had this nice little handwriting. She had the penmanship in the family.

So we started off on the art tip, collectively. And got off into different directions, but we stayed up on our writing strokes. Generally, everybody perceived us as artists.

DARIUS: What were some of your early publications?

PEDRO: Assorted. From high school and college papers, to freelance articles for some of the revolutionary Black magazines and newspapers of the day. They sprang up and died just as quickly.

DARIUS: What were the names of these publications?

PEDRO: There was this one mimeograph thing called *Black Rag.* And this other magazine, I forget the name, but it was put out by S.D.S. in the day. I did the most for *University Torch* at Rockefeller University. I had done some stuff for a magazine called *Encore* and it never hit the streets. Or maybe it did for one issue and then went under. I did a series for this other magazine called *The Informer.* On the serious tip, I would do stuff on the hot tops of the day. I did the debate about firearms; police control or lack of; observations of the

Courtesy of Photofest.

Penitentiary II

(1982)
[On Video]
DIRECTOR/SCREENWRITER/PRODUCER: Jamaa Fanaka.
CAST: Leon Isaac Kennedy (Martel "Too Sweet" Gordone); Ernie Hudson ("Half Dead" Johnson); and Mr. T. as "Himself."

Costing only $250,000.00 to produce, *Penitentiary* grossed over $13,000, 000, so M.G.M/U.A. put up a "sneeze budget" of $1,000,000 and Mr. T. for a sequel with what one writer described as "one of the longest title card prologues in film history."

Courtesy of Photofest.

Courtesy of Photofest.

whyte middle class. Political warrior stuff. I have a straight style of writing as well as what I call my pictographic style. Even if it was serious, I would put a lighter touch on it by illustrating it.

DARIUS: How extensively were you involved with playing the dozens when you were growing up?

PEDRO: Signifying? Wolf tickets? *I was about it.*

DARIUS: Tell me about it.

PEDRO: Back in the day, for biological reasons, I was somewhat of a "runt-a-tolla." If you were undersized, you had to learn three things: how to fight, run and signify. I started with signifyin' an' runnin'. Of course, one naturally follows the other. [Giggles.] In terms of signifyin' an' wolf tickets in the day, I spent my sixth grade down in Florida. That was real cool for one simple reason: it was separated down there but it was the first time I found out about Black history. And I picked up some of the southern-style of signifyin'. When I came back, Chicago was on the "poltergeist" tip as far as I was concerned.

I was usin' my Chicago style down in St. Pete; but, actually, I didn't have that many problems down there because most people thought Chicagoloids are gangsters. My size situation didn't make that much difference.

Chicago style was tempolized a lot faster and the cuss level was higher because in the South the parents still ruled. You couldn't play that. Parents would jump on your ass physically. To compensate, you had to have more of a story in your signifyin'. In Chicago style, you could get away with one line or two. In the South, you got props if you could hang a paragraph or a page on 'em.

There was these two radio DJs. They worked for WLS at the time. One was named Mort Krim. He was actually a radio journalist who had this real deep baritone voice. I don't remember the name of the other dude. He was just a DJ.

It was funny. They would have this little signifyin' session goin' on. It was such a high level of signifyin'. One dude would go ahead and pull all these multisyllabic words to talk about this other cat. He had this elitist manner, talked about his cultural distaste and used all these highfalutin words.

Meanwhile, the DJs got this laugh track goin'. And he's throwin' out this street-level stuff. I sort of liked that style. I could go 'head and cut high and cut low. There was a cat named Julius who also liked that kind of high and low signifyin' action. So we would go ahead and engage on that infidelic, adding these little 'loids, Latin prefixes or suffixes.

When I was up and coming, I went through a phase of studying history and dinosaurs. Also, my mother was a nurse. I would read some of her school books when I didn't have money to buy magazines, and developed a feel for the use of Latin prefixes and suffixes because of the medical terms. Pimp became pimpataurus. Infidel became infidelet. I just pulled suffixes and prefixes and lined them onto regular words. By the time The Funkedelic came along, I was already locked on how to go ahead and convert street into "Zeep-Speak."

DARIUS: Zeep-Speak?

PEDRO: The slanguage came first. The handle came later. Technology automatically causes the language to expand. At the other end, what happens on the street also causes the language to expand. The only thing I've done is merge the two concepts.

We've looked at how the irreverence of the signifyin' narrative style influenced the direction of blaxploitation movies, the pimpin' game, the actor's craft, stand-up comedy, hip-hop and the visual design of record jackets. And other than citing the novels of Iceberg Slim and Donald Goines, I haven't clearly pointed out how that style impacted on the work of Black writers in the 1970s. One such writer is Steve Cannon, author of the underground best-selling novel, *Groove, Bang and Jive Around.*

The novel was first published by Maurice Girodias's Olympia Press in 1969, during the second phase of the company's life, when Olympia Press was moved from Paris to New York. As Michael Perkins writes, in *The Secret Record,* the novels Girodias published during this period

Courtesy of Photofest.

Penitentiary III

(1987)
[On Video]
DIRECTOR/SCREENWRITER/PRODUCER: Jamaa Fanaka.
CAST: Leon Isaac Kennedy (Martel "Too Sweet" Gordone); Kessler "The Haiti Kid" Raymond (Midnight Thud Jessup); and Drew Bundini Brown (Sugg).

You haven't lived until you've experienced *Penitentiary III*'s hairless Tasmanian Devil—The Midnight Thud—at three o'clock in the morning on commercial Canadian television with a Labatt's hangover.

"used satire as a vehicle for comments on sexuality in American society." Also, considering Cannon's initial influences as a writer, it's not surprising that Girodias's father was Henry Miller's first publisher.

Like the majority of books published by Girodias, *Groove, Bang and Jive Around* was marketed as a d.b. or "dirty book." And it was. One of the filthiest. On close inspection, it's also a good deal more. In its narrative use of the toast structure, based loosely on the Temptation's popular song, "Runaway Child," it's one of the early examples of the neo-hoodoo aesthetic pioneered not only by Steve Cannon but by David Henderson and Ishmael Reed as well.

It sold one hundred thousand copies. It got one review. In *Screw*.

It is the story of a fourteen-year-old named Annette, who, by page forty, has fucked practically everyone in New Orleans, including the members of her family, and escapes to the Land of Oo-bla-dee (an Oz-like free zone founded by trumpeter Dizzy Gillespie). The following is an excerpt: chapter thirteen.

PAPA DOC JOHN'S
BULLDOG'S BONE

Courtesy of Photofest.

The Omega Man

(1971)
[On Video]
DIRECTOR: Boris Sagal; SCREENWRITERS: John William Corrington, Joyce M. Corrington; STORY: based on Richard Matheson's novel *I Am Legend*.
CAST: Charlton Heston; Anthony Zerbe; Rosalind Cash; Lincoln Kilpatrick; and Eric Laneuville.

As Criswell left a skid-row screening of *The Omega Man,* he predicted to his Angora-sweatered pal, Ed Wood, Jr.,— "In the future, Black Americans will mutate into uncolored, pink-eyed beings with white afros!"

Courtesy of Photofest.

A white-hot sun blazed down over the seven hills, valleys and cottages that dotted the countryside. The big silver plane, its nose red, the body looking black and blue drenched in the sunlight, circled the Land of Oo-bla-dee four times from an altitude of fifty thousand feet—and swooped down over the Hoo Doo Church.

Brothers on the block who were passing the pluck and telling dark tales, dug the action, commented on the wonders of Stevie, knowing he was a big bad navigator, and improvised lines about what he had brought back this time.

Last time out he had brought back the music, which the beast had

The Thing with Two Heads

(1972)
[On Video]
DIRECTOR: Lee Frost; SCREENWRITER: Lee Frost, Wes Bishop, James Gordon White; MAKEUP: Rick Baker; CREATIVE MAKEUP DESIGNERS: Dan Striepeke, Gail Brown, Tom Burman, Charles Schram, James Gordon White, Peter Peterson.
CAST: Ray Milland (Dr. Maxwell Kirshner); Rosey Grier (Jack Moss); Don Marshall (Dr. Fred Williams); Rick Baker (Gorilla); Lee Frost (Sgt. Hacker); and Albert Zugsmith.

Black Man Bugged By Talking Tumor's Bigoted Babble!

Courtesy of Photofest.

tried to steal, claim it was his, and placed it in the white-on-white-in-white museum-prison along with the statues of Paul Whiteman, Benny Goodman, Artie Shaw, Barbra Streisand and Janis Joplin.

The time before that he had brought back the dance: Vernon and Irene Castle frozen in the *cakewalk,* Ginger Rogers and Fred Astaire on celluloid, and a whole assortment of beasts, John Hawkins for the brothers, and placed them on thieves' row inside the white museum-prison.

No telling what he might bring back this time, maybe hard-rock blues, long stringy hair and black cat bones. Workin' Mojos.

But the brothers passed the pluck, putting the top back on after each sip, and conjectured anyway.

Foxes young and old sitting on front porches and in back yards along with dogs, cats, chickens and ducks, eating boiled shrimp, chitterlings and drinking java, rare wines and top-shelf booze, swapped lies back and forth as the big red-nosed plane disappeared over the northern part of the town. They were partying already, wasn't even waiting for the big blowout.

They eyed each other shyly but knowingly and told tall tales about his love life, since he was known by all the women about as a coxcomb.

Old blonde hags, blue-eyed monsters, stepped out of soul-sisters' kitchens where they'd been cleaning house, taking care of babies, washing clothes, making beds and cooking food, to catch a glimpse of the big black-and-blue red-nosed bird, and hear the news of Estavanico's arrival. Wringing their hands, some of them scared to death and already turned into witches—natural-born bitches—afraid that his arrival meant sudden death and evil possessions coming their way. But even this was better than being with the old fay-grey males on this day.

Children on roller skates, bicycles and tricycles, wearing tennis shoes, jumped with glee, kicking their heels, shouted, yelled and made up nursery rhymes about Estavanico's antics.

Like the time they told Estavanico to be cool, learn patience, lower his voice and stop all this complaining and stay in his place. Estavanico had got the mother's wife, daughters and granmo' too. Fucked them in the ass, the mouth, the ears, eyes, under armpits all up and down the White House lawn. Twelve o'clock at night. A full moon out. He made

Honky

(1971)
[On Video]
DIRECTOR: William Graham; SCREENWRITER: Will Chaney; STORY: based on Gunard Selberg's novel *Sheila*; MUSIC: Quincy Jones; SONGS: Quincy Jones, Bradford Craig (also Billy Preston performs "Hey Girl").
CAST: Brenda Sykes (Sheila Smith); John Nielson (Wayne "Honky" Divine); William Marshall (Dr. Craig Smith); and Lincoln Kilpatrick (The Drug Pusher).

As the wayward daughter of "the most hung-up spade in the country," it's *Brenda Sykes* who rebels against William "Blacula" Marshall and the comforts of her upper middle-class *Ebony* magazine background by taking a naive whyte boy as her lover, then leading him down the path to degradation, ruin and social embarrassment.

But to appreciate this story's true campiness you need the perspective of a *real* honky. So, with that said, it gives me great pleasure to introduce that lovely and talented lassie of the Canadian prairie—*Mr. Michael Will*—a man whose only contact with Blacks in the 1970s, prior to getting his lips greasy with a chicken dinner fried up by the followers of the Rev. Jim Jones, was through his stack of Motown 45s (see page 170).

WHERE I WAS LIVING IN 1972, **HONKY'S** "CONTROVERSIAL" THEME DIDN'T RAISE A SINGLE EYEBROW. WITH NO BLACK PEOPLE AROUND TO MISCEGENATE WITH, IT WAS ALL AS REMOTE AS SCIENCE FICTION. THE GEEKS IN THAT SHITHOLE GOT THEIR DAILY HATE FIX FROM THE NEARBY INDIAN RESERVE···

HAPPY TREATY MONEY DAY! DON'T SPEND IT ALL IN ONE BEER PARLOUR.

ALBERTA WHEAT PO

WHICH WAY GOIN

THAT NIGHT **HONKY** GOT OFF TO A BAD START. THE TITLE TEEN'S BLAND GOOD LOOKS AND STARK NORMALITY MADE ME FEEL INADEQUATE.

THEN THE CHARMING BREN LIT UP THI

SUNS

F

GO! TEAM! GO!

LOOK AT THE SUCKHOLE, ATTENDING A PEPPER RALLY.

PARDON.

SHE WAS *PETRANELLA DANFORTH!

*IN **BEYOND THE VALLEY OF THE DOLLS**, BUT I HAD HER MIXED UP WITH MARCIA McBROOM.

Courtesy of Michael Will.

Darktown Strutters

(1975)

a.k.a. *Get Down and Boogie*

[On Video]

PRODUCER: Gene Corman; DIRECTOR: William N. Witney; SCREENWRITER: George Armitage; PRODUCTION DESIGNER: Jack Fisk; ART DIRECTOR: Peter Jamison; COSTUMES: Michael Nicola.

CAST: Trina Parks (Syreena); Edna Richardson (Carmen); Bettye Sweet (Miranda); Shirley Washington (Theda); Roger E. Mosley (Mellow); Christopher Joy (Wired); Stan Shaw (Raunchey); and the Dramatics.

Darktown Strutters is a freewheelin' cinematic toast to that "other white meat"—*pig*. And it's got everything except the bow ties of the Nation of Islam condemning the eating of that wormy whyte flesh—red-robed Klansmen in women's lingerie; blackfaced minstrels performing traditional endmen routines; red-suited thieves in conkhead stocking caps; and Colonel Sander's Deep-Fried Genocide. Contrary to Gil Scott-Heron, this is the revolution televised, except these revolutionaries have taken over the set of "Peewee's Playhouse" with seltzer bottles and pig bladders.

As a gang of tri-wheeled hogridin' babes in Flash Gordon–style helmets (tricked out in fur, feathers and sequins) zoom along a stretch of highway, the film opens disclaiming any association with the story of Cinderella. They roll up to a beachside hot dog hut designed by an acid-crazed graffiti artist, have a pie tossing rumble with a group of lascivious marines, and end up at Sky Hog—a drive-in eatery "Where the Ribs is Bone-Suckin' Good" and you get a "Free Watermelon with Every Bucket."

Watch this after downing a pint of Thunderbird.

them get in line, down on all fours, bark like dogs, crow like roosters, neigh like horses and grunt. Pigs. Then he took his fourteen inches and shoved it down their throats.

"The FBI got pictures of the shit," a nine-year-old told a seven-year-old as he passed the juju.

"And J. Edgar Hoover sold them to *Time* magazine," the seven-year-old took a long drag, then snapped back, to show he was in the know.

"And all of them, Hoover and Company and the clowns at *Time,* use them to get their *johnsons* up!" interjected a five-year-old who was jumping rope nearby.

There were no cops, politicians or other lowly creatures in the Land of Oo-bla-dee. Hence, no welcoming committees or ticker-tape parades or speeches at city hall. The people ran their own lives.

Twenty years ago, when John Burks Gillespie was still playing with Charles Parker, commonly known as Yardbird or Bird, he took a breather for a spell and founded Oo-bla-dee. All the hip people got out of Media City and joined in the trip to this crazy retreat—where nothing but princesses and together brothers now come to lay back, relax, and T.C.B.

The pimps, shysters, tricksters and would-be police chiefs followed but were put dead in a trick bag. They were all tarred, feathered and kicked out of town, or lynched and hanged as weird ghouls, like they do the colored folks in West Hell.

But the only one who could remember the founding legends of Oo-bla-dee was Doc John who had made his dust and moved into semi-retirement by putting the man's business in the street, and telling the world about his evils.

He was seated in his pad, a wall-to-wall white bear rug on the floor, red, blue, green and yellow pillows all around, broads of all colors lying back in wraps and panties, smoking, sipping and bullshitting, watching idiots on dull quiz shows via satellite, the sound turned down. That's when the news hit the tubes.

"Hey, baby," Estavanico's voice vibrated from the plane into Pop Doc's sound studio.

"Yeah. What's goin' on?" Doc let a broad grin cover his face. Two broads got up and did a slow snake dance in the middle of the floor.

"We got the mothers, brother. Got um!"

"Solid. That's together. Was there any trouble? I mean, did you have to take any of them out?" Doc leaned back in the leather chair, dick hard, and signaled for Veronica.

A tall redhead with green eyes, freckled soft skin, big boobs, a wide behind and long well-shaped legs pranced over. She bent down, unzipped his fly, and mouthed his joint.

Doc John let his fingers run through the flaming hair as a big black bulldog growled in the corner.

"Just Miles Standish. The red-faced pecker is a real cracker. Thinks niggers don't know nothing. Pancho straightened his ass out. He's bound and gagged. I suppose we'll have to put his ass in the Zoo along with Maddox, Wallace and Ian Smith. Barney Rosset's *Evergreen*. Burn his ass in effigy, then scare him to death!"

Doc gave a deep guffaw. He leaned down and rubbed Veronica's soft shoulders and neck, feeling her hips on his knees, watching her head moving slowly back and forth, and checking out the contours of her behind.

Estavanico patted Annette's thigh, showed her the manors around on Oo-bla-dee, pointing out various pertinent places. She sucked out the marrow of the chicken bones, then started in on the sloe gin and vanilla ice cream.

Veronica was a Southern belle from down in Alabam', got a bad case of black eyes during the civil rights days. Dude screwed her in the barn, in the haystack, and in her mother's bed. She was only fourteen then.

The very next day, she cut out of town. She went to New Orleans and got put in two or three tricks with Voo Doo Dancers, Zulu Kings, and became a blues user's tool.

Cats out cattin' got the word on her ass and would drop by every day, different cats at that, and would take her through the changes, drag her through the paces, then leave her sitting there, pussy all sore, ass all aching, and breasts saggy with teeth marks and sweat.

In other words: they ate the bitch's food, drank the bitch's liquor, smoked the bitch's dope, fucked the bitch's hole, and took all her gold.

The funny thing about it is she enjoyed every minute of it. When Doc John found her she was wandering around Orleans and North Clai-

In Your Face!

a.k.a. *Akbar, the First Black Superman* (19??)
[On Video]
PRODUCTION INFORMATION: *Who cares?*

A Black doctor moves with his family into an all-whyte middle-class suburb. And his new neighbors can't git wid dat. The doctor and his family are greeted with "Coons Go Back to Africa!"–type picket signs as they move into their new home. The ugly news is broadcast by the local radio station and heard in the clubhouse of an all-Black motorcycle gang, which comes to the family's rescue. Scattering the jeering mob, the gang's leader stays on as the family's guardian.

Shortly, we discover the doctor's reason for coming to this community—he needs to be alone to work in secret on a serum that renders rabbits invulnerable to bullets. Anyway, he gives the biker brother some. And, well, hey, rent this absurd sucker and see what happens. . . .

Black Shampoo

(1976)
[On Video]
PRODUCER/SCREENWRITER: Alvin L. Fast;
DIRECTOR/SCREENWRITER: Greydon Clark.
CAST: John Daniels (Jonathan Knight);
Tanya Boyd (Brenda St. John); Joe
Ortiz (Mr. Wilson); Skip Lowe (Artie);
Gary Allen (Richard); and Jack Mehoff
([right . . .] Maddox).

I don't get it. I thought Warren Beatty
was already Black.

Courtesy of Photofest.

Nine-year-old girl and her eighty-year-
old pimp. In 3-D.

Black Lolita

(1975)
a.k.a. Bad Lolita
PRODUCER/DIRECTOR/SCREENWRITER: Stephen
Gibson (who the hell is Stephen Gib-
son?).
CAST: Yolanda Love (Lolita); Ed Cheat-
wood (Cleon); Joey Ginza (Buddah);
Susan Ayres (Shirley); Zenobia Wittacre
(Pearl); and Larry Ellis (Tinker).

borne—not too far from the House with Blue Lights—crazy as a loon: on the lookout for dudes, hot pants up to her crotch, tits hanging out of her blouse, trying to find any BODY who wanted some ofay pussy. You see, she was brought up in the sort of house that taught her that black men were beasts, hence she was convinced they all wanted her.

Doc John took the broad off the street, cleaned her up, and rapped with her for a few nights. He taught her how to shake ass when fuckin', work tongue when suckin', and eventually made her into a doll. Then he put her on duty at the best hotel in the city, pulling dignitaries who came to town for conferences, sent her to world fairs all over the globe, and before you could say WHO, she was bringin' in five G's a week. He set her up in her own bar at Washington and Galvez, then brought her to Oo-bla-dee.

"You still there, Doc?" Estavanico's voice boomed into the room.

"Still here," Doc answered, and added, "We'll fix him," with grim determination, glancing at the parrot who was watching Veronica's actions.

She had her head on his thighs, his joint half in her mouth, saliva all over it, and was fingering his balls. Doc was getting hot.

"Fox *who?*" It was Little Stephen again.

"The cracker. Miles Standish," Doc John answered, rubbing Veronica's shoulders, feeling the veins in his legs cord. His stomach muscles tensed. The bulldog growled. "How many's in the party?"

"Four of *us.* Pancho, and the other brother Chavez, a cute little chick from down home who I know you're going to dig, and myself." He glanced over the green hills, the valleys and the houses dotting the plains, then glanced at Annette. The sloe gin and ice cream were doing a job. She was *kite-hi.* "Then there's the Governor, Reverend Afterfacts, two strange broads, bulldaggers or something, Virginia Dare and Susan B. Anthony, and Reverend Afterfacts's old lady. Nine all told."

Veronica was busy nibbling around the head of his strong big cock, holding it in her right hand. Dock's dick-head was aching; it was getting ready to blast. He motioned for her to take it back into her mouth. Her eyes smiled, the lids went halfway down as she followed his instructions. Gobble. Gobble.

But Doc was still on the case: "Do they know?"

"No one knows but us four. Plus the pilots, of course; they know that something smells *fishy*. Same with Virginia." Then he rapidly gave Papa Doc John a synopsis of what had gone down inside the plane, bringing the case of Max Gordon up, and how Annette was there in the first place, and ending by saying, "And that's how Pancho and Chavez were able to take over the plane. Everyone was fucked."

Doc felt it coming. He reached down and grabbed Veronica under her armpits. She was a big strapping bitch. He slipped his back further down in the seat, sitting on his spine. The bulldog barked, the others watched, smiling. He pulled her up and down and she controlled his johnson till his seeds exploded. "Aaaah. Aaaah. AAAAAAAAAAH. Mercy Good Gawd."

"What was that?" Estavanico popped. Silence on the other end. He reflected for a minute. Watching the controls.

Doc was still trying to catch his breath as Veronica was still sucking on his member, lapping up all that was left. She had a mouthful now. She got it down in one gulp.

Sapphire came over with a bottle of cognac, her big breasts exposed, smiling.

Veronica took a plug. Coughed. Took another. Smiled.

Sapphire picked up a towel and passed it over to Doc John.

But the old man really didn't need it. Veronica had licked him clean, not leaving a single drop on his shirt, fly, pants—nothing. Veronica stood up, smiled in Doc John's face, and shook her behind and wiggled her hips on the way to the john.

Doc smiled and zipped up his fly. "Jes' one of my bad habits."

Estavanico caught it. "Yeah. I forgot about you and telephones. Gotta keep yourself busy. Entertained. Huhn? Hahaha! Look, we'll be landing in less than five minutes. Can you get the cars out here?"

Doc stretched, stood up with the phone in his hand, walked over to the bulldog and patted its head. It stuck out its tongue, licked its lips and rolled its eyes.

"Yeah. I'll send Coolout Williams and Steps in one Caddy, and Shit-face Turds and Asshole Jerk in the other. Need anything else?"

Doc watched the dark brown Siamese cat with emerald eyes arch its back, yawn, walk over near the parrot and sit on its haunches. It stared

Blacula

(1972)
[On Video]
DIRECTOR: William Crain; SCREENWRITERS: Joan Torres, Raymond Koenig.
CAST: William Marshall (Mamuwalde [Blacula]); Vonetta McGee (Tina/Luva); Denise Nicholas (Michelle); Thalmus Rasulala (Dr. Gordon Thomas); Gordon Pinsent (Lieut. Peters); and Charles Macauley (Count Dracula).

Yeah, y'all! One o' Pee-wee's pee-pee playin' playmates up in da playhouse was the original black bloodsucker his-self—Count Blacula! Or Blac-ka-la as we said in the hood.

Prince Mamusalde and his wife, Luva, travel alllllllll the way from Africa to Transylvania in 1790 to discuss an end of the slave trade with Count Dracula (this sequence might've been enhanced greatly had it included a discussion of Dracula's ideas on whether or not he believed Black people had souls). But Drac don't know nuthin' bout no nigra souls or slave trade. He thinks this is the set for *Mandingo*.

And tells the soon-to-be Count Blacula he wants to lay up with his wife like they do out in the shacks behind the big house. Blac gets all bent out of shape 'cause *he* thinks this is the set of some Brit-produced PBS *Masterpiece Theater* production. So Drac bites him in the neck.

Anyway, Count Blac ends up in Watts.

But what I want to know is—why didn't American International ever sue the General Mills Food Corporation for trademark infringement when they began stocking supermarket shelves with boxes of Count Chocula?

Wattstax

(1973)
[On Video]
DIRECTOR: Mel Stewart.
CAST: Carla Thomas; Rufus Thomas; Isaac Hayes; Johnnie Taylor; Kim Weston, The Staple Singers; The Emotions, The Dramatics; Luther Ingram; Rev. Jesse Jackson; Little Milton; Jimmy Jones; Albert King; Rance Allen Group; the Bar Kays; and, of course, Richard Pryor.

Woodstock goes to the ghetto. Imagine a dashikied Jesse Jackson dropping acid and bumping behinds with Rufus Thomas!

at the bird. The parrot flapped its wings and yelled: "Git away. Git away from here. You evil sum-bitch. Shoo!"

Doc cracked.

The parrot flew around the room in circles, cussing up a storm, and landed near the Crow's Nest. A sign hung down from the nest that read: HONEY-HUSH.

The big black crow raised its eyes, took the cigar out of its mouth, closed them again, then snapped: "Don't you start no shit, sister. Not today. I ain't in no kind of mood."

The parrot got in the wind, swooped down low over the bulldog, passed the cat, then landed on Doc John's head. "Tell that pussy not to be fuckin' with me, Doc."

Doc John busted his sides. He gave it a piece of popcorn, then pointed a finger at the cat. The cat meowed and stretched its paws.

Black Hawk's name exploded in Doc John's brain. He couldn't figure it out. He hadn't thought about that bad-ass dude in over forty years. Black Hawk.

"Jes' the colt. I wanna take this beautiful sister for a ride after we've landed."

"Right." Doc hung up the phone. He went over to where Sapphire was stretched out on the carpet cleaning her nails, rapping with Yoko—a down Japanese chick with long brown legs, silky, wavy blue-black hair, big eyes and a heart-shaped face.

The parrot swan-dived into Yoko's lap and complained to her about the cat. In Japanese, of course.

Bella Duh Zug, a big-boned Jewish chick, looking like she just stepped out of *The Brothers Karamazov* after having given a command performance as Grushenka, the WHORE, strolled into the room. She had dark brown curly hair, a rather pleasing but indifferent look on her face, a nice ass and size forty breasts. She sat next to Yoko, smiled over at Sapphire and looked up at Doc.

He gave the orders in a cool, relaxed voice. "Get Coolout, Steps, Turds and Jerk from the stables. Tell Asshole to get Estavanico's young colt ready, put it in the trailer and get out to the airport to meet the Jumbo Jet. He's back with a party of nine. Not counting himself. Take two of the cars."

The three girls started smiling joyfully, showing big eyes, gold teeth and excited faces. They got up off their asses, and headed for the stables. The parrot shot out of Yoko's arms, cussing in Spanish, and lit atop Doc John's head. "I wanna stay close. Fuck that cat."

Doc cracked, gave the parrot another popcorn, and mumbled through smiles. "Don't worry, little lady, Tom ain't tomming on you."

Bulldog Bone

Veronica walked back into the room buck-naked. Her body smelled of Love Potion Number Nine. Indian roses and magnolias. She held a glass of white wine in her right hand, a rose in her left. She stuck the rose between her teeth, looked up at the parrot on Doc John's head and started splitting her sides.

He looked into her eyes, searched her face for any telltale signs, saw a spider crawl out of her left ear, then pulled her to him. Veronica's body seemed to melt in his arms.

She rubbed her cunt slowly over his joint, which was stiff in his pants. He slobbered in her ear and kissed her on the cheeks.

The parrot got disgusted and flew back over to the Crow's Nest. "Beat it, Buster," the crow ordered, cigar still in mouth.

The parrot batted her eyelids, commented, "Ain't no peace, no peace in this world." And jumped back in its cage, locked the door, and went into a super-sad blues.

The cat meowed, arched its back, then lay back down.

Veronica said nothing, but purred and began breathing hard into Doc John's ear. She ran her hands slowly up and down his back, feeling the pressure of his sex against her. Hard.

She dropped down to her knees on the bearskin rug. She was expecting it.

Slowly he took off the Moroccan belt with designs of cobras and rattles all over it. Yawning ever so slightly, and remembering that this was a gig just like the others he had had when in Harlem—having to beat white folks' behinds for them to get a discharge, plus Marine sergeants who were sent to him by the government. *This*, with Veronica, com-

The Black Klansman

(1966)
a.k.a. *I Crossed The Color Line*
[On Video]
PRODUCER/DIRECTOR: Ted V. Mikels; SCREEN-WRITER: John T. Wilson, Arthur Names (Assistant Director); MUSIC: Jaime Mendoza-Nava; SONG: Tony Harris.
CAST: Richard Gilden (Jerry Ellsworth [John Ashley]); Rima Kutner (Andrea); Harry Lovejoy (Rook); and Max Julien (Raymond).

"He was black and joined the Klan! He dated the Exalted Cyclops Carol Ann!"

In sinister "We Are The World" tableux, a circle of robed Klansmen ring a blazing cross in a remote Alabama woods. A voice sings over the stark titles with such sorrow, you just *know* in your bleeding little heart, it's the same song Dick Cheney and friends sang on their doomed ride down to Mississippi:

THE KU KLUX KLAN KILLED MY LITTLE GIRL. . . .
I WILL DESTROY FROM WITHIN.
DISGUISE MYSELF
AND BE THE BLACK KLANSMAN. . . .

Thus begins this civil rights–era, black and white melodrama with a narrative based on a defining headline of the times. *The Black Klansman* is the B-side of the *Black Like Me* 45 (a 1964 film starring James Whitman as a real-

life whyte journalist who undergoes a radical color change in order to understand what it really means to be Black in whyte America. Despite the producers' best intentions, Whitman stil ends up looking like the blackface minstrel Charles "Andy" Correl of radio's *Amos-n-Andy*).

The Black Klansman's lead actor, Richard Gilden, is a wiry-haired goateed whyte man who portrays a colorless-complexioned Negro jazz musician named Jerry Ellsworth. As Ellsworth, Gilden puts a real twist on Norman Mailer's existentialist idea of the "White Negro," simulating "negritude" by talking whyte hipster beatnik jive. For example, the dialogue in a bedroom scene with his whyte lover, Andrea (Rita Kutner), consists of the kind of post-coital pillow-talk that might have inspired Whoopi to smear Ted Danson with boot-black and prop him in front of a Friar's Club mike:

"I'm still a *Negro*, baby! I'm still a Negro. You know what they say about one drop of African blood!"

We also know Jerry's down and black-identified because he—

1. carries a horn.
2. "braves" the 1965 L.A. riots with his kinky-headed, honky-looking self to snap pics for a drunken news reporter.

SPIN-WIPE to Delbert (Kirk Kirsey), a semi-literate black youth trudging down a dusty road in Turnerville, Alabama; who, after struggling through a newspaper account of the Civil Rights Act, is determined to sit down at Turnerville's "No Niggers Allowed" lunch counter and drink himself a nice hot cup of the whyte man's coffee ("It's the *law*, ain't it?"), careful to order it black

pared to that mess, he thought to himself, was light.

Sambo, the big black bulldog with red eyes, got down off the pedestal, its tongue touching the floor, and stood next to Doc John.

Sambo growled. Doc John patted his head. Suddenly Black Hawk's name startled his thoughts. Still, he didn't get it, assumed he must be getting old. Something.

"Are you gonna do it to me, Daddy?" Veronica was looking up at him, almost pleading. Sambo licked her face.

"Down, Boy. Down, Boy." The dog moved back and circled around Doc John, then sat next to his master. "Yeah, honey, the way you like it."

He looped the belt around his hand, tightened it over his knuckles, and snapped it a couple of times. "Put your head down on the floor. Your head forward. Spread your legs a little more. Come on, I ain't got all day."

ssssSSSSSMMMAAACCCCK. He hit her with the belt across the back. Sambo growled, rolled his eyes, bared his fangs. A two-inch welt rose on Veronica's back.

Veronica sucked air through her teeth. She refused to utter a word.

He hit her again. Harder than before—sssssSSSSSSSMMMAAAA-CCCCK!!! A three-inch wide blue-black and red welt rose from her backside and thighs like varicose veins. Veronica clutched harder at the bear rug and gritted her teeth.

"Come on, *nigger*. Get it over with. Beat me like you mean it. Like you hate me. Come on. Give it to me."

The crow knocked the ashes off its stogie, said: "Sheeeit, the bitch is nuts." Flicked on the set and watched the boob tube. He shook his head, flew over to the bar and got a Lowenbräu on tap. Sat before the set with legs crossed and checked out a talk show. Yawned.

Veronica was already hotter than the preacher's daughter caught in the closet finger-fucking.

Doc raised the belt higher. Sambo gnashed his teeth. The rhinestones and diamonds on its fangs showed. "What? What did you say?" Doc asked.

Through tears, she yelled, "Go 'head. *Nigger!* Go 'head."

Two alligators spied the action from the pond. They both shook their heads. Said one to the other, "Nigger's a bitch."

Doc thought for a second. He dropped the belt, walked over to the wall near a giant painting of Marie Laveau, Father Divine, Daddy Grace and Bumper Johnson, their eyes met on his eyes following him around the room, smiling really as he got a six-foot-long, ten-ply cord rope and began twisting it in his right hand. He paused at the bar and poured himself a Scotch and water. He poured a Bourbon for her, which she could have afterwards. The crow dropped a couple of ice cubes in the glasses for him and made a sign at his ear, circles, signifying that Veronica was out of her skull. Nuts.

"Yeah, I know. John Randolph had the same trouble with Virginia, that's why he went queer." He sipped the Scotch and water, and looked at her welted frame. Still fine. But strange. Blue-black red marks all over.

The crow spoke in deep tones, a whiskey voice. "Really don't know a damn thing about spooks, do she? Callin' you dem names." He puffed on the stogie and took a sip. "Well, back to the idiot box."

"Talkin' 'bout her mamma and don't know it. That's what it's all about." Drink in one hand, rope in the other, Doc John walked back over to Veronica, sipping the Scotch and looking at her body.

Veronica stayed in the same position, eyes closed, while images of a thousand boots and rods yea long, scuttled through her brain.

"Bitch, you keep callin' me names, fuckin' wid me, I'll put so much shit on your ass your hair will fall out, your teeth will turn black and fall down your throat, and you'll get the piles so bad you'll slide down your own asshole and drown in your own dung. Talkin' 'bout niggers. Shit!"

WWWWOOOOMMMMMP!! He hit her a lick, which caused her asshole to tingle.

This time she shrieked. She rolled over on the bear rug and started jerking and rubbing her body like she'd been stung by a nest of yellow jackets. She screamed. Cried. Yelled. Not words, but animal sounds! Grunts. Her eyes all bloodshot, face in such contortions, she looked like some mad dog with a wicked case of rabies. She threw her legs in the air, rolled on her back, exposing her privates—come juice oozing out her hole.

Doc John dropped the rope, patted Sambo's head (the dog barked), sipped the Scotch and stood looking down at her on the floor. Tears

because he knows asking for cream suggests he really wants to integrate his oversized body parts with those of a whyte woman.

What Delbert doesn't realize is that the good whyte folks of Turnerville don't know how to read none too well either and confuse the Civil Rights Act with the comics page.

"Niggers the same as whites? Where does Lil' Abner get them hare-brained ideas?! Har! Har!"

Naturally, Turnerville's local hooded pinheads decide it's time to put Delbert in his place—which, to their way of thinking, is located six feet underground. So, with a bullet fired through Delbert's skull, Turnerville's topsy-turvy social order returns to its proper balance, and the pinheads cap off their fun-filled evening by fire-bombing the town's black church; killing a six-year-old girl (who runs screaming from the church in a shimmering cloud of fairy-sparks and falls flaming to the ground. Kneeling churchwomen wail hysterically over a burning, stiff-legged doll).

Next, we're treated to a limp-lapped scene of interracial sex in a tawdry motel room. The telephone rings.

Drat! Coitus Interruptus!

I'd like to report that as Jerry reaches for the phone a jet of hot white sperm spurts from his jerking uncircumsized member and splatters his blonde bedmate, but I can't. This film was released in 1966. Cum shots didn't appear in wide-screen close-up in commercial cinema until five years later.

Over the telephone, Jerry learns that his daughter was murdered by the KKK. Consumed by beatnik Black rage, Jerry tries to strangle his mistress to death (all of this is quite permissible because the audience knows that Jerry is

really a whyte actor *pretending* he's a Black man fucking and strangling a whyte woman to death). As she recovers her breath, Jerry decides to go undercover as a whyte man in Turnerville, and joins the Klan and exacts his revenge.

The Black Klansman carries the distinction of being the first movie *I've* ever seen featuring Black people who don't know how to dance. I shit you not. In a scene with Whitman Mayo (Grady of *Sanford and Son*) polishing the bar top of a down-home after-hours spot, there are real conkolined Negroes shuffling across the dance floor with the same kind of stiff, zomboid movements Black people have traditionally laughed at in whyte people on *American Bandstand.* Subverting stereotypes is one thing but exploding myths people actually want to believe about themselves is quite another. I mean, do you actually believe you'll ever see Spike Lee pull his pants down on national television, wave his weenie at the cameras and shout, *"See, you racist shit-heads! Not all Black men have big dicks!"*?

I think not.

Max "The Mack" Julien makes an appearance here as a smooth-talking black militant from Harlem. Ted V. Mikels is also responsible for *Astro-Zombies* (1967); *The Corpse Grinders* (1972); *Blood Orgy of the She Devils* (1973) and that whyte trash crowd pleaser *The Worm Eaters* (1965).

rolled down her cheeks. She whimpered, turned over on the rug, and grabbed her huge breasts with both hands and started squeezing. Agony and ecstasy were written on her face. Doc John smiled to himself. It was time.

Without waiting for Doc's signal, Sambo, with his tongue hanging out, charged the rug, licked Veronica's cunt, then mounted her like some man: his flat ass and short tail down under. Sambo slipped his red dick straight into her hole.

Doc John laughed, shook his head, then thought to himself: I'm gettin' too old for this kind of carryin'-on. That's for them jitterbugs to do whose bitches got strange tastes. Shitface Turds and Asshole Jerk. They can have it. He settled back in his swivel chair and read about bloods cussing out Roi Jones because he had issued some kind of edict, tellin' them what to do. No good!

Veronica opened her eyes, smiled into Sambo's bright red eyes, saw the rhinestones and diamonds on his teeth and rubbed Sambo's head while he licked her face. She reached down between her thighs and grabbed his balls. The dog let out a bark, deep down and strong, then growled. But Sambo continued to work at a fast clip, humping away.

She tried to keep up with Sambo's pace, but her back still ached. She hugged the dog for all he was worth, kissed him on the nose, felt the tip of his tongue enter her mouth, saliva dripping all over, and sensed his long dick working out in her hole.

After about five minutes, Veronica turned on her belly and stuck her ass in the air. Now, she was about to find out what dog-fashion was really all about.

Sambo mounted her behind. He rested his paws on her shoulders, licked the back of her neck, and slipped his four inches up the crack of her ass.

"OOOO! OooOOOOH!" Veronica screamed! Sambo humped. She smiled, tears flowing down her cheeks. It felt so *good.* Good Gawd. Slippery, warm, hot-dog!

Sambo slipped his dick out her asshole, stuck it in her cunt; it got stuck. The pussy was so hot. So was his joint. Veronica stretched her legs. Sambo pulled it out. Breathing hard, his tongue bouncing off her back, Sambo impatiently got it back in, grinning from ear to ear like a mad Emmett Kelly. Clowning on down.

Doc John reached over, grabbed his 16-mm camera and got a few shots of the action. He was thinking about sending them to Veronica's old man. He was a Senator down in Washington, maybe give them to television news teams, for a price. Would cause more racket than the selling of the Pentagon. He played all angles, never missed a trick, nothing got away.

The parrot unlocked the gate to its cage, flew around the room a couple of times, humming a tune called *DOG BONE,* then perched itself atop Veronica's head, parroting: "Fuck Bitch! Fuck Bitch! Fuck Bitch!" then landed in the same place. "Fuck Bitch!"

The crow took the stogie out its mouth, leaned back in the chair, shook his head and with a cynical expression of dejection on his face, mumbled to himself. "I always knew the bitch had gone to the dogs—the day Doc brought her to the house. Old scraggly whore." He recrossed his crow's feet, and watched *The Dating Game* on TV.

Tom Cat, spying the parrot on Veronica's head, still yelling, "Fuck Bitch," blowing a stick of hash and sipping goat's milk, eased over near the two of them and began smelling Sambo's ass.

Sambo tried to kick it away. Tom meowed. Veronica swung again at the parrot; it circled her head, then landed again.

Sambo was working so hard on Veronica's hole, his mind deep inside his drives, he couldn't really pause to kick Tom out of the way. Besides, Veronica's cunt seemed to be getting tighter and tighter, reminding Sambo of that old white-assed bitch of a neighbor's dog he had just fucked yestiddy, and left for pregnant. Sambo yelped a couple of times and scratched Veronica's back. She spread her legs. His joint got out.

A vampire bat glued itself to the ceiling and listened to the sighs, moans and panting of Veronica and Sambo down below. Nuts, thought the bat, and vanished in the blackness.

Veronica jerked her head up in the air (the parrot lost its balance, fluttered, and flew back to its cage), screamed and cried as the bulldog worked overtime. She got a nut. It flowed from her cunt in jerks and spasms; she was rapidly losing control. Her mind in a daze, her head spinning, her body trembling, Sambo worked out harder, yelping and

Blackenstein

(1974)
a.k.a. *Black Frankenstein*
[On Video]
DIRECTOR: William A. Levy; PRODUCER/ SCREENWRITER: Frank R. Salerti; SPECIAL ELECTRONICS EFFECTS: Ken Strickfadden.
CAST: John Hart (Dr. Stein); Ivory Stone (Winifred Walker); Joe De Sue (Eddie Turner); Andrea King (Eleanor); Nick Bolin (Bruno Strager); Karin Lind (Hospital Supervisor); and Liz Renay.

"We plan to devote our full resources to making this 100th picture particularly outstanding."—Sam Arkoff

Produced in 1974, the movie isn't even listed in Arkoff's filmography at the back of his bio *Flying Through Hollywood by the Seat of My Pants.* Could this mean that *Blackenstein* is an outstanding *embarrassment* to Arkoff?

The square-headed brutha, Blackenstein, had no idea what was happenin'. He stomped, grunted an' farted in these clumsy-ass clod-hoppers. He tripped over the cuffs of his stove-pipe high-waters. And he hung out in discos. *Players* mag even cracked on m'man. Said he looked like Magilla Gorilla.

But he liked wastin' whitey though . . .

Ken Strickfadden, who created the electronic effects for James Whales's *Frankenstein* ('31), was even hired. So was gun-moll Liz Renay who later starred in John Waters's must-see *Desperate Living.*

As *Blackenstein* was a major cinematic metaphor on the exploitation of the Black man in Vietnam, for reasons lost on this writer, the two sequels *The Fall of the House of Blackenstein* and *Blackenstein III* were never produced.

In the end, it was a pack of dobermans that brought down Blackenstein. And the confused Joe De Sue was never heard from again.

barking, on her behind—paws clawing at her shoulder blades, scratching her back as his tongue licked at her neck and his squat ass moved back and forth.

Tom yawned, arched its back, and went and jumped into Doc John's lap. Doc John laughed to himself, set the movie camera down and rubbed Tom's fur.

Veronica sprawled out on the floor, her big red, freckled thighs spread out on the carpet, her hair all disheveled; she cupped her pussy in her right hand, shoved three fingers up her slit, pulled Sambo towards her face, his red dick dripping (hot and bothered, really going insane with this shit). She blew Sambo's Bulldog Bone.

And what a blow job it was! It really was!

Sambo barked, whined and tried to pull away. But he was getting excessively excited. He worked on her mouth the way he had her asshole and cunt, slipping his red dick between her juicy red lips—come juice all over, blended with saliva. Sambo got a charge. Veronica gulped and swallowed. Her body went into convulsions.

Sambo got up, slipped his dick back inside the skin and tipped to his kennel out in the backyard. Veronica lay panting on the floor, squeezing her breasts and cunt, her eyes rolling.

Sapphire, Yoko and Bella Duh Zug came back into the room. They were shocked, but not surprised when they saw Veronica cringing on the floor. The parrot gave a full report, perched in its cage. "Doc hit. Fuck bitch. Bitch fuck. Dog bit."

Veronica pulled at her stomach, like trying to rip her insides out. She tried to scream but nothing came out.

Sapphire looked at Yoko. Yoko at Bella. Bella at Veronica. No one said a word.

The Black Crow puffed on the cigar, gave them a passing glance, then got caught in the afternoon movie—something about buzzards and crows, jive studs and birds.

The cat purred and walked inside the circle of the three broads. And meowed. Yoko picked it up.

The parrot fluttered in its cage, cussing its fool head off about the essence of being, saying people are crazy, nuts, off their rockers, gone insane.

Veronica's face turned blue, her jaws ballooned and out of her mouth jumped ten black snails, five green lizards, teeny-weeny snakes; behind that, a brown frog jumped out. Veronica lay unconscious on the floor.

Sapphire and Bella got a gallon of vinegar and ammonia and washed her body down. The three of them picked her up and propped her up against some pillars in the corner.

Doc John yawned, drained what was left in his Scotch glass, chewed the rocks, gave Veronica a swift kick in the butt (she didn't even budge) and walked out the room. His mind was into getting Mama Dupre to make some rat soup for the unexpected guests—the crackers.

Sapphire didn't say anything; intuitively she knew Veronica had been fixed. Bella Duh Zug called it a hex. But Yoko knew it was a curse. They sat around on the bear rug eating grapes and smoking joints, discussing the merits of *being* and talking 'bout what they were going to wear to the Big Blowout.

Courtesy of Photofest.

ABBY
(1974) [Available On Bootleg]

EXECUTIVE PRODUCER: Samuel Z. Arkoff; **PRODUCER-DIRECTOR-STORY:** William Girder; **PRODUCER-STORY-SCREENWRITER:** Gordon C. Layne; **MUSIC:** Robert O. Ragland; **SONGS:** Carol Speed. **CAST:** William Marshall (Bishop Garnet Williams); Carol Speed (Abby Williams); Terry Carter (Rev. Emmett Williams); Austin Stoker (Cass Potter); Juanita Moore (Mama Potter); Charles Kissinger (Dr. Hennings); Elliot Moffitt (Russell); Nathan Cook (Taft Hassan); and Bob Holt (Voice of the Demon).

Blacula is **The Blacorcist**!!

This shit had me *rockin'!!* It's grand hoodoo camp with all the fixin's for a hit Off-Broadway musical.

Possessed by a *minor* West African Yoruba spirit (set loose during an archaeological dig in Nigeria), who *claims* he is Eschu, the great Orisha of sexuality, Abby doffs her closed-kneed minister's wife masquerade,

Carol Speed Factoid: In 1980, Holloway House published Ms. Speed's novel, *Inside Black Hollywood.* "A no-holds-barred account of an actress on the make."

A Change of Mind

(1969)
DIRECTOR: Robert Stevens; SCREENWRITERS/
PRODUCERS: Seeleg Lester, Richard Weston; MUSIC: Duke Ellington.
CAST: Raymond St. Jacques.

Depending on where you stand on the great Michael Jackson Vitaligo or Skin Bleaching Debate, some might say this film is the premise for most of the White-Socked Wonder's wetdreams: *a whyteman's brain is transplanted into a blackman's skull!*

The Beast Must Die

(1974)
a.k.a. *Black Werewolf* (video title)
[On Video]
DIRECTOR: Paul Annett.
CAST: Calvin Lockhart; Peter Cushing; Anton Diffring; and Ciaran Madden.

Opening with what looks like war games at an Aryan Nations' training camp (a chopper pursues a black man running through a dense forest with video cameras mounted in the trees and microphones planted in the ground), it seems that *The Beast Must Die* (that's *Black Werewolf* to you video renters) is speeding towards some bizarre combination of *The Prisoner* and William Pierce's "whyte pride" (that's "racist" to you multicultural gun-control advocates) novel *The Turner Diaries* with a dashikied werewolf tossed into the mix. But no such luck.

It turns out that this beast is some slow-moving mush about a billionaire Black man who can't imagine anything better to do with his money than to rid the world of werewolves.

Calvin "Reverend Deke O'Malley" Lockhart is the billionaire brutha with the affected Brit accent.

Ganja and Hess

(1973)
a.k.a. *Black Out*
a.k.a. *Black Vampire*
a.k.a. *Blood Couple*
a.k.a. *Double Possession*
(video titles)
[On Video]
DIRECTOR/SCREENWRITER: Bill Gunn; PRODUCERS: Quentin Kelly, Jack Jordan (a Chiz Schultz production).
CAST: Duane "Night of the Living Dead" Jones (Dr. Hess Green); Marlene Clark (Ganja) with Leonard Jackson; Sam Waymon; and Mabel King.

Written and directed by the late Bill Gunn (though you would never know it from the credits on some of the video releases), it concerns a scholar's investigation of a lost civilization of pre-Egyptian vampires located in Nigeria called the Mitherians. Supply yourself with lots of ganja to appreciate this one. Slow moving but interesting, especially in that its story prefigures today's AIDS crisis.

House on Skull Mountain

(1974)
[On Video]
DIRECTOR: Ron Honthaner; SCREENWRITER: Mildred Pares; MUSIC: Jerrold Immel;
SONGS: Ruth Taldmadge, Art Freeman, John Susan Welsh, Jaime Mendoza-Nava.
CAST: Victor French (Andrew Cunningham); Janee Michelle (Lorena Christophe); Jean Durand (Thomas); and Mike Evans (Phillippe).

In this would-be fright film directed by *Gunsmoke*'s associate producer, Ron Honthaner, a dying woman summons her relatives to her ("Skull") mountain estate for the reading of her last will and testament. *All in the Family*'s Michael Evans cribs moves from Richard Pryor's nightclub routine as an obnoxious Lothario; and the late Michael Landon's mortal sidekick on *Highway to Heaven*, Victor French, is a professor who discovers there's a drop o' black blood trickling through his arteries. There's more to tell but the most telling thing I can tell you is that I went to sleep thirty minutes into the tape.

Courtesy of Photofest.

Courtesy of Photofest.

Dr. Black and Mr. Hyde

(1976)

a.k.a. *The Watts Monster* and *Dr. Black and Mr. White*

[On Video]

DIRECTOR: William Crain; SCREENWRITER: Larry LeBron; STORY: Robert Louis Stevenson.

CAST: Bernie Casey (Dr. Henry Pride/Mr. Hyde); Rosalind Cash (Dr. Willie Worth); Marie O'Henry (Linda Monte); Ji-Tu Cumbuka (Lieut. Jackson); Milt Kogan (Lieut. O'Connor); and Stu Gilliam (Silky).

Bernie Casey develops a severe case of skin-ash in this tale about a doctor experimenting with a cure for cirrhosis of the liver. Volunteering at a Watts free health clinic, the good Dr. Pride tries his experiment on a patient, noticing a bizarre change. He eventually gets around to injecting himself with the serum, turning into an ashen, pale-skinned madman. The film climaxes at the top of the Watts Tower with the pitifiable, albino-looking brutha tumbling to his death.

J.D.'s Revenge

(1976)

[On Video]

DIRECTOR/PRODUCER: Arthur Marks; SCREENPLAY: Jason Starkes; MUSIC: Robert Prince; SONGWRITERS: Prince and Joseph A. Greene.

CAST: Glynn Turman (Ike); Joan Pringle (Christella); Lou Gossett, Jr. (Reverend Bliss); Carl Crudup (Tony); James Louis Watkins (Carl); Alice Jubert (Roberta/Betty Jo); Stephanie Faulkner (Phyliss); Fred Pinkard (Theotis); Fuddle Bagley (Enoch); Jo Anne Meredith (Sarah); and David McKnight (J.D. Walker).

This is a surprisingly well-done and entertaining Jekyll-n-Hyde timeshifter (with Prince in the music-mix) about the spirit of a 1940s gangster named J.D. Walker who comes back from the grave, takes over the soul of a young law student in 1970s New Orleans and wants to slash off a piece o' Lou Gossett's ass with his straight razor. The conkolined Glynn Turman be quite *dap* in his zoot suit.

Scream, Blacula, Scream

(1973)

[On Video]

DIRECTOR: Bob Kelljan; SCREENWRITERS: Raymond Koenig, Joan Torres, Maurice Jules.

CAST: William Marshall (Mamuwalde [Blacula]); Pam Grier (Lisa); Bernie Hamilton (Ragman); Bob Minor, Al Jones (Pimps); and Craig T. Nelson (Sarge).

It's really a pity a third installment of the Blacula series was never produced. Sam Arkoff could've struck a deal with Run Run Shaw in Hong Kong, hired Jim Kelly and shot a *Blacula Meets the Hopping Ghosts* Kung-Fu monster rally with *Blackenstein*'s Joe De Sue stumbling over the scenery.

Sugar Hill

(1974)

a.k.a. *The Voodoo Girl; Zombies of Sugar Hill*

DIRECTOR: Paul Maslansky; SCREENWRITER: Tim Kelly.

CAST: Marki Bey (Diana "Sugar" Hill); Don Pedro Colley (Baron Samedi); and Zara Cully (Mama Maitresse).

Voodoo-Mama Jefferson raises seventeenth-century slaves from the dead, who stumble into each other and eat some whyte folks. Now *that's* Black entertainment!

Courtesy of Photofest.

turns into a low-down and slatternly street-ho' and gets all kinda *niggerish* on mollyfockas.

Her panties get soggy over the sight of chicken's blood. She gives the church organist a heart attack, and throws up on the organist's replacement (it's not, as one expects, a congealed glop of pig tails and black-eyed peas), whom she later corners in a parked car.

With the new organist swooning under the spell of her "evil" funk, Abby cackles like Popeye on nitrous oxide, points her twisting ass in the air like a cat in heat and pumps his organ until his butt bursts into flames on the front seat.

Enter Bishop Garnet Williams (William "Blacula" Marshall) in the local "player's inn" (where all the pimps and hustlers go to profile and talk shit) waving a crucifix at the possessed Abby.

At this point, I'm thinking to myself *here we go again with more of that euro-honkie christian supremist bullshit!* Even Woody Allen knows a crucifix don't mean shit to a Jewish vampire. You gotta stop that muthafucka with a mezuzah! Hammer a hambone through his heart! Suffocate 'im in a kitchen filled with steam roiling off a pot of cooked chittlins!

But then Marshall, lookin' like Desmond Tutu, turns around and blows my mind by whipping some *deep* African shit on her ass. And the film's finale becomes a metaphysical struggle between real African spirituality and BlacNat bullshit.

The reason why *Abby* is only available on bootleg is because Warner Bros. claimed *Abby* copied too closely from *The Exorcist* and sued AIP. The film was withdrawn from distribution but not before AIP grossed $2,600,000 in domestic rentals.

But, frankly, I don't remember any scenes in *The Exorcist* with Linda Blair lickin' Louisiana Hot Sauce off her fingers and *friggin'* her afro-wigged twat with a plate o' fried chicken-wings.

INTERVIEW WITH THE LAST POETS' UMAR BIN HASSAN AND ABIODUN OYEWOLE

Philip Greenberg/courtesy of Rykodisc.

In 1970, The Last Poets released their first album (titled, ironically enough, *The Last Poets*), and dropped a bomb on black Amerikkka's turntables. Muthafuckas ran f'cover.

Nobody was ready.

Had 'em scared o' revolution. Scared o' the whyte man's god complex. Scared o' subways. Scared o' each other. Scared o' themselves. And scared o' that totem ot onanistic worship—the eagle-clawed *Amerikkkan greenback!*

That's a neat hat-trick in Amerikkka (*"I thought I was keepin' an eye on my money. And my money has been keepin' an eye on me!"*). Like

Right On!

(1970)
[On Video]
DIRECTOR: Herbert Danska; SCREENWRITERS: Felipe Luciano, Gylan Kain, David Nelson. PRODUCER: Woodie King.
CAST: Felipe Luciano; Gylan Kain; and David Nelson (the original Last Poets).

HEY, MOM! HEY, DAD! DO YOU WANNA *REALLY* TORTURE THOSE LITTLE "GANGSTA-RAP" BRATS HANGING AROUND THE HOUSE AND EATING UP ALL THE FOOD IN YOUR REFRIGERATOR?

Here's what you do: sit your kids down in front of the TV set. Go to the back of your closet, dig out those old dashikis lying under the mothballs and put them on. Next, put on a bushy black, red and green afro wig with a plastic clenched-fist pick sticking up in the back, and a cardboard mask of Sinbad attached to the front. Now, while your malt liquor drinkin' little crackbandits are absorbed by whatever the hypnotist on TV is trying to sell them, stand in front of the screen, and give them a really *looooong* lecture on how they "got no conception of their cultural roots" or "a sense of the *ideological* continuity of late twentieth-century radical Black thought." *Then* stick this cassette of the *original* Last Poets in your VCR. I'll bet a batch of "Free Bobby!" buttons that after watching ten minutes of this, your child, cheeks wet with tears, will be *begging* to watch a cassette of *Scared Straight!*

the twentieth century's two other great revolutionary heroes, Ho Chi Minh and Malcolm X, The Last Poets' birthdate falls on May 19. As a collective group entity, this means The Last Poets are represented by the sign of Gemini—mercurial and ever-changing in nature with a serious commitment to the evolution of mind and *revolution* of ideas.

And that's pretty much been the nature of the group. Names change. People change. Ideas change. And, frankly, I can't keep up.

At one time or another, the group has included David Nelson, Gylan Kain, Nilija, Jalal Nuriddin, Umar Bin Hassan, Abiodun Oyewole, and Suliaman El Hadi. Also, the lineup once included Felipe Luciano, a founding member of the revolutionary nationalist Young Lords, whose presence in the group not only marked the beginning of a heightened consciousness of *Black* Puerto Rican identity, but spoke to the fact that what is often considered Black urban culture is actually a synthesis of Hispanic and African-American ways of being (ask me and I'll tell you American Blacks and Puerto Ricans are the same people).

Whoever was involved, and at whatever time, The Last Poets could always deliver a smooth groove. The rhetoric made you mad. The drums made you pop your fingers. And the poetry made you sail on the cushions of a fine hashish high.

Most importantly, they made you think and kept you "correct" on a revolutionary level.

Even though my thinking was influenced by the ideology of the Panthers as a teenager, and the Poets' position was Nationalist, which the Panthers opposed, calling instead for "international revolutionary intercommunalism," I still connected. We all did. 'Cause it was a Black communal thing. Like the good vibes and paper plate of red-peppered potato salad at a neighborhood barbecue. The words and the rhythms were relevant. We joined together around the peace pipe and the drum. And when it came to the rhythms of the drum, the drum said, "Check your tired-ass ideology at the door."

When I arrived at publicist Bill Adler's offices, Umar and Abiodun were just finishing a phone interview with Canadian radio and, oddly, our conversation began with Huck's cousin, Michelle Gardine, a young woman who worked in the hair supply store below the dental office I occupied in New Haven in the mid-eighties. Shortly, our conversation turned to writing. They were curious about the nature of this book and, possibly, a little suspicious. They had not read my novel *Negrophobia* and had only heard rumors concerning its contents (rumors due to the hardcover publisher's exploitation [for the purpose of publicity] of one of its employee's good but misguided intentions to correct what she perceived as a racist cover). I showed them some pages from the book you are now reading and they commented that my prose evoked Baraka. It's a comparison I find amusing. Baraka and I are not mutual fans. Umar began the interview by relating how Baraka first came into his life.

UMAR: I was just getting into my Black nationalism thing. Givin' up my silk an' sharkskin suits. My lizards, cuzzins an' 'gators. I started wearin' camoflauge an' khakis an' dashikis. And I happened to look in the *Times*. This was when they were covering the riots in Newark. They had a picture of Leroi Jones.[8] That's what he was called at the time but it was Amiri [Baraka]. He was standing outside this Volkswagen bus. His head was bandaged because there was some blood and he had on this long jollopa. He had that patented Baraka scowl on his face. Under the picture was: Smash those jelly-white faces.

Me being a boy from Ohio, that's all I had around me was them hillbillies—*those jelly-white faces*. I said *Damn! This boy is on the money! I gotta meet this brother!* So when I came to New York, besides meeting The Last Poets and some other brothers, the greatest thrill for me was meeting Amiri Baraka. He's definitely different. He was like a mentor.

DARIUS: "Gash Man" was supposedly about Baraka.

UMAR: That was Abiodun's poem.

ABIODUN: I wrote "Gash Man" with Baraka as an influence. He was with me in Newark. He and I were sitting in a car. We were talking. And his eyes drifted off of me onto something on the street. It was a sister. I saw the sister, too. But we were talking at the time and I felt he was not being at his attentive, revolutionary best. I said, "Man, you ain't nothin' but a *gash*-man!" And he said, "That's a great line!

---

[8] In French, *le roi* means the king. So, loosely translated, Baraka was calling himself The Emperor Jones.

WHITE PEOPLE know your WHITE ROOTS! Take pride in your WHITE HERITAGE! Stand up and be proud of who you are—a WHITE PEOPLE with a WHITE HISTORY and a WHITE CULTURE!! There are GREAT WHITE FILMS to be seen! There are GREAT WHITE DIRECTORS making movies about the TRUE WHITE HISTORY of WHITE PEOPLE'S TRUE WHITE ORIGINS! And they were around LONG before Spike Lee's jungle bunnies humped in *She's Gotta Have It!* That's a TRUE WHITE FACT! The Boyz-n-the-Hood controlling the Hollywood Shuffle are a Menace-II-Society! They want WHITE PEOPLE to believe that they are nothing more than "grafted devils" spawned in Hell, only able to enter the earthly realm by pronouncing Pat Robertson's name backwards! In the following essay, WHITE FILM HISTORIAN, Michael Will, exposes THE TRUTH about the accomplishments of WHITE PEOPLE in cinema.

What could be defined as whitesploitation? A blaxploitation-type movie with Caucasian leads? If so, about the only one that comes to mind is the *Cleopatra Jones*–like *Scorchy* (1976), starring Connie Stevens. This sort of live action cartoon, with the ultra-hip killing machine pulverizing evil on the meanest of streets, is the one original formula to emerge from the blaxploitation cycle. The tag was given to any seventies genre item, from *House on Skull Mountain* to *Melinda* to *The Soul of Nigger Charley,* that featured a predominantly black cast. By theory then whitesploitation would have to take in a

You should use it in a poem!" The line was born at that moment.

I was just checking him out, watching the sister. She was fine. His eyes following her down the street. The gash-man syndrome came out of the fact that so many of us who were into the whole fire of revolution had time for the ladies and the ladies had time for us, that was a given, but sometimes we got carried away.

DARIUS: What's the history of The Last Poets?

ABIODUN: The group was born on May 19, 1968, in Mount Morris Park, which is a very famous park in Harlem. It's since been renamed Marcus Garvey Park.

David Nelson had asked me to join him in a poetry reading honoring Malcolm X's birthday. I was intimidated because I had never read poetry in Harlem. I was a kid. I was only nineteen years old.

I did not know what was happening in terms of how I was going to affect people from the stage in Harlem. Harlem always shook me up. It was a strong black place. Everybody seemed arrogant. Everybody seemed strong. Everybody seemed like we're about no nonsense. Everybody seemed like this is the power base.

"If you come here, you better be right! You don't come here with no sloppy shit! If you gonna come and try and talk to us you better know what the hell you saying because we know everything!"

I was totally wiped out with that.

I had come to Harlem about a week before we had this gig to get the flavor of what Harlem was about from a revolutionary point of view; just walking through, not talking, listening. And the line I heard mostly was, *"What's your thing, brutha, what's your thing?"*

That was the revolutionary line at the time. Everybody was saying, What's your thing? I think it was the Isley Brothers who did "What's Your Thing, Do What You Wanna Do." That was one of the code lines. And "What's Your Thing?" encompassed, What are you doing for the revolution? What are you doing with your life? What are you doing for the movement? Everything was centered around, what are you doing for Black people and the movement. Everything was geared towards that.

So I hooked a little poem called "What's Your Thing?", which was really a little propagandist piece more or less. It wasn't as much poetry as I understand poetry today, but it made the point because a lot of stuff we did at that time was propaganda. We tried to provoke and create more nationalistic understanding and tendencies.

I went to David's house—David Nelson lived around the corner from Mount Morris Park—he had another brother there named Gylan Kain, who he had met at a reading at Columbia University. And he [David] had said he was thinking about having him read with us. I said, "Cool, let's sing together."

And Kain couldn't sing—David doesn't sing that well either—but Kain *really* couldn't sing.

We knew we couldn't sing. So we said, "Okay, we'll go up on stage chanting." We went up on stage chanting a chant I heard at a Howard University demonstration. "Are you ready niggas? You got to be ready! Are you ready niggas?"

By the time we got up on stage, everybody in the park was chanting that. David had a poem entitled, "Are You Ready Black People?" I had a poem entitled, "What Is Your Thing?" And Kain had a poem entitled, "Niggers Are Untogether People." Those were our first three poems. The name came about three or four weeks later.

David was reading a poem by South African poet K. William Kgositsile in a book called *Black Fire*, edited by Leroi Jones and Larry Neal. The poem was "Towards a Walk in the Sun." In that particular poem the last part states, ". . . after this era of poetry there will be no more art talk. The only sounds that you will hear is the spearpoint pivoted into the punctured mouth of the villain and the timeless native son dancing like crazy to retrieve rhythms."

And David Nelson added, "Therefore we are the last poets of the world."

David summarized the poem into the title The Last Poets, saying that this is the last message, the last chance for the brothers and sisters who are unaware in consciousness, and not really with what was going down, to become aware and get with it, or to just perish in the holocaust, because we're definitely going to have a revolution—it's going to be bloody and heads will roll. We were trying to set that up.

solid percentage of all the rest of that decade's American films. Let's therefore be more literal and single out movies that, like the *Mandingo*s of blaxploitation's hardcore that sensationalize black suffering, caricature the extremes of white subcultural grotesqueries, and turn them into low, most often unintentional, comedy.

Quintessential is the spawn of *Poor White Trash*. This is the early sixties reissue of 1957's *Bayou*, a lurid backwoods melodrama dirtied up with some nudie footage to become a drive-in phenomenon for the next decade and a half. It and its scores of imitations, most of them regional cheapies that only ever played the small town and grind house circuits, tried to fill in the blanks left by *God's Little Acre* (1958). A bashful adaptation of Erskine Caldwell's smutty bestseller, it cheated audiences out of what they paid to see, namely cracked behavior at its most violent and lewd. That's just what Russ Meyer provided with his roughies *Lorna* (1964) and *Mudhoney* (1965), though it can be argued that these gals are merely Dixie variations of all those vixens and pussycats out in Meyer's California desert. Same antics, different landscape. Herschell Gordon Lewis, meanwhile, used the white trash genre to pioneer the splatter film. *2,000 Maniacs* (1964) is his bluegrass remake of *Brigadoon* (1954). The title populace magically reappears a hundred years after being massacred by Union troops, to take their revenge on a flock of Yankee tourists. As played by the residents of St. Cloud, Florida, there's nothing too ghostly or nineteenth century about their pickup trucks, greasy duck's ass pompadours and teased Leslie Gore flip

'do helmets. Gruesome fantasy, or cautionary travelogue for northern liberals?

Hollywood, whose own budgeted hate affair with the Deep South gave this junk a market, was by now past its fifties Hays Office hangover that had made such a yawn out of *God's Little Acre*. All that newly uncensored sex and violence became the stuff of epics. *The Chase* (1966) shows how just the right selection of too many cooks (extravagant Sam Spiegel, violent Arthur Penn and sleazy Lillian Hellman) can make the best mincemeat out of something as PBSy bland as a Horton Foote novel. The Texas trash in this one are upwardly mobile and all the worse for it. Led by snarling Richard Bradford and smirky Janice Rule, they start out the evening by guzzling whiskey and having a *La Dolce Vita*–style party, complete with suburban roulette and shooting off guns in the house. Then, just for the hell of it, they go out and stir up some real trouble. Along the way they spread vicious gossip, harass decent black folk, smash up the beer parlor, beat the sheriff (Marlon Brando) to a bloody pulp, cause a traffic jam, round up a lynch mob, start a riot, blow up the junkyard and commit a Ruby-like assassination in the town square.

Brando shows up for more eclectic abuses in *Reflections in a Golden Eye* (1967), John Huston's *Total Recall* of kinky southern gothics. This one's peacetime army base has enough debauchery to give any sleepy little town a run for its money. Staff Major Brando comes bursting out of the closet over a handsome young private who horseback rides in the nude (the seminude, rather: Robert Forster borrows Cornel

The members were David Nelson, Gylan Kain and myself. Later David left and Felipe took his spot. Kain and I had a beef between us. He left the group. He also wanted to pursue some other things.

The second phase of the group starts when Umar comes into the group and we do the album with Jalal. That becomes the next phase of The Last Poets which most people are familiar with because that album is what became popular.

DARIUS: That's interesting. When I was in high school, I was convinced there was going to be an armed revolution in America. I felt my time would be better spent preparing for that than going to college.

UMAR: We were very serious about revolution. We were serious to the point that when I first came into Islam and got locked up in its revolutionary fervor, I was going to strap myself with one hundred pounds of dynamite, walk into the 77th Precinct in Brooklyn, who were known for brutalizing black men, and *boom!*

But at that time, the Elders of Allah said, "Umar, I don't think you're ready for that, really. You might think you are but there are different things you need to learn not only about being a revolutionary or being Black or Muslim but you have to learn about yourself." A lot of brothers were very serious about revolution. I'm quite sure Huey Newton was very serious about revolution—

ABIODUN: *Absolutely!*

UMAR: —but look how he wound up. It's good that brothers like us can still be here and alive and even talk about revolution during those times.

ABIODUN: We have brothers like Ralph Featherstone and Che' Paine who are not here. They just happened to be in the other car up ahead of H. Rap Brown, whom we both know well. They thought they had blown up H. Rap Brown but they had blown up two other brothers.

Fred Hampton and Mark Clark, they're gone. Those brothers were very serious about the breakfast program. They had taken that whole Panther ten-point program and enacted every single point in

Chicago. And they were loved. They are loved to this very day.

When I go to Chicago, I hear people talking about how those brothers were loved. They weren't just a bunch of parading Panthers, runnin' around talkin' about "We Black Panthers! We baad! We Black!"

No. They [Mark Clark and Fred Hampton] were doing grassroots things. That kind of activity doesn't go on now. If they really showed some of the grassroots things that took place—because *Eyes on the Prize* is nice. It's really, really nice if you know what transpired during that period. There is a lot of blood that's unaccounted for.

DARIUS: What happened? Why did that kind of grassroots activism stop?

UMAR: The most extensive thing that happened was COINTELPRO [The FBI's counter-intelligence program, under J. Edgar Hoover, aimed at the nation's radical activist community]. Niggas who didn't like being niggas. Blacks who didn't like being black. Africans who didn't like being African. The whyte man found some people who would go against their brothers and destroy viable organizations. That was the first thing. Black people who didn't love themselves, who loved the whyte man and believed in the system more than they believed in the fact that we were of African descent.

The second thing was the drug thing. I had my trials with that. But not only I, there were other brothers who I could never believe would wind up going through it. I remember one day I was waking up on one of my little benches (I used to tell everybody I lived on Central Park West because I had a bench on Central Park West where I could crash. When I signed up for one of those little temporary jobs, I'd say Central Park West. Whyte people was like, "What? Central Park West? Lookin' like this?"), and right next to me was this brother . . .

We went through Moses Powell, a martial arts school. He was my martial arts instructor. Now, here was a brother who could take his leg and casually stick it straight up in the air, he was in such control of his body.

Matter of fact, he was a legend in Brownsville because one of his

Wilde's flesh-colored cod piece from the previous year's *The Naked Prey*). Jealous of the horse, Brando beats it senseless with a riding crop that his animal-loving wife, Elizabeth Taylor, later uses on his face, livening up an otherwise dull officers' smoker. Liz, who exposes herself to uptight and frigid Brando for kicks, flaunts her affair with the colonel next door, Brian Keith, whose own fey and neurotic wife Julie Harris (talk about offbeat casting!) has a penchant for mutilating herself. All leads up to a Day-Hudsonian climax of romantic mix-ups and bedroom shenanigans.

There's several such offbeat touches to the sex that seethes through Otto Preminger's wonderful *Hurry Sundown* (1967), which that year made everyone's Ten Worst list. Star Michael Caine, with a marvel of a Georgia accent, may be impotent but he gets some mileage out of it, as he taunts his sex-starved wife, Jane Fonda, with his saxophone, making her go down on it as foreplay then not even putting out. She should be thankful for that much attention as Caine, the soul of corruption, busies himself with nonstop double dealings with poor-but-proud sharecroppers, black and white alike, whose humble bits of land he wishes to seize and turn into oil patch. Nothing works, however, not even a session of kangaroo court with Burgess Meredith presiding. Burgess, here in his hissiest of Otto appearances, tries to force his attentions on demure schoolmarm Diahann Carroll and when she doesn't comply, he denounces her uppity northern ways to anyone who'll listen. Somewhat luckier in the sack is big-bellied sheriff George Kennedy, an oily bugger who looks the

other way when Caine, as a final resort, blows up half the county (which makes for the grandest of finales), but sneaks across the tracks to see his plump, jolly lover. In one enchantingly romantic scene she feeds him her prize-winning fried chicken and, with batter drooling down his chin, he leers at her and enthuses, "The blacker the berry, the sweeter the juice!"

Another fine law enforcer, Lee Marvin, is just as two-faced and full of dumb metaphors until he's morally blackmailed, by pissed-to-the-gills Richard Burton, into taking a stand in *The Klansman* (1974). That he takes it against rather than for his buddies in the hooded legion is about the full extent of this one's liberal posturings. Its Selma-like town spits toads over the arrival of northern demonstrators, which touches off a series of racist assaults. These, like the highlights of a slasher film, are clearly what the ridiculous plot is built around, and none is more sickeningly detailed than the rape of black leading lady Lola Falana. This puts the film in *Mandingo* territory and, like the shooting of Bambi's mother, casts a grim pall over the film's entire mood. Still, one's tempted to recommend *The Klansman* for some moments of exhilarating hilarity, like when social pariah Linda Evans takes on the shrieking hypocrites at her Baptist church, and when renegade sniper O.J. Simpson opens fire on a Klan funeral procession, stampeding the mourners and touching off a chain reaction of exploding hearses and limousines.

By the time *The Klansman* came out it was, despite its untempered 70s sadism, a throwback to the potboilers of the 60s, its "big picture" of silly

boys got jumped on in a pool room there. And he went over there—this is before the Uzis and nine millimeters, the most anybody would have would be a knife or a stick in their hand—and tore up about thirteen or fourteen brothers. I'm talking about *mutilated* them. I mean *discombobulated* them. Messed them up because of his boy.

So I woke up on this bench, looked over and said, "This can't be . . ." He said, "Yeah. It's me, Umar. I saw you layin' down and I thought I'd squat with you, brother."

And I thought—Damn! Me . . . This shit is deep. What's goin' on with this crack thing? What's goin' on? What's happenin' here?

He had got hooked up on it but what made it even worse, the young boys had him sellin' it in Central Park. He had turned into a prostitute for the drug.

I know sisters who used to be Muslims, sisters who used to be into the African thing, who were out there.

So that was the second thing—drugs.

At that time, man, the cities of America were burning. Black people were looking beautiful in their naturals and their dashikis. We looked strong to the whyte man, demanding power.

And the whyte man went, "Whoa! Waitaminnit, now! Y'all kinda scary now, we gon' have to find some way to break all that shit up!"

DARIUS: That's interesting, in that people, nowadays, conduct themselves in such a way as to make COINTELPRO unnecessary. They've become their own police.

UMAR: Basically, now, people are just trying to survive. The economy is in such a bad way, if you can find a job, you're lucky in America.

ABIODUN: We can't reenact another movement like we had in the sixties and seventies because there was a kind of blowup of ideas and attitudes and creativity for days and a lot of overt and whyte folks were intimidated if they saw brothers walking down the street giving the power sign. They'd say, "Oh, man! They probably gettin' ready to blow me up!"

What has to happen now is that there has to be some type of love and understanding that we're clearly moving into projects where we're doing things without all of the advertisement, without all of the parade, without all of the fanfare. We're going to have to be intelligent enough to make some kind of corporations among ourselves, among those of us who know what needs to be done and get the job done; to try and blow it up and get masses of folks to follow because that was always the thing—if we're going to have this revolution, we got to have the masses marching down the street to burn up city hall. It ain't like that.

The Spook Who Sat by the Door is probably one of the best messages that we can have for this period that we're dealing with right now. Because not only are we beside the door, we're in the door, we're behind the desks. We got the keys. And all we have to do is believe and have some reason to believe in what we're about. Umar made a statement, "Believe in our ancestors." Just believe in the fact that our folks who came before us died for some reason. That's the movement. That's what's got to happen.

All those things that Umar mentioned as to what happened, looking back, he just took me on a kaleidoscope. That's it. Drugs came in. "Man, I ain't got no job. I can't get a job. Sell these drugs? *Why not* sell these drugs if I can get everything I want with these drugs?"

I think we all remember the show with Gil Noble when he had a guy on there who can't live in the Black community because the Black people wanted to kill him and the FBI was looking for him because he was down with the Black Panthers out there in Watts, built a theater and burned it down. 'Cause he was gettin' paid. When people asked him why he always had eight hundred dollars a week in his pocket, he said he sells drugs. Then he had to go get drugs from the FBI to prove to the people in the group that he sold drugs. They had the whole thing worked out.

And that's just one story. You know if they paid for that one brother in California, how many brothers and sisters they had all over the country?

DARIUS: Were The Last Poets ever affected by COINTELPRO?

UMAR: *Are you kidding?* We can tell you an outrageous story about

small-town politics way out of fashion. South-set garbage had long since fragmented into so-called men's and women's pictures, the former typified by the bloody action heroics of the *Macon County Line* (1974) and *Walking Tall* films (1973 to 1977), the latter by such tepid teen romances as *Buster and Billie* (1974) and *Ode to Billy Joe* (1976), in which Robbie Benson made screen history with his line, "I'm downwind from you, girl!" Meanwhile an A-film return to the xenophobic horrors of *2,000 Maniacs* was made in *Deliverance* (1972), in which urban macho voyageurs are interfered with by horny hillbillies. A whole new genre was created here, but one that had more to do with tenderfeet on wilderness odysseys than the inbred geekishness of its first villains. The whitesploitation label can't really apply to *Whiskey Mountain* (1977), the cheapest and most direct *Deliverance* cash-in, with its cross-country dirt bikers running afoul of nothing more exotic than backwoods pot growers, nor to *Seasons in the Sun* (date unknown but yes, such a film actually exists), in which dying rock star Terry Jacks sails up B.C.'s eerie rain coast and smack dab into a cell of Russian spies. Closer in spirit, though taking a different whitesploitive direction, is Claude Jutra's *Surfacing* (1980), as trashy an adaption of pretentious Margaret Atwood as anyone could wish for. The laughs start fast and furious right with its opening theme, a Baez-like folk drone, in which dreary Kathleen Beller is described as having the "heart of a gypsy" as she peddles her ten speed through the pristine streets of downtown Toronto. From there she drags her sigh-guy boyfriend (Timothy Bottoms)

and another arty-academic couple out to the Ontario wilds to hunt for her missing archeologist father. Though they do have a run-in with some nasty moose hunters, mostly they're bashed around by Mother Nature and are themselves reduced to "savagery," which takes the form of pompous insults and kinky mind games. In one, co-star Margaret Dragu is coerced into doing a nude humiliation dance around a rotting heron corpse hanging from a pole, while her misogynistic lover R. H. Thompson takes home movies.

One would think that symbolism this subtle and politically astute would only crop up once in a very occasional film, but the adaptation of Thomas McGuane's *The Sporting Club* (1971) is just crammed with it. A satirical allegory of something or other, probably Vietnam, it follows the mounting tensions between upper crust swingers and squatting hippies at a Michigan hunting retreat. One's never sure what the verbose characters are talking about but plenty of cool stuff happens, like a realistic tar and feathering, exploding lodges, a bloody shoot-out and a climactic descent into mass sexual hysteria. A less action-packed but far funnier condemnation of the rich is the "Bergmanesque" backyard effort, *The Meal* (1975), a.k.a. *Deadly Encounter*. The perfectly cast Dina Merrill plays a snide socialite who gathers her associates, all of whom she's seriously sick and tired of, for a weekend at her country estate, where she plays Truman Capote with their dark dirty secrets then sits back to enjoy the carnage.

A much happier bunch, at least initially, is found in Franco Zeffirelli's *Endless Love* (1981). Don Murray and Shirley Knight play a fun-loving couple of blue-blood Bohemians who, having no friends their own age, provide a night after night party space for the

how we met our own agents, man!

Mine was a young college girl in Denver, Colorado. She met me after the show. Sisters and The Last Poets, y'know? It was one of my little conquests. One of the amenities of being a Last Poet, y'know what I'm sayin'?

She takes me up into the mountains, to one of these homes you wouldn't believe! Her mother is in state government. Her father is in state government. Her mother and father are gone for the weekend.

She's driving a little Japanese car. We're going up there into the Rockies. We come up to this house. She pushes a button. The garage door opens. She takes me upstairs through the garage into this sunken living room with the pile carpeting. And I said, "Damn! This is gonna be freaky! I'm gon' like this!"

She walks over to a wall and pushes a button. This curtain pulls back. I'm looking down into this valley, Darius. And the view is, like, "Shhoooo . . . !"

Now, dig what I do, I go up into the bedroom and grab the mattress off the bed. I said, "We gonna park it right here, baby! This is it! I'm gonna be poppin' that cootchie in front of all this stuff!"

Shit, she was down for like three or four hours! We went through the sweat an' the funk! Sweat was fallin' all off her titties an' her face. The lather was comin' out of the cootchie an' shit! It got so good—boom—we was like all day an' all night!

The next morning, she was fixing breakfast and real melancholy (y'know, after you hit that spot right, them sisters are in love with you, believe me), I say, "What's the matter? I didn't do it right?"

Like I hit the wrong hole. I was gettin' worried.

She said, "No. Come here and let me talk to you, Umar. Be careful. They're watching you. I was sent to get close to you and get information and find out what you were really about."

A tear came to my eye. She was crying, too.

I realized, no matter what the system has taken us through, that there will always be that thing between black men and black women that we're Africans—"I know you my man. I know you my woman." You could be with a whyte boy or a whyte girl but there always going to be that thing because once you get done with all that bullshit there is going to be nobody but us. It comes back to us. That's what happened. I was a young boy at the time, but I understood that. I stayed there a week with that sister.

About six months later, I saw her in Harlem. She was dressed in a dashiki with a hairpiece. I was wondering if she changed or was on another mission. But when I went up on her she had cut it all loose. She said, "Umar, that was a beautiful time we spent together. I'm trying to work for my people."

Being a black man in this society is hard sometimes, but once you find the beauty of it, there's nothing else you want to be. Yeah, we were looked after.

As a matter of fact, whyte boys came up on the stage with some axe handles at a little college in Oklahoma, talkin' 'bout [in cracker twang], "Y'all can't be sayin' all that stuff in here, goddammit, y'all got to go!"—with *axe handles,* man!

But, yo, it was cool! I had the mike! This was gonna be my Waterloo! But the campus police came up and chilled that shit out.

Yeah, we were in some very intimidating and provoking situations. It wasn't easy being a Last Poet.

DARIUS: It's clear you're aligned with Baraka and the Black Arts Movement. From listening to you talk, you make a real distinction between yourselves and the Black Panther Party. There's also the division which occurred among the writers in the Umbra group in the mid–nineteen sixties—the writers who regrouped uptown in Harlem as the Black Arts Movement and the bohemians who remained downtown on the Lower East Side. How do you view your relationship to those particular struggles?

ABIODUN: We had a place. We had a space. We weren't beholden to anybody. We had a place called the East Wind and out of that place came a lot of workshops. It was on 125th Street between Fifth and Madison. That was our home base. It was an L-shaped loft. A number of benefits for different conspirators like the Harlem Five took place there. Felipe got a chance to get off a lot of his political stuff because people discovered how well he could do his political rabble-rousing because he had a political workshop there. We were doing a

local teens. Their coolness is put to the test, though, when one of the regulars (Martin Hewitt), a nice boy but decidedly common, gets a shade too familiar with their patrician daughter Brooke Shields. It's no more parties for him, so in retaliation he comes creeping through the woods with a can of gas (to the hauntingly suspenseful chords of Blondie's "Heart of Glass") and sets their mansion on fire. Everyone manages to get out alive, so Hewitt's only sent to the mental institution for a scene or two. The day he gets out he's spotted, quite by chance, by the embittered and now destitute Murray, who comes running across a busy street to beat him up and gets struck down by a taxicab. Figuring the coast is now clear, Hewitt pays a visit to grieving widow Knight, with whom he's remained friendly, in an effort to worm his way around the restraining order and back into Brooke's arms. Knight, after confessing that she used to spy on him and Brooke while they were having sex, tries to put the make on him herself.

Had Hewitt shown more compassion and given poor Knight the tumble she craved, *Endless Love* might've been a different sort of film entirely. Brian Yuzna's *Society* (1992) is a first in that it seriously ponders the term "blue blood" and its possible connotations. A *Metropolitan* for the Fangoria crowd, its young protagonist tries to escape rather than infiltrate the ranks of the privileged, only to discover what he (and indeed we all) should've sensed all along, that they're not even human! They're an ancient race of obscene shapeshifters who actually practice the purest forms of incest to insure that each succeeding generation is all the more physically repulsive. As for their initiation rituals, they may be discreet but they're certainly not charming.

—Michael Will

The Spook Who Sat by the Door

(1973)
[On Video]
PRODUCERS: Ivan Dixon, Sam Greenlee; DIRECTOR: Ivan Dixon; SCREENWRITER: Sam Greenlee and Melvin Clay; STORY: based on Sam Greenlee's novel.

CAST: Lawerence Cook (Dan Freeman); Paula Kelly (Dahomey Queen); Janet League (Joy); J.A. Preston (Reuben Dawson); and Paul Butler (Do-Daddy Dean).

Along with *Pimp: The Story of My Life* by Iceberg Slim and the rare Vancouver, B.C., edition of *The Mini-Manual of the Urban Guerrilla* by Carlos Marighella (published by *N.Y.P.D. Blue* producer, Ted Mann, and distributed free on the east coast by the Black Panther Party), Sam Greenlee's novel *The Spook Who Sat by the Door* was required reading among my circle of homies in high school.

The novel and film are both concerned with a CIA-trained Black man with an agenda. Following the revolutionary's dictum *Know The Enemy,* Dan Freedman studies whytey's trickology up close, goes underground, and organizes a Chicago street gang into a unit of revolutionary warriors with knowledge of the Man and the Man's knowledge.

If there is one film from the seventies black film cycle that deserves a retelling for today's audiences, it's this one. Might give them Uzi-totin' dope-boys some *bright* ideas . . .

lot of things. There was always something going on. We did what we wanted to do.

One thing that we proclaimed as a group was that we were Nationalists, point-blank. We weren't coming from no Marxist-Leninist thing. There was always this friction between Cultural Nationalists, Marxist-Leninists, Progressive Labor Party people.

So when you're talking about downtown, we're talking about people who were more influenced by communism and socialism and all that stuff. We never had none of that. We were coming from a strictly Nationalist place and Marxist-Leninism was something that you had to read an awful lot of stuff and a lot of folks weren't going to take to a revolution that was supposed to be taking place in Germany in eighteen fifty and relate it to something in America in nineteen sixty-nine.

We all knew the dialogue. We read Franz Fanon's *Wretched of the Earth* and *Black Skins, White Masks.* We had to read *Blues People* by Amiri Baraka, Harold Cruse's *Crisis of the Negro Intellectual,* Chancillor Williams's *Destruction of Black Civilization.*

I was interested in the Yoruba religion because my name is Yoruba so I had to read *Muntu* by Janheinz Jahn. And there were books to be read.

You want to talk about reading?! These kids who are rappers and gangsters and all that nonsense now, a lot of them would be readers if someone would offer them some literature to read, but people aren't offering them the real literature!

UMAR: Plus they don't want to go get it because they don't want to change their own viewpoints of what they're rapping about! Though The Last Poets were clearly Nationalists, when you came to the The Last Poets' loft for a party or a poetry reading, we didn't give a fuck if anybody was a Nationalist or a Marxist-Leninist, you had to be family while you were in the East Wind.

ABIODUN: We didn't check for ID cards . . .

UMAR: We didn't ask your political or religious preference, if you black, you can come here and hang out. But you can't be coming in here proselytizing or try and get people to change into your beliefs.

You were there to be part of the family, to dance and listen to poetry.

DARIUS: So you basically had a creative collective which extended out into the community.

UMAR: You wouldn't believe who came out of East Wind.

ABIODUN: Jimmy Walker came out of our place.

UMAR: *We started Jimmy, man!* Jimmy Walker got his start at the East Wind. The first time Jimmy Walker ever got up on stage was at the East Wind. The truth was his jokes weren't funny, we just laughed at the way he looked! Very rarely will he tell you that.

ABIODUN: He'll mention that once in a while.

UMAR: Yeah, he'll mention it once in a while but not really all the time. I've known people who'll ask him and he'll circumvent the question.

ABIODUN: Because that makes him responsible for some thought he's not delivering now. But we let him tell his jokes.

UMAR: There's a lot of people who came out of East Wind.

ABIODUN: Nikki Giovanni. Nicky Grimes. Jackie Orly. Don Lee came through there. It was a place where people could be black and feel comfortable at.

DARIUS: Is East Wind still open?

UMAR: What's amazing is that the place closed down and has not been open since.

ABIODUN: It's like a tomb.

UMAR: In the future, we might be able to get it back open.

ABIODUN: Felipe has looked into it and got in touch with the owner but we haven't been able to follow through because there's money involved. We are in touch with the person who owns it and he's not unwilling to give it up, so that's a possibility. We just have to get our act together.

The Final Comedown

(1972)
[On Video]
PRODUCER/DIRECTOR/SCREENWRITER: Frank Arthur Wilson (Oscar Williams's *nom de cine*).
CAST: Billy Dee Williams (Johnny Johnson); Raymond St. Jacques (Imir); D'Urville Martin (Billy Joe Ashley); R. G. Armstrong (Mr. Freeman); Pamela Jones (Luanna); Maidie Norman (Mrs. Johnson); Morris Erby (Mr. Johnson); Billy Durkin (Michael Freeman); and Edmund Cambridge (Dr. Smalls).

Before Billy Dee stumbled through the door of his cheesy TV bachelor pad with a Colt 45 ho' snoozing on his arm, he once played the kind of movie militant that H. Rap Brown said, "Can't do wrong right." And this is the movie he did it in.

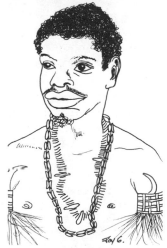

Courtesy of Joy Glidden © 1995.

Courtesy of Photofest.

Courtesy of Photofest.

The Black Godfather

(1974)
[On Video]
PRODUCER: John Evans; DIRECTOR: John Evans; SCREENWRITER: John Evans.
CAST: Rod Perry (J.J. [J. Johnson]); Damu King (Diablo); Don Chastain (Tony); Diane Sommerfield (Yvonne Williamson); Jimmy Witherspon (Big Nate Williamson); Duncan McLeod (Lieut. Joe Sterling); and Tony Burton (Sonny Spider Brown).

Put *The Black Godfather* in your VCR, swallow two quaaludes and I *guarantee* you'll go insane with boredom.

The Black Gestapo

(1975)
[On Video]
DIRECTOR/SCREENWRITER: Lee Frost; PRODUCER/SCREENWRITER: Wes Bishop.
CAST: Rod Perry (General Ahmed); Charles P. Robinson (Col. Kojah); Phil Hoover (Vito); Ed Cross (Delmay); Angela Brent (Marsha); Wes Bishop (Ernest); Lee Frost (Vincent); Dona Desmond (White Whore); Charles Howerton (Joe); Rai Tasco (Dr. Lisk); and David Bryant (Pusher).

Lee Frost is a 1960s "sexploitation" director, known for his ability to film flesh without showing actual genitalia. Neat trick. Trash film cultists consider *Love Camp Seven* his masterpiece.

On the other hand, *The Black Gestapo* represents the same fears reflected in *Birth of a Nation,* depicting a Black Panther Party–like paramilitary group as a gang of parasitic, Black-faced neo-Nazis. It's a pity Frost didn't have the balls to include a scene of his "Negro Nazis" eating buckets of KFC and picking their feet in a Congressional hearing room.

But, despite its abhorrent politics, if you like your Black-action flicks heaped with lotsa scenes of Black men beatin' up whyte women an' castratin' whyte men, jump on it.

Great sepia-tinted title sequence of Nazi parade.

Brothers

(1977)
DIRECTOR: Arthur Barron; SCREENWRITERS: Mildred Lewis, Edward Lewis; MUSIC: Taj Mahal.
CAST: Bernie Casey (David Thomas); Vonetta McGee (Paula Jones); Ron O'Neal (Walter Nance); Renny Roker (Lewis); Stu Gilliam (Robinson); John Lehne (Chief Guard McGee); Owen Pace (Joshua Thomas); Joseph Havener (Warden Leon); and Martin St. Judge (Williams).

This is a fictionalized account of the relationship between Angela Davis and George Jackson. After The Watts Monster, Bernie Casey's natural color returns to his cheeks just in time to portray George Jackson (or David Thomas here). Vonetta McGee is Angela Davis (or Paula Jones). David is sentenced to a prison term of one year to life where he is radicalized with the help of a jailhouse intellectual, who is later beaten to death by the prison's guards. And just as it happened in real life, David falls in love with a radical woman, and his brother is killed during an attempt to free him during his court trial. He himself is killed in a escape attempt. Seeing the movie is all very well and fine, but do yourself a favor, and read *Soledad Brother.*

Up Tight

(1968)
PRODUCER/DIRECTOR: Jules Dassin; SCREENWRITERS: Ruby Dee, Julian Mayfield, Jules Dassin; STORY: based on Liam O'Flaherty's novel *The Informer;* MUSIC: Booker T. Jones and the M.G.s
CAST: Raymond St. Jacques (B.G.); Ruby Dee (Laurie); Frank Silvera (Kyle); Roscoe Lee Browne (Clarence); Julian Mayfield (Tank Williams); Janet MacLachlan (Jeannie); Max Julien (Johnny Wells); Juanita Moore (Johnny's mother); and Dick Anthony Williams (Corbin).

Hollywood's first Black Nationalist production. Or so-called, anyway. It's a black-cast remake of the I.R.A. drama *The Informer.* Set in Cleveland four days after the assassination of Dr. M.L.K., Max Julien, Ji-Tu Cumbuka and John Wesley rob an arsenal, shooting a watchman during the getaway. It wasn't supposed to happen like that but it did 'cause the fourth member of their unit, Tank (playwright Julian Mayfield), got drunk instead. Anyway, black militant (and junior high school teacher) Raymond St. Jacques expels Tank from their organization. So Tank rats on everybody for a thousand bucks. Tank is one dead Negro. End of movie. The movie's soundtrack probably made more money than the movie. Booker T. and the M.G.'s "Time is Tight" is an R&B classic. It was even covered by *The Clash* on a collection of B-sides.

PANTHER

FOR RED ESTHER...

Courtesy of Photofest.

In the early seventies, the Black Panther Party's ideology, analysis and rhetoric gave definition to and provided a vocabulary for the anger, frustration and confusion I and others of my generation felt in the aftermath of the 1950s and 1960s civil rights battles.

Through elementary and junior high school, we had experienced the full trauma of the sixties. America's public institutions did not, and could not, provide us with the tools to understand the glaring absurdity of being Black in the exclusionary environment of mainstream culture. And our so-called "race-leaders" did not speak to us; instead, their language was tempered for the sensibilities of monied white liberalism. So

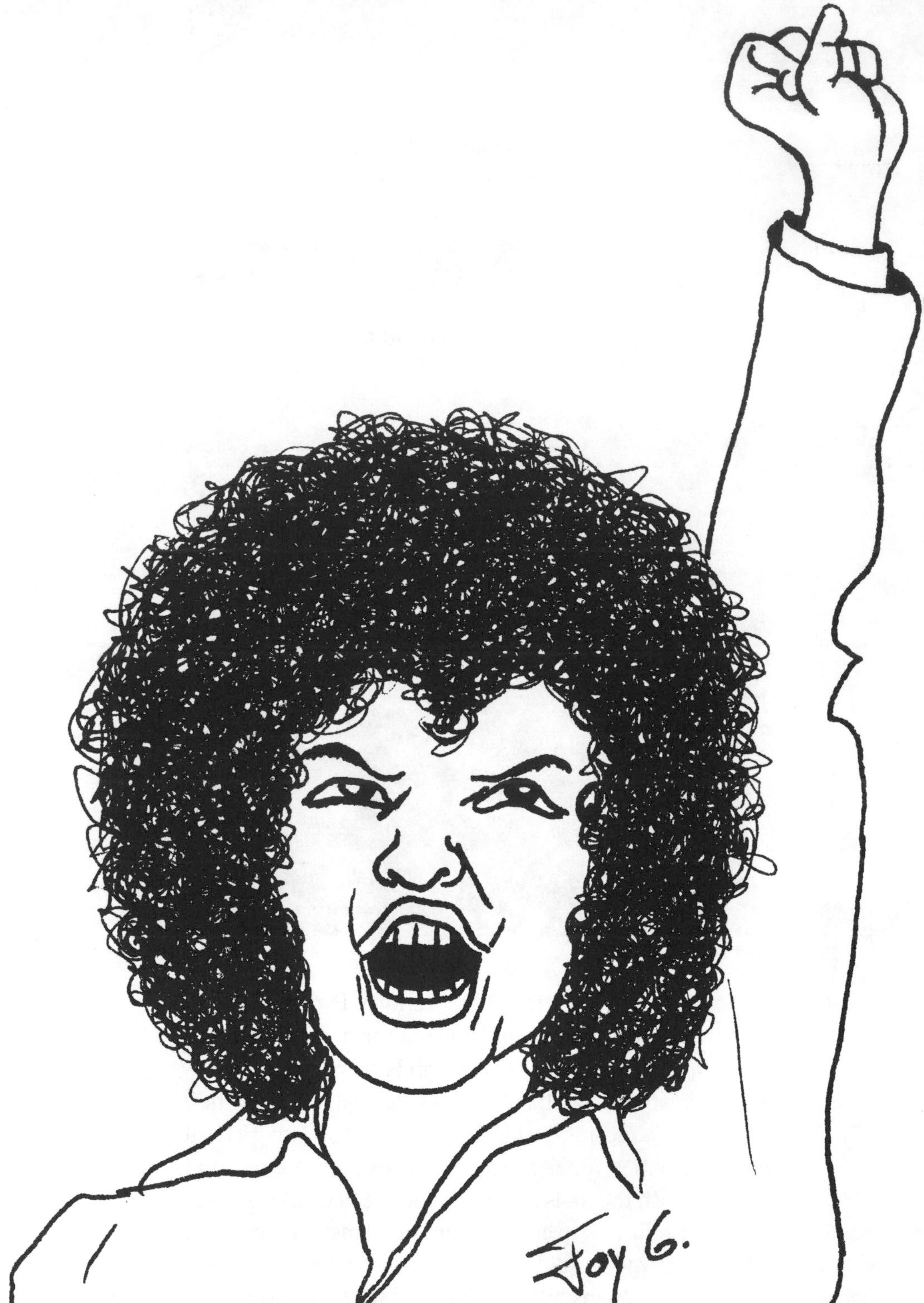
Joy G.

we sought self-illuminating significance elsewhere.

The tube signaled our first moment of deepening self-worth. It was the loud proud Black man who exclaimed, I *am* the Greatest!

He shocked America. Boojie black and whyte alike.

Who this nigger say he pretty? *Little Richard?*

Lawd! Who dis' nigga talk like dat in front all dem whyte folks? He g'wine git us *lainched* fo' sho'!

Our second was Kwame Toure's clarion call of *Black Power!* in Greenwood, Mississippi; followed by H. Rap Brown, in his way-cool Wayfarers, singing backup doowops on "Burn, Baby Burn." And the third was the whyte-ass-kicking antics of Kato on *The Green Hornet.*

Otherwise, we cast a cynical eye on the culture.

Once, a classroom discussion of a current events cartoon in *My Weekly Reader* nearly came to all-out blows ("Buffy the Bear be talkin' shit! What he mean 'get off the welfare'? We gon' bust Buffy in his fuzzy, honey-eatin' behind!") so our teacher decided a formal debate was best.

When called upon to choose sides, I raised my hand and, as the molotov cocktail–tossing cadres of doo-ragged doo-woppers, in those really cool shades, was a far more attractive choice than the nonviolent, spiritual-singing marchers I watched get head-whipped, fire-hosed and laughed at on television (which seemed like an awful lot of trouble to go through for the right to sit down next to the whyte man in a desegregated toilet stall), joined the all-black, pre-teen pro "militant" squad; proposing we pooled resources with our red-skinned sistern and brethern, and take back the *whole* red, white and blue muthafucka!!!

I first suspected something was up in the fourth grade.

Amerikkka began to smell funky after Dallas. I understood, though, the bullet in Kennedy's head.

The man was a sitting duck: his teeth clenched in a big Pepsodent smile; his arms waving like a mechanical dummy encased inside a glass booth at a seaside arcade; seated in the back of a stretch limo with the roof down; exposed to thousands of people—

Then bulls-eye!!!

Spicy brain bits spilled all over Jackie's pillbox.

But Oswald? *Shot? On national television?* Surrounded by hundreds of *cops?*

Ted & Venus

(1992)
(On Video)
DIRECTOR: Bud Cort; SCREENPLAY: Paul Ciotti
and Bud Cort; STORY: Paul Ciotti; DIRECTOR
OF PHOTOGRAPHY: Dietrich Lohmann;
MUSIC: David Robbins; MUSIC SUPERVISOR:
Swamp Dogg.
CAST: Bud Cort; James Brolin; Carol
Kane; Rhea Perlman; Martin Mull;
Woody Harrelson; Kim Adams; and
Pamela DePella.

What I look for in a seventies flashback flick is that sudden, dislocated sensation of a wad of Silly Putty sticking to the roof of my mouth followed by a shimmer of fairy dust. Most films in the flashback genre don't do that. Instead, they codify their period reference points with no more than clod-hoppin' platforms, ill-fitting afro wigs, and god-awful soundtracks. Watching *Crooklyn*, for example, I had hoped Spike would serve up an eerie sense of déjà vu with his dysfunctional family shenanigans but all I got for my two-fiddy was a group of lil' cullud *chirrens* singin' how dey woke up dat mornin' in love with David Cassidy's trademark shag. Matty Rich's paper bag club comedy, *The Inkwell*, was about as meaningful as "The Jackson Five" cartoon show. And, unbelievably, *Dazed and Confused*'s Richard Linklater actually tried to recre-ate Texas in 1976 with *one* peripheral black character and *no Mexicans!* (What happened Rich? Everybody get *lynched?*). Until someone buys the film rights to this book (for, say, four-to-five hundred thou), and produces the sev-enties equivalent of *Cooley High*, there's only one film currently sitting on the shelves of your neighborhood video store with the flashback potential

I WASN'T BUYIN' IT!

To my nine-year-old brain, it seemed Kennedy had been dead only but five minutes before some red-nosed peckawood hauled Oswald out in front of the news cameras, talkin' bout—"This man killed the presi-dent!"

I was watching television, pissed off I was missing my afternoon Popeye cartoons, snacking on a chocolate duck-doodle, staring at this squinty-eyed peckawood in the fucked-up cowboy hat, and the only thoughts I had were, How you know? and, How you find him so fast?

I might have been a peasy-headed, cartoon-watchin', grape Kool-Aid–drinkin', monster model–makin' little "colored" boy chumped into thinking he was actually a werewolf by a five-dollar set of plastic dog dentures, but I wasn't a goddamned fool!

Oswald said, "I didn't do it. I've been set up. I'm a patsy."

I believed him. Then he was shot. In the "protective custody" of the police.

In watching Oswald's murder, I experienced the same horror, the same fear I felt the first time I saw photos of Emmett Till's corpse in *Ebony* magazine.

Unconsciously, the two images transhaped in the suffocating detail of dreamscape: the charred, mutilated genitalia of Till's corpse with Os-wald's winded death-fall.

For a Black male child experiencing the world before the Civil Rights Act and the Voting Rights Bill were even signed into legislation, whistling at whyte girls was tantamount to killing the president—*castration anxiety,* indeed!

After the country's "official" period of mourning, and the nation re-sumed its business, the authorities in my elementary school made an attempt at dealing with the emotional trauma this public tragedy might have on our young psyches by inviting a psychologist from the city's De-partment of Public Health to conduct classroom discussions on the president's assassination.

The health department's visiting psychologist was escorted into the classroom by Miss Fishbox, the school principal, an elderly whyte woman with the cold war's A-bomb shelter mentality.

Miss Fishbox and I had had a run-in the year before. My mother was called in for a conference. The problem was this: I'd been assigned to write an essay entitled "Why I Loved America"; but, after watching the evening news report that hundreds of Blacks were mauled by vicious police dogs, and washed away by high-pressure fire hoses, I wrote the opposite.

The psychologist looked like a dim-witted gym instructor. He had a conical, barrel-chested build, like a turnip on steroids, his look of dimness emphasized by a swollen Joe Palooka jaw. And he wore his hair in that by-product of Kennedy's Peace Corps liberalism—the "folk-a-nanny" crewcut—hair that said *Burl Ives is hip!*

He smiled and tried to initiate discussion.

Understandably, my classmates, confused and numbed with shock, sat in silence.

Though saddened by the president's passing, I raised my hand and voiced my fears regarding the suspicious circumstances of Oswald's murder.

The psychologist grinned in open-mouthed disbelief. His tongue protruded to the right and his eyes cut to the left.

Miss Fishbox's liver-spotted face pinched in hostility. Then she told me to *shut up!*

I was just the "attention-seeking" class crackpot, a "crackpot" spawned of "bohemian" parents, who wasted his time tinkering with nightmare face makeup in his father's sculpting studio, brought in photos of his experiments for show-n-tell, and made his classmates puke a bilious mixture of undigested cornflakes and chocolate peanut-butter cups on their wooden desktops.

Miss Fishbox's face turned a mottled high blood-pressure purple. She wagged her finger.

I was that "colored" child who watched violent monster movies in a musty basement and thought he was a werewolf. What possible "trauma" could he suffer watching that pathetic communist Lee Harvey Oswald get what he deserves on national television?

Her face returned to its normal shade of jellyfish gray.

The psychologist's brow lumped in furrowed concentration. His tongue shifted to the left and his eyes rolled to the right. Then, brightly, he reminded me that this was still America and not Russia.

Courtesy of Photofest.

of a hit of four-way brown dot blotter. And that's Bud Cort's *Ted & Venus*.

Based on real incidents reported in *The L.A. Weekly*, and set during Nixon's exit from the White House in 1974 (which makes this film the perfect counterpoint to *Shampoo*), the story concerns a poet infatuated with a woman he first observes emerging from an early-morning swim in the Venice Beach surf. The poet's infatuation for this comely bosomed young woman quickly turns into obsession. And, oscillating between moments of real tenderness and owl-eyed obscenity, his obsession degenerates into full-blown psychosis—a mental state that leads him to the asylum, prison, and finally, death.

Through more than merely paying attention to period detail, and confining itself to Venice Beach and its poetry scene, with a wonderfully giddy and quirky performance by Ms. Pamela DePella, marking her a winning candidate for *Pam Grier: The Next Generation*, *Ted & Venus* successfully captures the contradictory essence of the seventies 'tude with an expert blend of astute directing, imaginative acting, and an emotionally-complex script. By Hollywood's bloated budgetary standards, *Ted & Venus* was shot for nothing, a little over a million dollars, but the end result is remarkable—a film that is black, transgressive and *smart*.

In Russia he said, po' liddle cullud kidz like me can't grow up with the same equal opportunity to become the first colored werewolf President of the United States like we do in America no matter how much of the whyte folks' welfare money we cullud folks done spent.

"Let me ask you somethin'," he said. "Do you like vodka?"

"Huh? Uh—*no!* My daddy drinks *rum!"*

"Well," he continued, "you're gonna learn to like it if the commies ever take over. 'Cause that's all you're gonna get! No more fried chicken and 'gator-ribs with corn-liquor gravy or whatever it is you people eat! Just vodka! Breakfast, lunch and dinner!"

"In a *communist-controlled* America," he said, "baseball cards would be replaced by 'Heroes of the People's Revolution!' trading cards; you'll be passin' around pictures of that butcher, Joe Stalin, instead of Willie Mays! Popeye would be carted out in tar and feathers, denounced as a lackey dupe of the military-industrial complex! And his cartoons would be preempted by the wacky misadventures of *Mao Tse Tung!"*

My classmates shivered with the fear of God.

"Not only that, you'll own just one pair of cloth shoes, manufactured in Communist China; wear scratchy clothes made out of burlap and work eighteen hours a day, including Sunday, 'cause goin' to church will be against the law in Communist America, punishable by death! And do you know what you'll be doing during those hard, eighteen hours a day? Wanna take a guess?"

I shrugged my shoulders. "Nope."

"Makin' vodka! And that's what that weasly little commie Oswald was tryin' to do! Take over America and force poor little colored children like you to be alcoholic-slaves to the *State!"*

By 1970—stoned, cynical and Apple-Jack capped—we had wiped our asses with the pages of America's history books. And we saw this country for what it was: *a lie.*

Amerikkka could tongue our ink-stained rectums.

It was because of the legacy of Malcolm X,[9] which formed the basis of the Black Panther Party, we could perceive, analyze and articulate the ways we had been hurt by the lies perpetuated in those institutions.

Through Malcolm, the Black Panther Party had given us a language

---

[9] I'm often asked what I thought of Spike's *X.* And I reply I'm waiting for the sequel, *XII*—starring Bo Derek with an extra pair of tits!

to clarify our circumstances, an arsenal of ideas to guide us towards an understanding of who we were, a "revolutionary" sense of self in the face of an oppressive culture.

For many, including myself, it was the first time in our lives we spoke with authenticity.

Pick Up The Gun! and *Off The Pig!* was the language we spoke.

For nineteen-seventies black youth, the Panthers served the same critical function as rap music for today's hip-hop young. The Black Panthers were our Public Enemy, so to speak, both figuratively and literally, declared so by that shame of the American transvestite community, (giving) FBI head J. Edgar Hoover.

The Panthers weren't academics, coffee-house intellectuals or opportunists with six-figure record deals. The Panthers were a product of the streets. The Panthers spoke the language of the streets, whose words were reinforced by deeds.

And, through their deeds, they were intent on responding to the needs of the people in the streets.

Huey Newton and Bobby Seale began the Party as a direct result of their disgust with the theorizing, inactivity and coffee-house rambling of the Merritt College African American Association's armchair revolutionaries.

Together, they spoke to Oakland's Black community in order to determine their exact needs and desires; and, on October 15, 1966, finalized the Black Panther Party's "declaration of black empowerment," the *Ten-Point Program and Platform—What We Want, What We Believe.*

As restated, in brief, by Elaine Brown in *A Taste of Power,* the Black Panthers demanded "restitution for slavery, food, education, decent housing and land for black people . . . constitutional guarantees relating to 'justice for all' be enforced for blacks; the exemption of blacks from the military service; the release of all black prisoners and the granting of new trials by juries of their peers." And, lastly, it "stated that blacks in America had the right to self-determination and called for a UN-supervised plebiscite to establish this claim." It was published on the back page of each issue of the Party's newspaper.

On the Bay Area college circuit, they met with resistance in their drive to recruit membership for the Party. Huey and Bobby found their

Farewell Uncle Tom

(1972)
[On Video]

Written and directed by Gualtiero Jacopetti and Franco Prosperi, the two Italian filmmakers who blessed us with the perverse documentary *Mondo Cane.* I hadn't heard of *Farewell Uncle Tom* when Pedro Bell first described it. And it wasn't listed in any of the film books in my library. Then, browsing one idle afternoon in one of my favorite shops in the East Village, See/Hear Books on E. 7th, I came across a description of the film in Steve Puchalski's outstanding 'zine of the outre' and obscure, *Shock Cinema.*

According to Puchalski, *Farewell Uncle Tom* opens on a southern cotton plantation in the 1800s . . . *with a film crew circling above in a helicopter!* In the explicit Mondo-Cane style, what unfolds is "two full hours of debasement . . . brandings, enemas, rape." The movie ends with what Puchalski describes as "a cool Kill Whitey scenario!" My kinda movie.

greatest support on the street. "Lil' Bobby" Hutton was their first recruit.

Seventeen months later, three days after Martin Luther King was assassinated on the balcony of a hot-sheet motel in Memphis, Lil' Bobby was gunned down in a battle with the Oakland police.

He was only seventeen.

I was thirteen the first time I came in contact with the Panthers. I had written a play. It was an abstract history of black oppression in America, culminating in the formation of the Black Panther Party. It was called *Panther.*

I'd been encouraged to write the play by a graduate student in Yale's School of Drama, Walter Dallas. He in turn introduced me to Black Panther Erica Huggins, widow of Black Panther John Huggins, captain of the Southern California chapter of the Party.

John Huggins was murdered by a member of the United Slaves' Simba posse at U.C.L.A. He was killed two days after a dispute between the Black students of U.C.L.A. and United Slaves, over who would determine the direction of the new Black Studies program in 1969; a program United Slaves' leader, and architect of the faux-African holiday, Ron Karenga, attempted to usurp.

I remember Ms. Huggins as a tall, regal and charming woman.

She smiled. And I flirted. We talked about my play. She said it was a counter-revolutionary product of cultural nationalism.

"—but I can *correct* that, young *bleed!*"

She escorted me to the basement of the local branch of the Black Panther Party, gave me a stack of the Party's newspapers and told me to read them. I did.

One week later she was in jail, charged with murder.

After that first encounter, and throughout my first years in high school, I sold the Party's newspapers; collected contributions for the Panther's free-breakfast program and legal-defense fund; organized "political education" workshops; and was busted for burning a nineteen-cent American flag.

Eventually, the FBI's Fred MacMurray look-alikes bugged my phone under its COINTELPRO program.[10]

But, in the summer of nineteen-seventy, before entering our fresh-

---

[10] *And logged hundreds of hours of my failed attempts to bed the enchanting Melissa Marlowe!* Obviously, since it was costing the American taxpayer thousands of dollars in equipment and man-hours, what I did with my circumsized teenaged penis was a matter of grave security to Nixon's United States. Had I successfully penetrated the moist floral folds of that lithesome, buoyantly bosomed fifteen-year-

man year in high school, Huck, Pete and I camped on the lawn of the New Haven Green, across the street from the Superior Courthouse, attending daily prisoner-support rallies for Black Panther Lonnie McLucas, who was on trial for the kidnap, torture and murder of suspected police informant Alex Rackley.

We lounged in a stupefying fog of cheap wine and pot smoke: I strained my eyes staring at the nipples of braless hippie-women; Pete pondered the life of Ho Chi Minh; and Huck complained about "the songs."

It was the same song he said, playing over and over again.

"Which one?"

"'Sugar Sugar' by the fuckin' *Archies!*"

Huck pressed his palms against his cheeks, scrunching his lips. *"Fuckin song won't go away!"*

He balled up his hands and pounded the sides of his head with his fists in frustration.

Huck intercepted phantom radio signals. It was a peculiar side effect he experienced after smoking pot. This never happened to him after he dropped acid or nodded out on reds. His teeth were in great shape, so he couldn't attribute it to the metal fillings in his molars. How else could he explain the voice of the Arizona John Bircher he once heard buzzing in his skull through a wall of white noise, accusing a prominent black civil rights leader of being a puppet of the International Zionist conspiracy?

It had to be the pot.

I'd just returned to New Haven after spending two semesters in a boys' boarding school in the woodlands of western Massachusetts. As I was not the kind of Negro who knew how to dribble a basketball; nor did my family have any money (I was a pearl-diving kitchen slave on financial aid); and, too, given that I flashed during my preacceptance interview (much to my mother's dismay) a vinyl-covered copy of Mao Tse Tung's *Little Red Handbook* of quaint communist quotations, I have no idea why I was let loose among these people.

But there I was, in the thick of starched white and blue-blazered New England Preppiedom, higher than a Chinese box kite, spouting the incendiary rhetoric of armed insurrection with my shapely teenage tes-

old, my penis might have saved America! Sadly, it was not meant to be. Melissa brought me home and introduced me to her vacant Mom and stiff-back, workingman Dad, two figures in a Norman Rockwell still life with the mentality of his brother George. "He's a *genius!*" she said. *"But he's black!"* they said. *"And that's the end of that!"* I said.

Space Is the Place

(1974)
[On Video]
DIRECTOR: John Coney; SCREENWRITER:
Joshua Smith
CAST: Sun Ra and his Arkestra

This is another of Pedro's faves. A flying saucer lands in the ghetto. Jazz legend, Sun Ra, steps out. And, visiting a community recreation center, he tries to persuade a group of neighborhood kids to leave planet Earth with him and re-colonize other worlds. Sounds like the premise of a George Clinton album. Hmmmm. But that's only a snippet of this convoluted story. There's more. Lots more. Tarot card fights in the desert. Gov't wiretaps. Kidnappings. Cosmic musings by the master himself on the "Caucasian power structure." Only I haven't seen any of it.

Again, *Shock Cinema* saved my butt. This 'zine is devoted to all the out shit, frequently unearthing gems on video—blaxploitation and otherwise—that's completely out the box. I wouldn't have known about *Akbar: The First Black Superman" (a.k.a. In Your Face!)* if not for this 'zine. It's hand-made but brilliant. The man is devoted, his descriptions are trustworthy and he's usually on target. Y'all should come out y'pockets for this at four bucks an issue (five dollas overseas): *Shock Cinema* c/o Steve Puchalski, P.O. Box 518, Peter Stuyvesant Station, New York, N.Y. 10009.

ticles dangling from a hole worn through the crotch of my denim bell-bottoms.

The school's headmaster was a stern, silver-haired, New England WASP in horn-rimmed glasses, whose head, because of the pockets of sagging muscle on his face, looked like a rubber shoebox set between the shoulders of a really cheap suit.

He lurched across campus with the aid of an aluminum walker, his movements punctuated by a grunt and a fart, his deadened legs dragging behind him like snail slime.

I asked this crippled Mr. Chips, one week before fifteen-thousand demonstrators gathered on the New Haven Green, Mayday weekend, 1970, for what promised to be the American Left's answer to Woodstock, if I might visit my family, adding "and, oh yeah, attend a lecture by *Jean Genet!*"

Listing on his walker, he studied me with an enigmatic smile.

Finally, in the voice of a bullfrog strangulating on a lungful of sand, he said:

"I'll have you know, young man, when I was headmaster at Worcester Academy in the nineteen fifties, I gave that hooligan, *Abbie Hoffman,* five dollars *and made him get a haircut.* So, in answer to your question—*no!*"

So, making up for moments missed Mayday weekend, I sat, that summer, along with Huck-n-Pete, under the Viet-Cong–colored banner of the New Haven Wino Liberation Front, in the circle of wine-n-reefer annointed acoyltes of "Professor" Herman Wilson.

"Professor" Wilson—tall, brown and bald with a scrub of knappy salt-n-pepper growth on his chin—conducted, while copping spare coin for "the revolutionary's weapon of choice"—a *cold* pint of Thunderbird wine, open-air lectures, or to the uninitiated, "free-form harangues," on the insidious ensnarlments awaiting the Black man in Amerikkkan society.

"Lightbulbs, got any ideas where the expression 'the wellsprings of wisdom' comes from?"

"Uh . . . a fountain of knowledge?"

"That's simply another cliché for the same idea. How 'bout you other *wattless wonders?*"

He searched our faces. And found nothing.

"Give up? Okay, let's look at the word 'academe'—" Then he turned around to address a businessman, pointing his finger with spittle gathered under his lower lip.

"Hey, you in the glasses! Yeah, I'm talkin' to you!"

The businessman stopped. Frightened.

"It's my official responsibility, as designated by the group you see gathered around me, to raise your reduced consciousness to this one hard revolutionary fact o' life: it's your duty and obligation to both our sacred mother planet, and to the future of the human race, to contribute whatever monies you have to a special slush fund for this coterie of fine young revolutionaries. *Or we'll kill you.*"

Herman continued, counting quarters.

"For the ancient Greeks, the place of learning was a grove near Athens called an 'academe' (or, as I prefer to think, where Plato drank wine, got wasted and talked shit). This 'academe' of trees and flowers surrounded a body of water.

"So, the distinctive feature of an academy is that it surrounds a body of water. It supports and nourishes *life.* Thus, the expression 'the wellsprings of wisdom'!"

He pointed to Yale's Old Campus across the Green.

"Now look at that stone fortress across the street. Do you have any idea what lies in its center? What makes up its heart?"

We stared. Our expressions blank. Our eyes red.

"A Goddamned *cemetery!*" he spit. "Yale University is built around a *boneyard!*"

"A graveyard? Ain't dat som' shit? I bet dey ain't got no niggas layin' up in dat muthafucka eitha! Now git som' Thunderchicken, Herman. *We thirsty!*"

"Don't you lightbulbs see the implications? Grove . . . *grave?* The founders of Yale University were *necrophiles!*"

"Git da wine, Herman! And stop talkin' crazy!"

"Fuck the wine! This is a lesson in the revolutionary's first code of conduct—'***Know Your Enemy***'!"

"But we don't be unnerstannin' what you be sayin, Herman! Break da shit down fo' us!"

Courtesy of Joy Glidden © 1995.

"*Break the shit down! Break the shit down!* Do I have to spoon-feed you simpletons? What I'm saying is this—those freakish, Dr. Strange-love muthafuckas coming out of Yale are going to control the world's major corporations, commit mass genocide and *fuck the corpses!*"

"Huh, Herman? You still talkin' crazy!"

"Why do you think there's so much secrecy shrouding that 'deaths-head-in-tuxedo' Skull-n-Bones cabal? Do you think it's only a cover-up for frat boys having fun with the sororities' underwear? Use what brain you have left! It's bigger than that—*it's conspiracy!* From Nixon on down! *They want us dead so they can fuck us all!!*"

"I hear you, Herman!" I piped. "Cause if you remember *Dracula*—"

"C'mon, Herman! We don't wanna hear dis shit! Git us som' *grape!*"

"Let the brutha speak, picklehead!"

"But da nigga's talkin' 'bout *Count Dracula*—!"

Huck-n-Pete looked at each other and howled in laughter.

"—an old, dead, pasty-face, stoop-shoulder, float-across-da-floor, *Max-Schreck* lookin' Nosferatu muthafucka!"

"But you don't understand!" Pete said. "You talkin' silent *Dracula!* Movies can talk now. Not like when you was a boy. *Talkin' Dracula is clean!* Da wimmins be goin' crazy for his *bad-ass* cape! They be faintin' an' shit, wantin' to give it up to *Drac!*"

"Yeah." Huck agreed. "Not Wolfman, though. Wolfman's raggitty. Who you know wanna give him some? Wolfman be at a party or sump'in, tryin' to get som' play. An' th' wimmin take one look at him an' say, 'You better get your stank-breaf' outta my face an' go chew on a Milk Bone dog biscuit!'. Right, *Wolfman?*"

Huck looked at me and grinned. *Wolfishly.*

I blushed.

Herman came to my rescue. "Stop embarrassing the brutha so he can make his point."

"Well, uh, if we apply a correct Marxist analysis to Stoker's text, who I believe was associated with both the Fabians, and the Golden Dawn, understanding its occult, as well as its Socialist shadings, you'll see that the aristocracy, or the military-industrial complex's capitalist ruling class of Dracula's time, are a class of walking dead, feeding—*vampiri-cally*—on the life's energy, or blood, of the peasant-lumpen classes."

"Dis nigga crazier'n you, Herman!"

"Shut up! Let him speak!"

"Now we need only extrapolate on Stoker's basic theory of the vampiric nature of the ruling class, and look at the class structure of the Undead (the vampire being the capitalist taskmaster; the zombie being the exploited worker; and the ghoul representing the lumpen underclass), then concretely apply his theory to our current condition of oppression, vis-à-vis—Yale's *boneyard*—and take proper revolutionary measures."

"Right on, young brutha! I'm sure you'll be gettin' plenty o' wimmins wid dat rap! Now git da wine som'body, *please!*"

Courtesy of Photofest.

"Goddamn, baby! You best give up eatin'
them pig tails and black-eyed peas
I been cookin'!"

CONTRIBUTORS

. . . .

Joy Glidden is a multitalented figurative painter who has exhibited throughout Canada and the U.S. In addition to painting, her extensive background includes dance and film. Some of her drawings also appear in the paperback edition of *Negrophobia*. Currently, she is choreographing a ballet utilizing construction-site cranes. She has large, sparkling Bette Davis eyes.

Micheal Will is a writer, cartoonist and actor. He has authored numerous works including *I Have Seen the Wind*—a wide-eyed and sensitive look at his prairie boyhood in easy-to-read words and pictures; the play "The Peebles Method"; and the Peter Sandmark film *Cult of the Nuclear Brain Dead*.

Steve Cannon is the hougan of the Lower East Side Gathering of the Tribes gallery, theater and magazine collective.

Francois Gaudet is an occupational therapy assistant in Nova Scotia, designing artificial limbs for medical conditions no standard prosthesis will fit.

Rick Trembles. Robert Crumb had this to say about Rick's work: "I thought my perversions were weird—God, that guy is *really* out there. But it made me happy that somebody is even more twisted and weird than me. Way more, he's way out there." For those of you who've seen the Crumb documentary, you *know* that's quite a mouthful. Chester Brown has also cited Rick Trembles as the inspiration for his early Yummy Fur strips. In addition to cartooning, Rick is an animator, 3-D model builder and singer/guitarist for the world's oldest nontouring punk band, The American Devices. For copies of his comix Sugar Diet, American Devices' t-shirts and recordings, send international money orders to: Rick Trembles, Box 693, Tour De La Bourse, Montreal, Quebec, Canada, H4Z-159.

THANKS AND ACKNOWLEDGMENTS

. . . .

To George W.S. Trow for the loan of his extensive library of stills and promotional materials; Kim Sykes for arranging my meeting with Pam Grier; Fred Braithwaite for putting me together with Melvin Van Peebles and granting me permission to use portions of his interview with Iceberg Slim; Peter Donald for the necessary numbers leading to Antonio Fargas; Dael Orlander-Smith, who keeps me in raucously high spirits with her great humor and tasty fried chicken-n-potato salad platters; Jenna Laslocky for her warm support, expertise and barbecue lunches; Bill Adler and Roberta Magratti for The Last Poets; Marty Arno, Dawn Algieri; Jody Whitcomb and Lisa of Two Bridges Video in Brooklyn; Ted Mann for not only the Rudy Ray Moore tapes but also for publishing The Mini-Manual of the Urban Guerrilla; Penny Pattison for locating it; David Mills for putting me on to Cap'n Draw; Alan Drogan and Celia Lehar for upgrading the technology; Rob Simpson for *Shaft Among The Jews*; my sister, Jeri Collette, for taping hours and hours of television; Joy Glidden for transcribing hours and hours of tape; Lisa Blaus-Child for the Michael Jackson Swiss Chocolate Bar; and the usual crew of suspects: the E. 3rd Street Stoop Crew; Tracie Morris; Rob Hardin; Jenny Seymour; Joe and Connie Razza; Heidi Berg; Marc Shapiro; Ansel Parkison; Donald and Barbra Howie; Michael Gonzales; Ronald Judy; Thomas Adcock; Lou Stathis; Judy McGuire; Ronald Hansley; Debra Bergman; Chuckie Williams; Terry Southern; Gail Gerber; Nelson Lyons; Bud Cort; Elaine Angelopulous; Meagan Fraser; "Elf" Holdridge (star of the unaired *An Old Fashion Holdridge Family Christmas* special); Marc Ewert; Nemo; Snoop; Todd Ivey; Gabe Tolliver; Cheryl Hardwicke; Chris Dowd; Hod David; Morley Kamen; Nehar Oza;

Diamanda Galas; Peter Kleinman; Greg Moore; Sarah Ferguson; Steve Pink; Tyrus Coursey; Roberta Magrini; Joel Rose; Paul Dennis; Catherine Texier; Flip Barnes; Merry Fortune; Kay Anderson; Steve Assetta; Jamie Delman; Emily Carter; Maggie Estep; Tim Beckett; Ian Tannenbaum; Leslie Pitts; Angela Lucakin; Michael Powell; Barry Secunda; Sandy Choron; Buddy Meisler; Wadia Gardner; Sean Kelly (who actually wrote: *"Sometimes I feel this whole world is a sharecropper's shack. Some of us are niggers. And the rest of us are black."*); Nigel Cox-Hagen; Jim Jarmusch; Jackie Geller; Josh Whalen; Barbara Seaman; Ben McManus; Mary Mitchell; Stuart Constantin; Gunter Blank; Michel Vezini; Asher Lack; Jean Stein; Debbie Treisman; Ian Stephans; Lynn Suderman; Ishmael Reed; Robert Downey, Sr.; Lech Kowalski; Patricia Winter; Jane Rein; Khalid Lum; Zulu Nation, D.C.; Jake-Ann Jones; Nat Estes; Ann Milburne; Emily XYZ; Bob Holman; Faith Childs; Dennis Cooper; A Gathering of the Tribes; Gilles Vaugeois; Tracy Freissen; Elizabeth 'Biz' Mitchell; The New Orleans Kali Krewe; Ben Mapp; Hal-n-Vicki; Stephanie and Suzanne Jones; Jennifer Jazz; Peter Conte; JoAnn Wasserman; Gillian McCain; Jim Fitzgerald; Tori and Jori Leanza; Eve Greenbaum; Monica Gregor and Lucas Hall; Nancy and Mark Jacobson; Aron Vandoorson; Miranda Ford; Imani Tolliver; Erik Maas; Bruce Benderson; Ricardo Cruz; Fredrique Pressman; Dennis Giron; Samantha Courbel; Uncle Butch McAdden; the steff/squat in Karlsruhe, Germany (Keep makin' the revolution happen!); Ralf Keller; Torsten Liesegang; Tree at Nu Yo; Claudia Basrawi; Mario Mentrup; Andy Helfer, Jim and Debbie Goad; Stewart Home; Howard Mandelbaum; Mark Zero; Pam Snead; Simone Salitter; Carmine D'Intino; Jack Tilton; Earl McGrath; and the great granddaddy of Black Bohemia, Ted Joans; and the hundreds of other folks I know I'm forgetting.